D0560848

BIO LOGIC

BIO LOGIC

Designing with Nature to Protect the Environment

• *Revised Edition* •

DAVID WANN

• *Foreword by Frederic Krupp* •

Johnson Books: Boulder

David Wann works for the U.S. Environmental Protection Agency, but the views and opinions in this book do not necessarily represent Agency policy or priorities on particular issues.

Cover design by Bob Schram/Bookends
Special Focus logo by Sue Simmons

"For the Children" from *Turtle Island*, © 1974 by Gary Snyder. Reprinted by permission of New Directions Publishing Corporation.

Revised Edition
9   8   7   6   5   4   3   2   1

Library of Congress Cataloging-in-Publication Data

Wann, David.
    Biologic: designing with nature to protect the environment / David Wann; foreword by Frederick Krupp.—Rev. ed.
        p.   cm.
    Includes bibliographical references (p. 263) and index.
    ISBN 1-55566-122-X
    1. Environmental protection.   2. Environmental sciences—Philosophy.   3. Environmental protection—United States.
4. Environmental engineering—United States.   I. Title.
TD170.W358   1994
363.7—dc20   94-2328
                                                         CIP

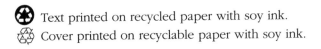

Printed in the United States of America by
Johnson Printing Company
1880 South 57th Court
Boulder, Colorado 80301

We must learn to think not only logically
but biologically.
— Edward Abbey

A thing is right when it tends to preserve the
integrity, stability, and beauty of the biotic
community. It is wrong when it tends otherwise.
— Aldo Leopold

Dedication:

For Julie, Colin, and Libby, who put up with me; for my parents, who always counseled not to tear anything apart until I was ready to suggest alternatives; and for my sister Susan and brother-in-law David, whose support came at just the right times.

CONTENTS

FOREWORD

In this book, David Wann succeeds at nothing less than describing and giving texture to a new environmental ethic. His choice of the word "biologic" is perfectly in keeping with this ambition. At first glance, the word is a lighthearted, rather obvious pun, but it also points to an important idea—that the organic and artificial, intuitive and rational, poetic and technical aspects of human problem-solving have too long been seen as mutually exclusive.

Biologic attempts to synthesize these opposites. Using nature as a touchstone, it guides human intelligence within the clear limits imposed by our involvement with and dependence upon the rest of nature. Rather than overlay human inventions on natural systems, it studies those systems as models for efficient, sustainable ways of organizing our energy use, food production, housing, transportation, and recycling of wastes. Instead of a disruptive force to be dominated—at best a source of romantic inspiration—nature is revealed by biologic to be an endless wellspring of practical information.

This book makes clear that throughout our history we in the United States have consistently ignored the lessons of nature. Yet Wann's critique of American mass-engineered, earn-and-spend, throwaway "monoculture"—while devastating—is not malicious. As a pioneer nation with vast natural resources in the midst of seemingly unlimited land, water, and air, we found it possible to get rich without worrying about the consequences. This wasn't really surprising, he says, although it was foolish. We may have not had much understanding, but we had power, and we used it. Now our car-driving, TV-watching, energy-gluttonous lifestyle has become untenable. It's time to change.

Using biologic, we must rethink everything from energy use to the way we advertise our products. As the paradigm of our culture, we must replace the unwavering arrow of "forward progress" (an illusion) with the continuous loop of recycling (the way nature actually works). To do this, we must make use of every available tool—from free market mechanisms to government intervention. Only by making an unstinting effort at every level of society can we make the changes that will allow us to prosper and not just survive.

Happily, Wann's idea of change is not to renounce everything we enjoy, put on sackcloth, and glumly eat our Brussels sprouts.

Just as he has enlivened his dry and sometimes grim subject matter with a prose full of fresh metaphors and sparkling humor, the process does not have to be unpleasant. In fact redesigning our culture—more humbly this time—should be exciting and satisfying because changes will be local and specific, not generic and imposed from afar.

Many of these are not new ideas, but Wann pulls them together in an argument that is optimistic without being naive. He understands the magnitude of such threats as global warming but refuses to be gloomy about it. In the United States today there is a consensus that we must change our ways. We are a can-do people—the same smart, vital people who subjugated the wilderness—and we can harness our creativity and will to learn to "fit in" with the natural systems we formerly (and mistakenly) thought we were above.

This is the business of the 1990s and beyond. The heart of this book lies in the fascinating, exhaustively researched examples of biologic that have already sprung up throughout the country. Clearly this is not a movement of the future—it is already well under way.

Much remains to be done, of course. National, state, and local politicians must rally the public to change, pass laws that are good for the environment, and see that government bureaucracies adhere to biologic. Corporations must change their production processes and products (something it is increasingly in their financial interest to do). Consumers must change their buying and living habits.

Each of these actions will provide positive feedback for the others. As more consumers demand environmentally sound products, more such products will appear in the stores, and it will become easier to find and buy them. As people make, for example, recycling a part of their lives, they will expect politicians to propose up-to-date, efficient programs. As politicians make curbside and apartment collection of recyclables the standard, it will become even more convenient for citizens to participate.

Of course, no matter what systems we are able to devise, there is no substitute for every individual adopting an environmental ethic. This excellent book gives us the philosophical framework for such an ethic and a myriad of down-to-earth ways to achieve it.

FREDERIC KRUPP, EXECUTIVE DIRECTOR
ENVIRONMENTAL DEFENSE FUND

INTRODUCTION

Remember in the old Westerns, the unshaven, determined band of soldiers holed up inside the besieged army fort? They were down to their last fourteen bullets, a plug of tobacco, and half a canteen of muddy water. Then suddenly (inevitably), the cavalry rides onto the screen in a coordinated last-ditch rescue effort.

Luckily, there are some fresh new ideas and designs blossoming in America which resemble that cavalry, but without the fanfare and cinematic clouds of high plains dust. Some innovative responses to nagging, fifty-year-old questions are popping up like prairie wildflowers.

We're recycling and redesigning our entire culture, nothing less. In a country filled with both excess and opportunity, we're learning to take advantage of the opportunities, finding more coherent ways of getting things done. We've discovered that it's often possible to convert a can of worms into a container of live bait. The sign is up on the door: *Gone fishin' for new ideas.* From energy sources to consumer goods and manufacturing processes (from blueprints through molecular structure), our country's inputs are being completely rethought so the outputs will have fewer impacts. This is a huge step for a pioneer culture to take.

The opening premise here is that our years of excessive consumption and poor design were pretty much inevitable. When you *have* a lot of stuff, you *use* a lot of stuff, and good design gets lost in the midst of abundance. Before we could get a handle on overconsumption, we had to agree on two things: that we had a major environmental problem, and what the sources of that intertwined problem were. And we had to slow our cultural vehicle down before we could expect to change directions.

From an ecological perspective, it's also inevitable that we will progressively become more organized, more cooperative, and more ingenious because that's the way nature works. Natural systems move from disorganization and inefficiency toward balance and stability, and we're part of a natural system (even though we sometimes pretend we're above it all). The same notion has been expressed by economist Kenneth Boulding, who foresees an inevitable shift from Cowboy Economy (with limitless resources) to Spaceman Economy (ingeniously designed for efficiency and recycling).

It's been said that "people and nations behave wisely once they have exhausted all other alternatives," and America, at least, has already gone through a good many.[1] We're last century's gold miner, blasting whole mountainsides away with concentrated jets of creek water; we're the 1990s sports car driver, top down, accelerating right up to the stop sign; and we're the newly gigantic suburban teenager, hanging on an open refrigerator door, gazing blankly at brightly packaged superabundance and griping that "there's nothing to eat." We're the nation that uses 1/750th of its electrical power (one huge coal or nuclear plant) to run millions of television sets *while they are off,* since many silent sets draw 1.5 to 8 watts of standby power for remote control, electronic tuning, and instant-on features.[2]

Undeniably, we're filled to the brim with "American gusto"— that curious, oblivious, yet somehow forgivable blend of rugged individualism and mass hysteria. Young and disorganized as we were, we rapidly learned how to reach commercial consensus, particularly when it meant that everyone would get a larger slice of cake.

North America!

Topsoil, timber, and ore, the icing on the cake of North America, were at the center of a banquet table set exactly five centuries ago, right before Columbus rang the doorbell. And we did what came naturally—we went after them with gusto, because cake is cake. Do bacteria control their appetites in a petri dish full of agar? Do lynxes keep a yearly census of their prey, the snowshoe hare?

Our evolving fast-food mentality—very similar to the resource-gobbling now underway in Latin America and elsewhere—has come to be an American trademark. The saving graces were that despite our bungling naiveté, deep down we were well intentioned and we did love our land, even though we didn't completely understand it. How could we, since we didn't really *know* it? The new continent was as unfamiliar to us as Disney World must be to a Brazilian tribesman.

Of course, it was when some Pennsylvanian stepped in a puddle of oil in 1859 that all hell broke loose: here was energy, food, and a storehouse of profitable molecules all in one place. From that point on, we didn't need to go out; we could just order room service.

Using overall vigor as a yardstick, it really can't be disputed that we've thrived in the New World and the products of it, very much like the handful of hardy English rabbits set loose in Australia that quickly multiplied to several hundred million. By God, we got rich! The thing is, you need a plan, or at least a series of goals. America still doesn't have an itinerary, only an open highway, littered with burger wrappers and billboards. The road signs are set up to be readable only if progress is forward, a very limiting, tunnel-bound approach.

Boomerang–throwing Lessons

The most important lesson for Americans to relearn is that life is a loops-and-cycles arrangement. Our preoccupation with "forward" reinforces a mind-set in which resources continually go out but never come back, like a boomerang poorly thrown. When we go out to buy something, it seems obvious that we should also have unused resources to return. Wherever we see waste, we need to develop a way to scavenge it, turning it into nutrients just as an ecosystem does. We've incorrectly assumed that the supply of resources on the input side of the conveyer belt is limitless, and that resource acquisition doesn't harm the environment. Because resource extraction (as well as waste discharge) takes place in a scattered way, we've preferred not to perceive the full effects.

The physicists' symbol for infinity, a sideways eight, seems to be an appropriate way of looking at resources and the stuff they're made of. As long as there's life on earth, there will be recycling. Either humans learn how to recycle, or we can count on *being* recycled as a species.

An elementary school teacher I know once mischievously left the globe in his classroom turned upside down. His students couldn't stand it; as soon as he left the room, several ran up and returned the earth to its standard orientation. When he came back, he explained to the students that there really *is* no "upside down" from a cosmic perspective. Similarly, there is no "right-side up" to our common worldview. We need to be looking at things from all angles, not just one. Fortunately, we *do* have some guidelines we can rely on, and natural systems are right at the top of the list.

Futurist Hazel Henderson suggests "morphogenesis" as the most appropriate natural analogy of our society's growing pains. Like a chrysalis turning into a butterfly, our society is experiencing the breakdown of old structures and the creation of bright new structures at the same time. And just as the butterfly uses genetic information supplied via the tissue of the caterpillar, we need to make sure our best cultural information is passed along while everything that is not relevant to the butterfly state is jettisoned for recycling.

It's also useful to think of human society as widely dispersed components of a thousand different ecosystems because *that's what we are.* Mythologist Joseph Campbell observed that the distinction of "tallest structure" belonged in turn to the church steeple, capitol dome, and corporate high-rise as the focus of our civilization changed. The cultural changes yet to come may be even more dramatic. Our search for fossil-fuel substitutes that will reduce our dependence on polluting combustion represents nothing less than the deliberate "undiscovery of fire" (in Amory Lovins' words), just as our quest for nature-compatible design will have enormous historical significance (the "domestication of technology").

No Room Service in the Twenty-first Century

This book highlights ingenuity, American style. We're learning, slowly but steadily, that ecological design—what I call "biologic"—can be very productive, very challenging, and very *American.* Despite our resource-eating disorder, we *do* take care of our problems, and we will this time, too, once we're convinced the noisy, raucous party is over.

What we need right now is not prefabricated, media-fed environmental scare stories but a sense of momentum. We're tired of CFCs, PCBs, acid rain, traffic jams, and all the rest. We just want to figure out how we can effectively rearrange the "furniture" and start to feel better about getting out of bed each morning. We know by now what we *don't* want: pollution, cancer, and stress. But what do we want, and how do we get it, using our basic tools of experience and imagination?

I propose that we abandon the excess baggage of guilt and stupefaction, and get on with it. Let's assume we're about where we should be, and that we're prepared to move on. There are billions of useful designs out there in the natural world already, and we can come up with many more if we start with the right materials and the right attitude. This book challenges traditional assumptions, highlighting new concepts from biological wastewater and hazardous waste treatment through design upgrades in cars and appliances. New ways of recycling are explored, along with bioregionalism, "negawatts," and other ideas now ripe for harvest.

Suit Coat or Straightjacket?

Our highest conceptual priority is to design and tailor a "new suit." We've been wearing this same old suit backwards for centuries, and we didn't even realize it! We let the world be defined by our inventions, which was very clever, but not nearly as clever as finally knowing enough to put the suit on frontwards, letting ingenious inventions be defined by the natural world. Ecologist Aldo Leopold had his suit on frontwards when he wrote, "We abuse land because we regard it as a commodity belonging to us. When we see land as a commodity to which we belong, we may begin to use it with love and respect." It's the same with our fellow species that we rely on more than we realize—they don't belong to us, they belong *with* us.

The basic issues under discussion here, from my own perspective of compost-crazed grassrootser, bureaucratic meeting-goer, and part-time instructor in an environmentally blossoming college classroom, are the infallibility of natural systems and the expansion of human understanding.

We stand at the gateway to an exciting transition that we can make either intentionally or under police escort. The "limits to growth" we kept hearing about are coming into focus now as resource scarcity and environmental brick walls. It's no longer up for debate.

We've run out of land for waste disposal in New Jersey and New York. We're running out of water in the West, out of breathable air in Los Angeles, and out of tolerance in our immune systems for the chemical substances that have invaded our world. There are cost limits on how clean we can get a given Superfund site and engineering limits on the combustion efficiency of an automobile or solid-waste incinerator. One critical atmospheric layer is disappearing while another expands in direct proportion to the flames fanned by human activity. The message is clear: we need a *better understanding of natural limits, and designs that creatively coexist with those limits.*

Humorist Woody Allen may have overstated the historical implications when he said, "More than at any other time in history, mankind faces a crossroads. One path leads to despair and utter hopelessness, the other to total extinction. Let us pray we have the wisdom to choose correctly." Our situation may not be quite *that* bleak, but there are a good many ecologists and scientists who believe that we may be the most important humans that have yet come along because, environmentally, we can either "make it or break it." Why not *make* it?

The basic proposition offered in this book is that environmental deterioration is a lack of relevant information. This simplifies things because we can use the same thought process to help answer many different kinds of environmental questions. We need to understand living (and nonliving) systems and adjust our behavior to fit in with them, just as lions blend in with the savanna and flowers knock themselves out to attract bees. We need to extract *information* instead of just ore and oil from our environment, transferring it into the products and processes we live with so they'll fit better.

A perfect example is the clever, informed control of agricultural pests using biological methods. Once we've established through skillful observation exactly who our pest is and what its habits are, there is a whole universe of gadgets, traps, and maneuvers available to control its impact on our crop, without destroying the crop or in effect shooting ourselves in the foot with pesticides.

The exciting news is that we are adopting this biologic approach in many different areas, such as water conservation, hazardous waste management, product design, energy use, air and water quality control, and the use of land. By reducing the amount of and the manner in which excess "stuff" moves through our mega-systems, and by tuning up the mega-systems themselves, we can maintain the same level of social satisfaction with far less effort and far fewer negative impacts.

Rather than monolithic, one-size-fits-all types of solutions, we are devising more customized, diverse ways of meeting our needs, just as an ecosystem's countless partnerships and interdependencies give the system its overall vigor and resilience.

The Paradigm Sneeze

Is there a definitive way of telling from the way we are what it is that we want? Not always. In the case of American culture, even an objective observer might not perceive that all the typical American really wants (beyond a hot shower and a cold beer) is peace of mind. The reason Americans have been "trained" to settle for dissatisfaction and poor design when far better is within reach is simply that if we were content with what we have it would be bad for business—we wouldn't need to *buy* anything. So we're paying two household salaries and more in order to achieve commercially engineered dissatisfaction. I always assumed that wants were somehow beyond needs. Once you got the basics taken care of, you could then progress to the luxuries. But it seems that many of us do not yet have the basics—we've just skipped over them, trying to forget about them by indulging as many wants as possible.

The biggest change our society will experience in the near future will also be the hardest to document or quantify because it will be an *internal revolution*. A new ecological ethic is beginning to come into blossom, flower by flower—one that acknowledges this elemental, universal quest for peace of mind. This ethic acknowledges that peace of mind is not an extra, but an essential. We need coherence and harmony like we need food and water.

All the little environmentally destructive decisions we make for approval, convenience, and short-term gratification are becoming unacceptable and rather foolish. Our peers are expecting better of us. We're realizing that since the appearance of wealth is not really a prerequisite for peace of mind, we may as well quit tearing things up in order to have that corner house or sleek, sexy car. At last, we're becoming adept at "connecting the dots"—recognizing cause and effect. We are realizing it was the monosodium glutamate that gave us the headache, and the four hundred million cars, worldwide, that have severely damaged some of our most valued forests.

This ethical metamorphosis, however, won't be immediate or automatic, and in the meantime, we have to get busy using those institutions and systems of exchange that are already in place. Referring to the threat of global warming from "greenhouse gases," scientist Steven Schneider has warned, "You don't wait until you are sick to buy health insurance because they won't sell it to you then."

It's as if we are answering for the ills and abuses of the past twenty or thirty years in a doctor's office. The doctor asks, "Where does it hurt?" sensing that something is genuinely wrong. "It hurts in my rain forests, Doc," we respond, "and it hurts in my rivers. What can you give me to make the pain go away?" The doctor is sympathetic, but his well-meaning prescriptions are insufficient, and he knows it. He's been in the habit of selling "fixes," even though he realizes intuitively that the most effective cure by far is prevention.

We need to use the preventive approach of traditional Chinese physicians, who got paid for their services only when patients were healthy. If our rivers and wetlands remain intact, along with our vitality and well-being, *then* we can pay ourselves.

Through our consumer choices and our politics, we need to select which social organisms we'll tolerate and which we won't. Those industries and processes that don't make the cut get recycled, along with all the nutrients and resources they contain.

This book reports on some of the good, nature-based design already being implemented in America—not always for the purest of reasons, since our ethic is still evolving. But at least the rational side of our culture is beginning to realize the power that the intuitive side has, and each side continues to understand and accommodate the other a little better. We're looking now at a merging of the two: intuitive and rational; philosophical and pragmatic; New Age and Old Guard; frugality and extravagance.

This "open moment in history" reminds me of that disoriented, out-of-control feeling that precedes a sneeze and the physiological recognition that everything else must take a backseat to that sneeze. In the 1960s and early 1970s, we thought we were going to sneeze, but it went away. In the 1990s, the feeling is back, and this time it's going to happen. The authors of future history books will no doubt have their hands full trying to make sense out of our transition era, but I predict they'll offer us a figurative "gesundheit!" at the very least.

DAVID WANN

CHAPTER 1

This is a book about a new way of thinking. In a sense, the potentially apocalyptic environmental crisis we face is in our heads! We've tended to look outside ourselves—at the polluted lakes and brown clouds over our cities—and regard those impacts as the problem. Recently, we've begun to see the environmental crisis in a more holistic way: pollution is a collection of symptoms of poorly designed products and processes that don't fit natural systems.

The fundamental problem is that our brains—and technologies—are still evolving. Although part of nature, our intellects brashly decided to go their own way, decoupling from the reality of biology. In recent times, an industrial alliance between physics and chemistry walked all over the still-evolving field of biology like a herd of cattle.

The result was runaway chemicals, overburdened immune systems, disappearing species. The truth is, until our brains come back home to nature again, the environmental crisis will continue to escalate. Fortunately, there are signs that our brains are finally responding to nature's cowbell! We have new knowledge about biology that will help us design our technologies and our lives in a more integrated and satisfying way.

For example, we know the basics of how chemicals move through living systems, from human bodies to regional and global ecosystems. We know that all healthy systems rely on fundamental qualities such as diversity, interdependence and flexibility. And we have a better understanding about the interplay between living things and their non-living support systems, such as the ozone layer and weather cycles.

What do we do now? We change our minds, and our designs. Instead of whirling completely out of control, we try a new, very accessible strategy: fitting in. We resolve to become experts rather than remaining beginners. The fact is, in the next generation, we all have to be designers, insisting that technical and behavioral rules follow natural rules. That's what "biologic" is about—the incorporation of environmental knowledge into the things we design and use. When the flow of energy and materials through human systems matches or complements their flow through natural systems, we'll have a civilization we can live with, on a sustainable basis.

Like the master gardener in each of our neighborhoods, we need to become attuned to our natural world, and learn how to help it come into blossom. As frenzied as we have become lately, we'll still take a few extra minutes to walk past the neighborhood's master garden, where we see expertly chosen tree species offering shade and maybe even a secluded spot for a hammock. Flowers, fruits, and vegetables contribute a mixed ambience of colors, shapes, and scents. Everything fits, and it feels good just being around the garden.

What makes that yard and garden work is informed design. We sense that the owners are keenly aware of the interplay between environment and people, ingeniously meeting the needs of each. They have surrounded themselves with plants that won't need pampering, because of natural compatibility existing conditions.

This definitely isn't the case with our twentieth-century industrialized landscape, which all too often surrounds us the way a bombed-out battlefield surrounds a military general. In our world, things rarely fit together; our products and creations battle each other and their mutual environment. Our GNP may be rising, but our peace of mind is shrinking right along with our resource base.

The good news is we can do better, if we just go back and follow the directions. That's what this book is about—following natural rules so our design strategies—and our lives—will be more integrated and coherent. For starters, I propose that we adopt a master gardener's approach toward the resources and materials that move through our world, in the things we buy, use, and manufacture. We need to perceive and seize opportunities: wherever there is pollution, there are opportunities for better design.

When you think about it, poor design is responsible for many if not most of our environmental problems. We leave "muddy footprints" behind ourselves in the form of pollution and environmental/social impacts because we have not in effect taken our shoes off at the door. Our brains just don't get it.

Cars pollute because they're not designed well and use inappropriate fuels and materials. People find it difficult to ride bicycles to work because bikepaths are not designed into community plans. Toxic chemicals are discharged into rivers and into the air because manufacturing processes are poorly designed; wastes move right along with the product and then become toxic orphans in our environment.

The environmental headlines of the late 1980s were different than those of the 1970s. They told us, "The Hunt Is on for CFC Substitutes," "Alternative Fuels Studied by Bush Administration," and "New Sources of Energy Needed to Cool Greenhouse Effect." What's different about these headlines is that they've shifted focus from the *effects* to the *causes*. Instead of focusing on air pollution and water pollution, we're starting to home in on transportation schemes that are in alignment with the reality of land use; mandatory recycling programs that mimic the way nature does it; and industrial innovations that make use of existing molecular structures. We're looking at entire *systems* rather than individual pipes and containers. After half a generation of debate, we've agreed we have a problem, and that—just as in health care—prevention is preferable to hit-or-miss correction.

It's high time we looked at this "other side" of the environmental kaleidoscope: the *design* side as opposed to the *discharge* side. We look more closely here at avoiding causes rather than patching up effects, using solid, nature-compatible designs and inputs instead of clumsy, out-of-tune ones.

The field of engineering takes a few well-intentioned jabs in this book because of its bias for trying to reshape the world to fit geometric and budget-obsessed "specs." Nature-compatible design, or biologic, is suggested as an alternative approach, although I do not mean to imply that the substitution will be automatic. We are looking at a whole series of multi-dimensional challenges or puzzles that will need some creative, often intuitive focus.

Using a Better Recipe

Because of abundant supplies of raw materials and a continuous stream of resource-hungry innovations, what goes *into* our processes and designs is sloppy, in a big way. As a result, what comes out is also sloppy. Each flaw on the production side becomes one of many pathways for pollution. So many of the designs we tolerate are out of scale, energy addicted, and filled with unnecessary, harmful ingredients. We won't put up with crabgrass or dandelions on our front lawns yet we'll pay good money for products that are full of "weeds." And the industrial processes we settle for remind me of putting green wood on a campfire: we get as much smoke as heat. What's the lesson? Don't put green wood on to begin with.

The input/demand/design side of our economy is cluttered with toxic-laced paint ingredients, building materials, and cosmetics; products like throwaway razors that maintain their structure for hundreds of years even though the intended use is only a day or two, and energy sources that "cut butter with chainsaws" by supplying sixty-eight degrees of heat with thousand-degree nuclear reactions. We wear gas masks and gloves when dealing with many of our products, transporting them in isolating containers. We haven't surrounded ourselves with a "garden" of good designs and ideas—far from it.

The old vaudeville team of Supply and Demand gets a weak review here, too. The act may be indispensable but the billing has always been backwards—it should be known as "Demand and Supply," with Demand appearing on stage first and making just as good a living as Supply. Too often, Demand ends up paying for drinks that Supply obliviously spills all over the place. Though Supply still has lots of potential talent, its performance is overconfident, undisciplined, and full of flaws. (The music that comes out of its poorly tuned "banjo" is the pollution coming out of our poorly tuned factories, tools, and procedures.)

Demand needs to get tough and insist that Supply sober up: in water use, power use, packaging, product quality, and tolerance of "runaway chemicals." The act should be based on ecological reality rather than convenience, habit, and short-term profit. Of course, Demand's not perfect either: demand-side thinkers explain the energy crises of the 1970s not in terms of too little supply, but too clumsy a demand: naive, inefficient, and greedy.

Learning to Live with Reality

As overwhelming as the situation sometimes seems, it is far from hopeless. We have native intelligence on our side, plus a collective imagination that won't quit. Just as immature information got us into this mess, it seems quite possible that more seasoned, savvy information can get us out. (Refer to criteria discussed in Chapters 3, 4, and 5.) In many cases, it's not raw materials we should be mining from our environment, but *information* about how that environment works, to be infused into our designs and devices.

Our technologies are direct extensions of our bodies. They're not alive, but like birds' feathers, we need them if we expect to fly as a species. Overly heavy technologies, however, never really get off the ground. And they make a feathery mess out of things in the attempt.

What do we do well? What motivates us? What gives us a genuine sense of fulfillment? For example, what exactly is it that makes gardening, fishing, or skiing so special? In addition to a craving for contact with nature, aren't we drawn by the challenges and limits presented? Why shouldn't we make our design strategies, businesses, and lifestyles a little more like recreational challenges? Wouldn't a few nature-based guidelines make our chaotic world a whole lot more *livable?* For example, a skier tests his or her ability to convert snowpack and gravity from adversaries to allies. For a mountain climber, the constraints are different: you reach the summit by using top-quality equipment, a well-chosen route, and a good pair of lungs. A golfer uses dexterity and concentration to challenge the natural forces of roughs, sand traps, and the physics of ball flight. And a fisherman either knows where they'll be biting by knowing the ecosystem or he gets lucky—or he sneaks past the supermarket fish counter on the way home.

Similar constraints exist in the "real world." We live with limits and natural guidelines such as gravity, friction, soil fertility, microbiological capabilities, sun, thermodynamics, genetic information, life span, and the ability to communicate. We need to use these guidelines and our own equipment to accomplish the major purpose of the game: a balanced *marriage between nature and culture.* More than anything else, what our world needs is careful, thoughtful design that can integrate the three stocks of wealth mentioned above (material, biological, and cultural). We need sturdy houses that face the sun, chemicals that decompose when their useful life is through, products specifically designed for multiple lifetimes, energy-efficient components in our appliances and industrial equipment, transportation systems with a higher ratio of people-to-vehicle, and so forth. The first question we need to ask is, "What do we want, and how can better design help us get it?"

Back on Track

"Within natural law is total freedom," technology expert Tom Bender writes, "because it defines the realities through which we must move."[1] The last century or so has been a detour—a petroleum-subsidized spree—that permitted us to defer good design in favor of quick-hit consumption. We let pollution leak into our environment the same way we stuff monthly bills into a desk drawer, hoping that somehow they'll just go away.

But for the last half of the century-long spree, we've been getting red-letter overdue notices on the bills: health effects, lack of space for waste disposal, resource shortages, and deterioration of ecosystems (so that, for example, a lake cannot bounce back from toxic discharges). In startled response, Congress pounded together Rube Goldberg-like regulations that try in vain to contain pollution within the boundaries of economics and politics. We're trained to think of these boundaries as bottom lines, below which nothing important exists, but we sense that beneath these temporary, sometimes arbitrary boundaries lie the roots of life itself—awesome, organic, magic. Collectively, these fundamental roots make economics and politics look pretty insignificant.

Having just taken a thirty-year crash course in ecology, we now know enough to begin doing some *real* designing. From this point forward, we can start getting very creative and integrated with our environmental laws, insisting that they reflect fundamental ecological and social realities.

Our culture needs to put its tested strategies to work before oil, stored water, and minerals become so inaccessible that it costs more energy to *get* the resources than they are worth. Enlightened architecture, alternative sources of energy, innovative political mechanisms, and highly efficient gadgets that get twice the work for half the electricity are sustainable strategies that can endure over the long haul, without running down, spilling over, or running out. One by one, these strategies are being sent into the game, and they're working. In the new way of thinking, it's not a question of the economy vs. ecology; the truth is, the two are interwoven. Our economy is simply a strand in the environmental tapestry.

Inputs, Outputs, and Throughput

Ecologist Eugene Odum believes that "technologists and politicians are approaching pollution problems from the 'wrong end.' Attention for years has focused on increasing outputs; that is, yields. From both environmental and monetary standpoints, attention now needs to be shifted to the input side of agriculture, power plants, industrial plants, and other production systems." By increasing the efficiency of these inputs, Odum suggests, pollution and excessive "throughput" of resources can be reduced without sacrifice. (Some yield decrease is tolerable because costs are generally less due to a reduction in input costs.)[2]

This input/output strategy will keep us busy for a while, but when we have upgraded our overall efficiency, we can then proceed to an even higher objective, "*humans* as output." Organic farmer Masanobu Fukuoka expressed this goal when he said, "The purpose of agriculture is not simply the production of food, but the cultivation and perfection of human beings."[3] Similarly, the purpose of *culture* is better humans, who are less stressed and more connected with natural reality. Logic is not good enough, since it's often separate from its support systems. We need *bio*logic.

A Few Principles of Biologic

1. Understanding basic physical concepts—like gravity, nutrient cycles, and the flow of sun, wind, and water— so decisions can be based on what's really here rather than what can be done with the "mirrors" of once-only energy.

2. Using resources on a sustainable basis, taking only the "interest" out of our ecological savings accounts rather than dipping into the principal.

3. Using the right tool for the right job. We need a diverse toolkit of solutions, and in many cases we'll have to use more than a single tool. As Mark Twain observed, "When all you have is a hammer, all your problems start to look like nails." And as Amory Lovins instructs, "Don't try to use monkey wrenches to repair Swiss watches."

4. Carefully monitoring and streamlining what goes *in* so that junk will not come out along with the intended product. Less waste means less cleanup, less regulation, less conflict, and fewer taxes.

5. Developing the habit of tracing the origins and future route of each physical interaction so that something enjoyed in the present doesn't leave a hole in the future, and nothing discharged or thrown away here becomes a compounded problem there. We're right in the middle of a product's past and its future.

6. Acknowledging the uniqueness of each location and its suitability for *certain uses only*. Conversely, acknowledging that a single prescription will not work in all cases.

7. Using the *simplest* process or product to get the job done so the environment benefits as well as the manufacturer. For example, packaging has more than one mission: it needs to fit in the environment like the product fits in *it*.

8. Using software (information) rather than hardware whenever possible to reduce inevitable collisions between imprecise human design and "custom-fit" natural design.

9. Using design solutions that accomplish three or four things at once, such as native vegetation plantings that conserve water, reduce erosion, soak up greenhouse-forming carbon dioxide, and have a cooling effect on an urban landscape, all at the same time.

10. Accounting for costs with the full lifetime of the product in mind. How much soil was lost to produce that supermarket full of food? How much energy did it take to acquire that barrelful of oil? What are the hidden costs of owning that shiny automobile?

What would happen in our world if we actually began applying these principles? What if companies started using fewer solvents in response to regulatory demands and our insistence that manufacturing expenses reflect *total* costs, including ecological impacts? What if we learned how to make the same amount of electricity or water do far more work for us, reducing pollution dramatically and permitting natural resources to remain in place? What if farmers spent less money for chemicals and therefore didn't have to produce a cumulative surplus to eke out a living? What if every time we generated industrial steam, we also produced electricity and vice versa?

What if we each began to take responsibility for literally "designing the hell out of our world," by tolerating only those devices, designs, and processes that come full cycle rather than having a short, obsolescent stay in our world and then rudely remaining as junk? What if each of our environmental regulations was designed to prevent pollution, rather than just contain it?

If we can imagine it, we stand a good chance of designing it.

Biologic: Benign Design

Biologic is applied ecology, and there's no way we can design things correctly without understanding the fundamental dynamics of natural systems.

The word *ecosystem* has a very fuzzy sound to it, I realize that. So what if the big fish eats the little fish? Why do we care? We're not fish—we've got oil. The reason why the concept bugs us is that it encompasses *everything*. How can you learn about everything? But the fact is, until we've taken "everything" into account and incorporated the findings into our culture, we've got no business bringing new designs into the world at all, just like a couple has no business having a baby unless they're prepared to take care of it.

Ecology is a storytelling kind of science. We learn by studying and conveying context and by direct observation. The business of design relies on how good the storytelling is. We may have a great design sitting in bench-scale on our lab table, but unless the context of the design's *destination* is understood, the inventor has no right to set it loose and consumers have no right to use it. If our laws are lax enough to let that lab door remain open so the design can get out, we need to insist on better-constructed laws. Our federal pesticide and toxic substances laws ("FIFRA" and "TSCA"), for example, have all too often left the lab door open without adequately previewing the consequences.

Ecosystems are important for two critical reasons: they are inherently valuable in and of themselves, and our technologies need to fit them. That's the crux of our environmental situation—our designs don't fit. Many are as unsuited for their surroundings as a loaded gun would be at our kids' birthday parties.

The fundamental rules in the design game of biologic pivot around three basic questions, posed by Wendell Berry in *Standing by Words:*[4]

- What is here?
- What will nature permit us to do here?
- What will nature help us to do here?

The Way Ecosystems Do It
(Adapted from E.P. Odum)

Immature Systems	Mature Systems
Inefficient nutrient utilization (wasteful)	Highly efficient nutrient utilization
Competitive, cutthroat	Cooperative, mutualistic
Poor resistance to outside stresses	Resilient, "unsinkable"
Low information quality	High information quality
Food chains mostly linear, grazing	Food chains weblike, use all available wastes
Nutrients "extrabiotic"	Nutrients "intrabiotic"
Low species diversity	High species diversity
Niche generalists	Niche specialists
Short, simple life cycles	Long, complex life cycles
Fast nutrient turnover rate between organisms, environment	Slow turnover rate between organisms, environment
Production emphasis: quantity	Production emphasis: quality

We know from observing other ecosystems that they move from a highly productive yet highly wasteful "pioneer" state toward a "climax" state that is highly *protective*, using nutrients very efficiently. This is exactly what's happening to us.

According to Odum, "We observe dog-eat-dog competition every time new vegetation colonizes a bare field. The immediate survival premium is first placed on rapid expansion to cover the available energy-receiving surfaces. The early growth ecosystems put out weeds of poor structure and quality, which are wasteful in their energy-capturing efficiencies, but effective in getting growth . . ."[5] As ecosystems mature, they become "smarter," as well as less cutthroat. They emphasize protection rather than production, become highly structured and full of useful, interlocking information, and learn to control their own growth by "knowing" that bigger is not necessarily better—that enough *is* enough.

It may not be flattering to our national self-concept, but the present American culture is still the bare field full of colonizing weeds, struggling toward something more sophisticated, interwoven, and permanent. Until now we've consistently chosen the resource-hungry path of least resistance. Yet to assume that we will remain a "dog-eat-dog" kind of society is to misunderstand the idea of "survival of the fittest." Ecologists such as Odum instruct that the phrase should be, "survival of those who *fit.*"

The overall theme of nature is *not* bloodthirsty competition, but carefully crafted interdependence. Ecosystems move toward a balanced, imperturbable condition by building on the efforts of the pioneers. Shade-loving Douglas fir trees are able to get a start by taking seed in the moist shade of the ponderosa pine. A sloping meadow becomes covered with columbines and delphiniums thanks to the soil-holding capabilities of colonizing grasses. A small recycling company benefits when a railroad is constructed right past its warehouse, which in turn helps the entire recycling industry preserve the country's resources.

There *is* a goal—mutual success and stability. By the time an ecosystem is old and wise, it is living proof that cooperative arrangements within and among species do work. With evolved wisdom comes a foolproof system to recycle the minerals and nutrients available, since no new supplies will be forthcoming; a highly efficient method of sharing the solar energy income; and a complex, tried-and-true system of checks and balances, so that if there is a major challenge to meet (such as a volcanic eruption or a stock market collapse), the interwoven structure of the system can act as a safety net. *Something* will survive to throw out a lifeline for something else. A good illustration of this is the dynamic rebirth of the Mount St. Helens ecosystem, which is bouncing back from volcanic holocaust much quicker than expected.

In a nutshell, our best course of action is to find pathways to sustainability and mutual success, using better design and ingenious technologies that get more results for the same effort. To use the jargon of such ecological economists as Herman Daly, we need to minimize "throughput" (the resources moving through our culture) and obsessive output while maximizing quality, diversity, and durability.[6] We need to radically cut back on the amount of wastes that escape from our factories; we need to design products expressly for reuse and recycle; and we need to reduce the "vehicle miles traveled" in and around our cities, without *depriving* ourselves in any noticeable way. These changes for the better will require persistent, informed demand.

In some cases, this "cultural tune-up" will necessitate completely new designs for processes, cities, and products. Now that's exciting! And far from being some distant, Oz-like fantasy, the transformation is already well underway.

Biologic in Bloom

Birth control is a good example of biologic—we arrived at an understanding of what causes conception, and we learned to prevent sperm from completing its determined marathon to the egg. The only losers are the detoured sperm and the stood-up egg. We can live with that, far more easily than we can live with famine or global demolition.

Agricultural pests can be detoured on a sexual wild-goose chase, too. For example, the grape berry moth is successfully controlled in vineyards by using sex pheromones, or natural attractants, to confuse male moths so they're unable to find a mate. It may seem like a dirty trick, but then so are most pesticides.

High-tech windows are another great example of biologic. The evolving generation of glazings is selective rather than indiscriminate: windows coated with a seventy-atoms-thick metal layer can now let light pass through while turning heat wavelengths away. This biologic converts windows from a design liability that has to overcome nature with imported energy into an energy asset that pays its own way. The Seattle Museum of Flight, for example, is mostly transparent, but because "low-emissivity" windows are used in the structure, the design passed the energy conservation standards of Seattle's rigorous building codes.

The design of a certain aerosol spray bottle uses biologic by taking advantage of pumped-in pressure and the elastic properties of rubber. Responding to the need for an aerosol container without ozone-depleting CFCs, the Exxel Company invented a mechanical pump spray bottle. Company president Peter Gould describes how it works: "The pressure it takes to force the product into the plastic bag is used to stretch the rubber, and the rubber more or less acts as a battery in the conservation sense. As you depress the activator button, the pressurized rubber pushes the product out." The company's brochure highlights one design advantage of the bottle, citing the experience of a vinyl and furniture care product company. "These products frequently were applied to hard-to-reach areas such as the underside of sofas and chairs. As cans were inverted, propellant loss and consumer complaints quickly followed." When the company switched to the Exxel sprayer, sales increased tenfold.

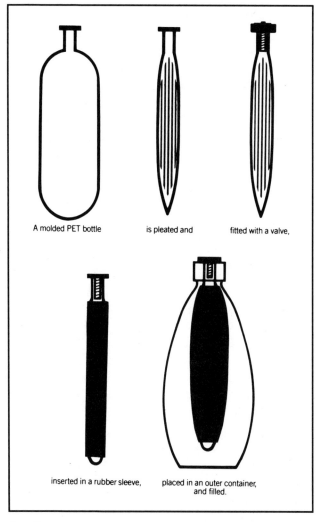

A molded PET bottle   is pleated and   fitted with a valve,

inserted in a rubber sleeve,   placed in an outer container, and filled.

Exxel's spray bottle design uses no chemical propellants. Instead, a rubber bladder expands when the product is injected into the bottle, and releases pressure when the button is pushed. *Photo courtesy of Exxel Container, Inc.*

Biologic is a harmony between the past and the future; between our natural endowment and what we intend to add. As a species, we're designers, and we need to take some pride in our designs. We've gotten into the "fix-up" habit in the last forty years—tacking on air scrubbers, catalytic converters, and chemical treatment plants at the end of our discharge pipes. Biologic audits what goes in at the *beginning* of the process. For example, if careless logging results in stream sediment that ruins fish habitat, we don't need bulldozers to dredge streambeds, but rather more sophisticated, less wasteful logging techniques, as well as more effective recycling downstream, to minimize the trees we have to cut.

Life Cycle Analysis: A Foundation for Good Design

A fresh concept has recently come into the environmental mainstream. Called Life Cycle Analysis, it's a way of getting a theoretical handle on the impacts caused by a particular design or activity. Although this technique is now used by EPA, National Park Service, corporations and others, the American Institute of Architects has led the way concerning materials use. Its subscription-based publication, the *Environmental Resource Guide* discusses the impacts that materials such as aluminum, glass, wood, and paint have throughout their entire relationship with humans. The typical building material is mined or harvested, consuming energy and possibly causing ecological impacts such as species depletion or water pollution. It is then transported to a manufacturing site, using more energy and creating more pollution. During its installation and use, there may be further impacts such as indoor air pollution. At the end of its life cycle, there may not be a designed-in provision for reusing the material, and its disposal will result in *more* energy use and *more* environmental impacts.

Innovative architects are now applying the concept of "embodied energy" to their designs, very much aware that the flow of materials is inherently connected to the energy and technology expended to make them flow. On a pyramid-like hierarchy of energy intensity, we spend 56 times as much energy per pound to bring aluminum into our buildings as we spend for drywall. Glass, though it's made from very basic elements, requires 6 or 8 times the energy as drywall to reach its destination in buildings.

The flow of materials through our designed world is an evolutionary process: trial and error. The goal is for an evolution

PAINTS AND VARNISHES

	GENERIC MATERIAL		INITIAL PRODUCTION				INSTALLATION/USE			RESOURCE RECOVERY		
Material	Contents/Process	Energy KWH/LB	Major Non-Energy Environmental Impacts	Recycled Content	Raw Material Reserves	Installation Hazards	Indoor Air Pollution	Maintenance	Recycla-bility	Reuse	Notes
"All Natural" Water Base Paint	plant resins, fillers, mineral pigments, water	?	minimal air and water pollution, renewable materials except minerals	nil	renewable	minimal risk, all low toxic contents	minimal	some are washable	nil	nil	performs like latex, range of colors from manufacturer
Casein Paint "Low Tox"	milk protein, mineral pigments, water	?	minimal air and water pollution, renewable materials except minerals	waste milk	renewable	minimal risk, all low toxic contents	minimal	not washable	nil	nil	prone to mildew
Water Base Paint	petroleum resins, fillers, pigments	9	moderate air and water pollution, petroleum depletion	nil	petroleum limits	less toxic contents than conventional	minor after dry	limited washability	nil	nil	latex without the biocides, limited colors
"All Natural" Oil Base Paint	linseed oil, driers, mineral pigments, may contain odorless petroleum solvent	?	moderate air and water pollution, possible petroleum depletion	nil	renewable	some fragrant citrus oils or low risk solvent	minimal after dry	very durable, interior or exterior	nil	nil	performs like alkyd but without odors, range of colors from manufacturer
Conventional Latex Paint	acrylic and latex resins, fillers, pigments, preservatives	9	moderate air and water pollution, chemical risk to workers from preservatives, petroleum depletion	nil	petroleum limits	ammonia, gases from solvent, biocide hazard	minor emissions for prolonged period	semi or gloss are durable	nil	nil	

This matrix illustrates the life cycle impacts of paint, providing a tool for choosing the product with the best environmental report card.

towards increasing efficiency and biological compatibility, but some of the trials inevitably become errors. Asbestos, CFCs, PCBs, lead—all these are species that have gone extinct, for our purposes.

The fact is, the materials we use in buildings are gradually becoming more information-rich, using less mass and less energy per unit of service provided. We're also seeking out "biologically smarter," less toxic materials, often substituting knowledge and better design for chemicals.

Life cycle analysis in effect puts the spotlight on weak links in the chain of human ecology. Companies who want to avoid future liabilities will do well to perform LCA's on their products because where there are identifiable impacts, there is the potential for surcharges, taxes, and other disincentives. Several states already have mandated that utilities must consider remote impacts—or externalities—when planning new power plants. The federal Clean Air Act amendments of 1990 have similar stipulations. These laws will "level the playing field" to favor design that doesn't result in environmental impacts, since comparatively clean technologies, like wind generators, will receive tax incentives.

The next few pages discuss a few more examples of designs that optimize resource use throughout their full life cycle.

Industrial Ingenuity

Instead of removing paint from jet airplanes with thousands of gallons of highly polluting paint stripper, why can't a system be devised that blasts the paint right off with recyclable materials? At Hill Air Force Base in Utah, that's exactly what *was* designed. The problem with chemical strippers was the contamination of large volumes of rinse water, as well as worker exposure to the chemicals.

After years of after-hours experimentation using everything from walnut shells to button fragments, now-retired air force employee Bob Roberts devised a method to remove multiple layers of paint at much lower cost, with much less pollution, and with savings in plane down-time. Plastic fragments, he finally discovered, were soft enough not to pit the planes' metal or break down into dust, but hard enough to strip the paint. Good design had been substituted for toxic chemicals.

Biologic also proved successful at a 3M Company electronics plant where copper circuit boards are made. An employee,

Engineering technician Bob Roberts invented a better way to strip paint from jet airplanes than using conventional hazardous chemical paint strippers. Recyclable plastic beads are fired at the paint surface, eliminating pollution and cutting costs at the same time.

inspired by the company's focus on "Pollution Prevention Pays," invented huge "toothbrushes" to clean the boards. The "toothpaste" was non-toxic pumice—far more desirable environmentally than the toxic spray that had been used.[7]

The Brulin Company in Indianapolis is marketing a new line of nonhazardous industrial cleaners called Worksafe. Based on naturally occurring citrus oils, the cleaners contain no chlorinated or petroleum-based solvents. Both worker safety and disposal costs were cited as incentives for the product's development. According to company spokesperson Janet Cleery, "Our customers—mostly industrial—were spending $2 to $3 a gallon to buy floor strippers with compounds like methylene chloride in them, but anywhere from $60 to $600 a gallon to dispose of the hazardous wastes after the stripper's use."[8]

Smarter Than Bugs

An entomologist, when asked to rid a library's books of small insect pests, discovered that simply stowing the books temporarily in a frozen meat locker would do the trick. A colleague prefers microwave ovens (the cookbook method) to get rid of pesky "bookworms"; the recipe calls for one minute per book or magazine. Still another method being tried is boiling water, sprayed on fields to destroy weed seeds as well as insect pests. These remedies may seem amusing but trivial, but hold on: a recent *Business Week* article (April 1989) describes how Tanimura & Antle, the second largest lettuce producer in the country, is using a technique just as amusing and saving lots of money by doing it. Pests are *vacuumed* off the lettuce with gigantic six-row vacuum cleaners, which don't stunt the growth of the produce as some pesticides will. (Many of the beneficial bugs reportedly avoid being sucked up).

Any Starport in a Storm

Another interesting illustration of biologic is an airport design by designer Jim Starry. Though not yet out of the blueprint and 3D model stage, the design is sure to be closely scrutinized in the future because of its ecologically sensitive design. The runways fan out from a central hub like the arms of a starfish, eliminating the usual miles of walking to and from planes. The truly ingenious aspect of the design is that the arms of the "starfish" have inclines built into them. When planes take off, Starry envisions, they will taxi downhill, saving large quantities of fuel. Likewise, when they land, they won't need to use fuel-hungry reverse thrusters because they will be going uphill. Because of the radial pattern of the runways, landings and takeoffs can be arranged to accommodate wind patterns, reducing the influence of weather on both fuel consumption and flight schedules. The runways are kept free of ice by the heat generated under the inclined runways where parking and terminal facilities are located. And the contaminating de-icer, ethylene glycol, now routinely used on arriving airplanes, can be collected for recycling as it trickles down the inclines. There are a few wrinkles to be worked out, such as the effective removal of air pollution from the terminal space, but my basic reaction to this design is, "why not?"[9]

Solar Cooling

One of the most appealing applications of solar electricity is for cooling, since it works best exactly when it's needed. Several car companies, including Saab-Scania, have prototypes that include

ENVIRONMENTAL PROTECTION DESIGNS
JIM STARRY
P.O. BOX 1939 BOULDER CO   80306

The Starport design would save fuel and reduce pollution by being compatible with natural elements such as gravity and weather conditions. Landing "uphill" and taking off "downhill" and in the direction the wind is blowing could cut airport fuel consumption in half, according to designer Jim Starry.

rooftop solar cell panels to run exhaust fans while the car is parked. On a hot day, temperatures inside a parked car can reach 200 degrees, which places a considerable burden on the energy-intensive air conditioning system when the driver returns. But solar-powered exhaust fans can cut those temperatures in half, making use of otherwise wasted cartop surfaces.

Similarly, imagine a solar fountain, as conceived by John Todd: "The fountain can be powered by solar cells that drive the pump which lifts the water in the air. The brighter and hotter the sun, the higher and faster the plume."[10]

Renaissance Trees and Porous Pavers: Pollution Controls That Are Living

The informed use of trees and other plants may well be humanity's single best biologic-based strategy for energy, water, and soil conservation, as well as pollution reduction.

At the United States Department of Agriculture (USDA) labs, researchers are focusing on a wide variety of useful industrial

Biologic

Why not use automobile roof surfaces for solar panels? These panels can
power devices such as exhaust fans to keep interior temperatures cool when
the car is parked. *Photo courtesy of Saab-Scania of America, Inc.*

applications of plants, ranging from natural adhesives to time-
release organic pesticides. One Amazonian tree, the copaiba, produces burnable fuel of diesel quality in much the same way that
maple trees produce syrup—except the fuel doesn't need to be
boiled down! A fast-growing bamboo-like plant, kenaf, shows
great promise as a more efficient source of wood pulp than commonly used pine or fir.

In urban environments, trees are the Renaissance men of the
landscape, providing natural air-conditioning, air-pollution filtra-
tion, soil erosion control, and aesthetic backdrop all at once. The
average tree, according to Worldwatch Institute, absorbs enough
carbon dioxide in its life to offset driving a car 26,000 miles. In
Stuttgart, West Germany, city planners made use of trees and pre-
vailing wind patterns to "funnel" air pollution out of the city. Along
Colorado highways, trees are being used as "living snow fences"
to keep deep snow accumulations from drifting onto roads and to
keep snowmelt on ranch land where it can do some good.

Another new idea in urban ecology is that of "porous pavers" for
roads and parking lots. Enlightened city planners have discovered
that road materials with a high porosity (such as asphalt containing

large aggregate, making the pavement into "peanut brittle") can do several things at once: permit water to soak into the ground beneath the road or parking lot, prevent the rapid runoff of chemical-containing sediments into city waterways, and prevent flooding. Several companies make "turf blocks," which allow a surface to be part concrete, part grass. Turf blocks aid water infiltration and also help anchor a city's runaway summer temperatures.

Going with the Flow Is Cheaper

What's the common thread in these design strategies, from radial airports to living snow fences? They conserve energy and resources by using natural systems effectively. They have very few negative impacts on humans and ecosystems. They go with the flow. The examples given throughout this book are not necessarily panaceas—a given challenge may require a whole cluster of them, woven together like a tapestry. The illustrations offered here are only a small selection of some of the available threads. Because of their color, vibrancy, and natural compatibility, they are *useful, satisfying* solutions. We'll do well to use strategies like these because we can stay out of trouble with them. But the fact is, they are also money-savers, and as market analyses continue to reveal, their potential as money-*makers* is wide open. As Ted Flanigan of the Rocky Mountain Institute explains, "People don't yet realize that an investment in some of these technologies—like compact fluorescent bulbs and low-flush toilets—has a payback which out-competes stocks and bonds." Watch the stock market in coming years: Recyclers, organic produce suppliers, renewable energy companies, and small companies with "smart" gadgets will do well. (Chapter 5 looks more closely at the economic opportunities of biologic.)

The manufacture of products, the control of insects, the conservation of water, and the treatment of waste products all need to move toward a goal of *natural compatibility*. In each of these areas, there is some good news to report. For example, a recent *New York Times* article reported that the number of biological pesticides approved by the EPA for the market has doubled since 1981 to more than forty. In 1988 the USDA for the first time registered more biological pesticides than chemical ones. Industry analysts predict sales of biologicals might total $55 million in 1995. In fact, the total sales of three companies (Mycogen, Eco-

City pavements permit pollution to run off into streams and rivers, killing wildlife and contaminating drinking water supplies. "Porous pavers" allow precipitation to go into the ground where microbes can break down the chemicals. This design can also help keep a city cooler. *Photos courtesy of National Concrete Masonry Association.*

gen, and Crop Genetics International) that use a bacterial pathogen, *Bacillus thuringiensis*, are already approaching $40 million. Meanwhile, sales of chemical pesticides fell from $4.6 billion in 1982 to $4.1 billion in 1987, according to the U.S. International Trade Commission.[11]

Out Standing in Their Fields

Wes Jackson, a veteran of alternative, biologic-type thinking, has devoted his career to finding sustainable ways of farming that don't result in erosion, pesticide runoff, and soil depletion. One of the more promising developments at Jackson's Land Institute in Kansas is his work on perennial grains—which wouldn't have to be replanted every year.

Jackson believes that wilderness is the standard against which we should judge our agricultural practices. By creating a low-input "polyculture," wherein a prairie-like natural system could be harvested on a sustainable basis, we could achieve some very desirable goals:

- Virtually eliminate soil erosion (by keeping the soil covered year-round).
- Reduce energy consumption for seed bed preparation and cultivation.
- Reduce the need for pesticides and fertilizers (due to the broad genetic base and natural disease resistance of polyculture).

Several growers in the Practical Farmers of Iowa are experimenting with a different kind of polyculture: strip inter-cropping. This technique brings the diversity of the vegetable garden out into the fields. Instead of planting huge rectangles of a single crop, strip cropping takes advantage of natural synergies by planting six or eight rows of legumes, a second strip of small grains such as oats, and a third of corn. Because there are so many "outside rows," the sun-loving corn crop grows more productively, benefitting the following year by growing in the nitrogen-rich soil prepared by the leguminous crop. Far from being a factory, strip cropping is an ingenious, biologic system that controls pests, conserves water, prevents erosion, optimizes sun and nutrients *by design*.

With these visionary concepts, Jackson and the Practical Farmers are really only one step beyond the many blossoming fields of low-input, organic farming, a movement that a recent *Wall Street Journal* article characterized as "back to the future." (See Chapter 3 for more on sustainable agriculture.)

The Pollution Prevention Path: Biologic in the Mainstream

Remember the marching broomsticks in Mary Rodgers' "The Sorcerer's Apprentice"? The word *design* is the incantation that can stop those bucket-carrying brooms, because if we design smart, we can get just as much water (or energy or consumer satisfaction) by carrying fewer buckets. Less bucket-carrying means less effort and less pollution.

Even the mainstream Environmental Protection Agency, until now a "fire-fighting" agency by necessity, has recently formed a forward-looking Office of Pollution Prevention to focus on tracking pollution back to its source and getting rid of it using modifications in design, process, and product. As ex-EPA Administrator William Reilly summarized, "Pollution prevention will increasingly become the measure against which all our policies and regulations are judged." EPA has recently implemented a program called "Design for the Environment" that examines such industries as printing and dry cleaning and looks at viable substitutes for hazardous inputs.

World Resources Institute president Gus Speth envisions a completely new approach in the protection of the environment in the United States:

> Imagine an Environmental Protection Agency organized not strictly by air pollution, water pollution, pesticides, and so on, but by transportation, manufacturing, agriculture, energy, and housing. Today, EPA stands outside, imposing external "pollution control" standards. In the future, EPA must come inside, and environmental factors must be integrated into the basic design of our transportation, energy, and other systems.
>
> A new type of cooperation among the private sector, EPA, traditional Cabinet agencies, and environmental advocates must be forged. Together, they must work "upstream" to change the products, processes, policies, and pressures that give rise to pollution.[12]

A New Recipe: The Leaning of America

The same society that places a social premium on health and slimness is beginning to admit to obesity in the society at large. In effect, the culture itself is poorly designed, to consume quantity rather than quality. Yet if we resolve to jam less "junk food" through our economy, we can instantaneously be leaner and less prone to diseases (and pollution) without having to fret over it. Pollution control equipment is the environmental equivalent of expensive home exercise equipment. To a certain extent, each accomplishes the same design goal—to trim away fat and pollution. But this type of solution is really too much work, and it arrives too late, like a doctor caught in a traffic jam. It makes more sense, we're discovering, to monitor the ingredients: junk food in, poor health and obesity out. Any process that permits pollution to move right along with the product or service is out of shape.

Good intentions are like ice cream—they melt quickly. If we are going to make a difference, we have to *act* on our new design ideas, not just have them. To act, we'll have to overcome certain social barriers. For example, one reason we are still overweight as a culture—despite our good intentions—is that we've become biased against design simplicity. In order to make money, many products and services have complexity intentionally *added to them*. The fact is, simple goods and services have a hard time making huge profits on a per-unit basis. For example, it's difficult for farm supply companies to get excited about marketing the natural enemies of agricultural pests, since after they are set free, they "manufacture" themselves. But instead of selling just one product (such as pesticides), why can't companies make their money by marketing *expertise* that anticipates and identifies pest outbreaks and prescribes a whole spectrum of biological and physical controls?

A basic media-fed bias against simplicity in design is that if something is simple, isn't it old-fashioned? As if fashion should honest-to-God be the major criterion when we are facing globally scaled disasters, such as the loss of one planetary species or more per week, and the carbon dioxide "quilting" of the earth's atmosphere! The only kind of fashion we really need recognizes the genius of simplicity. (Once a simplified, ecological design ethic is more fully evolved, fashion and function will once again be partners, and our society can be powered by peer pressure alone.)

The most compelling reason for encouraging design simplicity is not to save energy or to spare ourselves minor inconvenience, but to avoid fouling up the inherent complexity of natural systems. (We haven't seen inconvenience yet!) We simply don't know enough at this stage (and probably never will) to second-guess nature—tinkering with nutrient cycles, using inappropriate farming practices, blithely reconfiguring genetic material, and causing the disappearance of species by a wholesale eradication of their habitat. As ecologist Aldo Leopold reminds us in the classic, *A Sand County Almanac*, "The first rule of the tinkerer is to save all the pieces."[13]

We tend to look at future-planning as an altruistic activity: since we won't be here, we really only make these kinds of decisions to be kindly ancestors, right? But we may need to be a little more selfish in our approach to make sure it actually happens. So we're not designing a good future for our descendants—we're doing it for *ourselves*. By living and designing well in the present, we automatically provide for the future.

When the Going Gets Tough, the Tough Go Shopping

The "leaning of America" means lean, informed input—less money and fewer materials expended to do a given job. Conceptually, we've got to get beyond the notion that it's less sophisticated to use already here to meet many of our needs. Things like solar energy, natural pest control, and naturally existing molecules are not primitive—our understanding of how they work was primitive. Now that we're looking at things more systematically and comprehensively, it makes sense to tap into resources that have already had significant energy and natural intelligence built into them.

Until just recently, the trend has been completely in the other direction—how can we re-engineer nature to make it more profitable? Just as ecologically wise agriculture degenerated into agribusiness, our culture degenerated into nothing more than business. In the last forty years, annual advertising expenditures in the United States have skyrocketed from $3 billion in 1950 to $30 billion in 1975 to over an estimated $100 billion in 1990.[14] An estimated 62 billion pieces of third class junk mail found their way into American homes in 1988, along with millions of "catchy" TV and radio commercials.[15]

The ecological significance of this is staggering. In effect, this deluge of "junk information" is separating us from directly experiencing the environment and from making quality decisions about it. There's a double message in American-style advertising: the good life is *out there* (we can see it right there on our screens), but it can't be attained unless we buy precisely the right mix of products. And we can't do that because the products keep bobbing up and down, like multiple targets in a penny arcade. Enough is never enough.

Wendell Berry writes, "By inducing in them little panics of boredom, powerlessness, sexual failure, mortality, paranoia, Americans can be made to buy (or vote for) virtually anything that can be attractively packaged."[16] Commercial success, American-style, *demands* helplessness. Advertising intentionally jams our signals so we'll remain dependent on products rather than nature and our own resources.

The economic reshuffling of America is graphically reflected in rising insurance premiums and taxes. For example, between 1970 and 1987, state and local taxes skyrocketed from $136 billion to $656 billion, while total federal tax receipts went from $193 billion to $909 billion. These hidden costs are picking up the tab for environmental cleanup and the other effects of a hyper-society.[17]

Backwards Progress

In the same forty-year post-war period that saw the explosion of advertising, taxes, and insurance, pesticide use increased fifteen-fold, yet crop damage remained about the same. Furthermore, insects had the evolutionary opportunity to become resistant to many chemicals. In 1938, only seven insect and mite species were known to be resistant to pesticides, but by 1984 that figure had climbed to about 450, including most of the world's major pests. Herbicide resistance in weeds was not really a factor before 1970, but since then at least fifty weed species have become resistant. (Both insects and plants have millions of years of experience when it comes to chemicals—substances like caffeine, nicotine, and opium are simply plants' evolved innovations to deter pests. The insects, meanwhile, have evolved the ability to tolerate compounds like caffeine. Like certain misdesigned pesticides, these natural compounds just seem to give them an energy boost as they buzz through their workdays.)

In the 1930s, U.S. production of synthetic organic chemicals for things like plastics, solvents, and various product ingredients was around one million tons. By 1985, that output had increased to 250 million tons, and it is doubling every seven or eight years.

One of the more visual illustrations of the changes that took place after World War II are the observations of cultural historian Thor Heyerdahl:

> In 1947, when the balsa raft Kon Tiki crossed 4,300 miles of the Pacific in 101 days, we on board saw no trace of man until we spotted an old wreck of a sailing ship on the coral reef where we landed. The ocean was clean and crystal clear. In 1969 it was therefore a blow to us on board the raftship Ra to observe from our papyrus bundles that entire stretches of the Atlantic Ocean were polluted. We drifted slowly past plastic containers, nylon, empty bottles and cans. Yet most conspicuous of all was the oil. The surface was littered with small clots of solidified black oil, ranging in size from that of a pinhead or a pea to that of a potato.[18]

"Ill-logic" is not a rare commodity in this country. Our food packaging industry, which now makes more net profit than do the farmers who *grow* the food, invented a plastic masterpiece of a package that will permit a shelf life of six months, a microwave cooking time of two minutes, and a landfill lifespan of two hundred years or more. The disposable diaper that will be used for two hours is engineered to withstand the presence of ammonia and uric acid, but as a result, its structure may remain intact long after baby's great grandchildren are dead.

We have spent untold billions on nuclear energy subsidies, yet we can't muster the political will to effectively subsidize renewable energy sources, fibers and fuels derived from agricultural surplus, or sensible transportation schemes. For all the research and development of renewable energy, we currently spend less than one-third of the projected cost of a single Stealth bomber. Simply by reaching consensus on what is socially desirable, we can remove counterproductive subsidies and institute socially and ecologically positive ones. That's the overall aim of this book—to discuss what's socially desirable and technically achievable.

At a recent conference on nuclear winter, Carl Sagan lamented that during the course of the U.S./Soviet Cold War, ten trillion dollars was spent on military infrastructure by each country. When asked by a conference participant what that kind of money would have bought in terms of buildings, schools, hospitals, and farms, Sagan responded, "Everything."

Our misguided expenditures carry through to almost every sector of our culture. We spend millions on biotechnology research to engineer "better" life forms, but very little for the inventory of *existing* species that have evolved nature-certified solutions to pest control, medical, and many other problems. We spend billions on space research, but very little to research "alien" locales right here on our own planet, such as the oceans, Antarctica, and the rain forests. These earthly wildernesses play *major* roles in planetary dynamics, yet we know very little about them. (We know more about moon rocks than about many of the earth's species.)

The ill-logical list goes on forever. We all sense that it is longer than we really have lifetimes or patience to learn about. It's a list filled to the brim with contradiction, cross purposes, vested interest, wasted effort, and short-sighted goals.

Carrying Capacity: The Buck Stops Here

Our environment is being destroyed not by "*them*," but by *us*. It's not *they* who must protect things, but *we*. The small choices and demands we make on a daily basis accumulate to create the nearly unmanageable mess we now live with. One person's decision to drive to the park rather than walk seems insignificant, but what if everyone simultaneously makes the same decision? The park is no longer a pleasant place to be—it's a traffic jam surrounding a crowded park.

In a classic 1968 essay entitled "The Tragedy of the Commons," ecologist Garrett Hardin presented this highly relevant concept in terms of a village commons, where grazing has always been uncontrolled. Each additional animal has in the past resulted in a small increase in individual profit. The destruction of the commons from overgrazing is *shared*, however, so there is little incentive to stop destroying it. Each family keeps adding one more cow, even though it doesn't fatten up quite as quickly as it used to.

Look around you; there are tragedies such as these everywhere: acid rain, noise pollution, and urban sprawl. All of these result from small, oblivious decisions, magnified to a mega-monster level. To use ecological terminology, the carrying capacity of the commons is being violated. The central theme in many environmental problems is "too much of a good thing," without any thought of the consequences. Economist/futurist Hazel Henderson compares the obliviousness of the U.S. experience to a colony of termites in one beam of a house. Operating completely on beam-geography, beam-physics, and beam-assumptions, the termites eat their way into the sunlight just in time to see the house cave in. There was far more to the universe than just the beam, and there's far more to our environment than just a source of profit.[20]

According to Lester Brown, founder of the Worldwatch Institute, a critical global boundary was crossed thirty years ago when "the yields of the three basic biological systems (forests, seas, and grasslands) expanded less rapidly than population."[21] What has expanded to take up the slack is an increase in per capita use of fossil fuels and their by-products, such as fertilizer. Yet, as ecologist F.H. Bormann explains, petroleum is a very poor substitute for the services performed at no cost by natural systems. With the loss of solar-powered ecosystems, writes Bormann, "We must find replacements for wood products, build erosion control works, enlarge reservoirs, upgrade air pollution control technology, install flood works, improve water purification plants, increase air conditioning, and provide new recreational facilities. These substitutes represent an enormous tax burden, a drain on the world's supply of natural resources, and increased stress on the natural systems that remain."[22] These engineered substitutes are expensive, and they are generally far less effective. Isn't there a better way for people to make money than tearing things apart and building imperfect replicas?

For far too long we have naively relied on the rejuvenating capacities of soil, air, and water, right up to the boundaries of natural tolerance. When we ask nature to digest unnatural substances such as DDT or PCBs, we end up with Superfund sites, devoid of all life.

 **SPECIAL FOCUS**
Beefeaters

The eating habits of humans are almost as critical environmentally as the eating habits of microorganisms, but unlike microbes, humans have the capacity to be illogical. (Writer Wendell Berry has commented that humans are the world's only species with the capacity to do more in our own behalf than is necessary.)

We ingest fifty tons of food per average lifetime. The pathway of that food from field to table is one filled with environmental horror stories, when fertilizers, pesticides, antibiotics, soil erosion, transportation, and water use are all factored in. American agriculture represents a tremendous opportunity for applied biologic. The recent trend away from cholesterol-heavy red meat in response to medical data indicates that lifestyle changes *can* play a major role in reducing environmental destruction.

But there's still plenty of room for improvement in beef production and use. A single pound of beef, for example, represents the pass-through of 2,500 gallons of water. Roughly one-third of North America is the exclusive domain of cattle; more than half of the water consumed in the U.S. goes into livestock; and two-thirds of the cropland produces animal feeds, such as corn, soybeans, and alfalfa.[23] About 40 percent of the antibiotics used in the United States are fed to livestock.

Before World War II, most beef came from grass-fed animals, an effective use of a resource that human stomachs can't digest directly. But since the 1940s, the cattle industry has been in the habit of feeding "people food" to cattle to fatten them up quickly and meet the labeling requirements for "USDA Choice Grain Fed Beef" (requirements based largely on palatability rather than nutritional value).

Today, cattle are typically housed in crowded feedlots for an intensive four-month period and treated to a pre-slaughter eating spree that is stimulated by growth hormones and antibiotics. Feedlots cause surface and groundwater pollution from stockpiled manure, and they misuse U.S. farmland. The protein content of the grains that are force-fed to cattle would be eight times more efficiently used if humans ate them directly. In addition, grain production for feed uses over seventy million pounds of pesticides and twenty-one million tons of petroleum-based fertilizer per year.[24] The cow's impact is not limited to North American feedlots. In South and Central America, huge areas of rain forest are being cleared to provide cattle pasture that remains usable only for three or four years. According to Worldwatch Institute's Alan Durning, "Every time an American eats a Honduran hamburger, he or she effectively cuts a kitchen-sized swath in the jungle."

More than a billion humans could be fed by the grain and soybeans eaten by U.S. livestock. Worldwide, cattle-ranching makes a major environmental impact. *Illustration by Kevin Bachman.*

In many tropical forests, the majority of an ecosystem's nutrients is contained in the trees and vegetation. When the plants are burned off to clear farmland (adding carbon dioxide to the atmosphere), the remaining soil is depleted and forms a hard, concrete-like surface. Species are disappearing faster than they can be identified. (Burning the forest for several years' grazing is a bit like using a Picasso painting as fuel for a Sunday afternoon barbecue.)

In Africa, the impacts from cattle are no less dramatic—deserts are expanding in the Sahel region and elsewhere on the continent, and cattle are largely to blame, as Paul Ehrlich explains in his excellent ecology book, *The Machinery of Nature:*

> Cattle must walk daily to a water supply to drink. This consumes a good deal of energy and slows the rate at which they gain weight. It also results in the trampling of valuable grasses and compacting of the soil surfaces, especially around water holes. On the other hand, wild herbivores have much less need to drink. Some probably do not have to drink at all, obtaining all the water they require from the vegetation they eat.
>
> Most native African herbivores also conserve water much more efficiently than cattle. For example, nearly all of the moisture is extracted from the intestinal contents of gazelles before their dry feces are released. Cow pats, in contrast, are produced moist, and they quickly lose ammonia (a gas containing the vital nutrient nitrogen) to the

atmosphere. Cow pats also dry rapidly in the sun and heat up, killing the bacteria and fungi that might speed up their decomposition. The flat, dried cow pat also kills the grass beneath it. On the other hand, the dry fecal pellets of antelopes are roughly spherical. They fall between the grass blades, do not heat up, and retain their nitrogen. Rather than tending to create a "fecal pavement" as cattle droppings do, the pellets are readily broken down by decomposers, returning the nutrients to the soil.[25]

Ehrlich's study of ungulates' habits and even their dung is highly relevant to this book's theme for several reasons. First, it is a graphic illustration of the need to fit culture to nature. Imported cattle are simply not a good biologic choice for these dry African regions. Second, the native African animals offer a model of efficiency for our own society, which needs to move toward complete use of all resources. We need to mimic these native species, which ingeniously conserve resources and pro- duce "intelligent wastes."

Because of the innate, evolved superiority of native animals in "living lightly on the land," various experiments in ranching them have been conducted in Africa. On the 20,000-acre Hopcraft ranch near Nairobi, a mixed population of gazelles, elands, antelopes and other quadrupeds has been fenced in and harvested on a reg- ular basis. Besides ecological sustainability, game ranching offers clear-cut cost savings in water supplies (and wells, dams, piping, and so on) as well as measures to prevent parasites and diseases to which native species have evolved resistance. However, Ehrlich points out that if game ranching is to be successful, a market must be created for such products as antelope jerky, which he describes as "addicting."

Similar experimentation is underway in Latin America, where indigenous species such as alligators are being farmed to provide a feeding efficiency of one pound of meat produced for each pound and a half of food consumed. This ratio compares favorably to cattle's inefficient ratio of 1:7.

In the United States, we may not be quite ready for gatorburgers, but we have been expressing consumer interest in leaner beef and chemical-free "organic" beef. Mel Coleman, a rancher in Saguache, Colorado, has established a $19 million niche in the marketing of natural beef from range-fed cattle that are not fed any chemical addi- tives "from conception to consumption."[26] Coleman's impetus came from the complaints of his daughter-in-law, who wanted to be able to buy meat free of chemicals and hormones.[27] Although the natural beef industry comprises less than 1 percent of the total beef industry, Coleman's success demonstrates that consumers are willing to pay more (25 percent more in Coleman's case) for a product they perceive as superior. The biologic of natural beef is clear: range feeding is what cattle have done for millennia, it results in fewer costly inputs, such as antibiotics, and it avoids water pollution as well as human consumption of potentially toxic compounds.

The natural beef market is also an example of a positive change that reflects consumer tastes rather than available technologies and constrictive standards. Yet because the cattle industry is so closely linked to the USDA grading system that favors "marbled beef," and because 70 percent of the nation's beef comes from three agricultural conglomerates, significant change will almost certainly be very slow. As Coleman expresses it, "It's like doing a 90-degree turn with an enormous ship; it can't move that quickly."[28]

Wrong Side Up

The poultry industry has many of the same characteristics as the beef industry. About 90 percent of our eggs come from a few large companies that raise one species of bird—leghorns. What happens if this single "basket of eggs" falls victim to a virus for which leghorns have no immunity?

As for crops, out of a potential 80,000 edible species, humans routinely use only about thirty, with the "big four"—wheat, rice, corn, and potatoes—meeting more than half our nutritional needs.[29] It doesn't appear that we're exercising our options. In fact, we are limiting them unalterably by erasing unused species from the face of the earth. Several years ago, some horticulturalists came across a genetic gem in Mexico: about an acre's worth of wild perennial corn, which could unlock the door to a corn crop that would not have to be reseeded every year. But that acre was surrounded by land that had already been cleared. Who knows how many useful species have gone under in the last thirty or forty years for the sake of teakwood coffee tables and super burgers?

Using land for its appropriate purposes is fundamental to the notion of biologic. Recent history is littered with experiments that didn't work, from peanut growing in Eastern Africa to the importation of the kudzu vine into the southern United States, where its voracious appetite is infamous. Misuse of land in the Great Plains created the Dust Bowl of the 1930s, as Stewart Udall pointed out in *The Quiet Crisis*: "Many regions west of the 100th meridian should never have been plowed at all: the familiar pattern of farming in the East was out of place in a region of little rain. In this country of half steppe, half desert, the soil was anchored to the land by grass. Once the plains were plowed, the dry, upturned soil had no protection against the driving winds."[30] Put simply, we weren't using biologic. Wes Jackson of the Land Institute tells the story of a Sioux Indian watching settlers "unzip" the prairie sod a hundred years ago. "Wrong side up," the native is said to have commented, shaking his head.

Jackson noted that corn grows best east of the 100th meridian (which cuts the Dakotas, Nebraska, and Kansas into halves) where *tall grass* prairie had evolved before humans intervened. West of that meridian, wheat is better suited, as evidenced by the climax of *short grass* prairie in that region.

Reading the physical and cultural features of a region is a discipline that now has a name, and is rapidly gaining a following in America. What *bioregionalism* can do for us is turn the tide on this country's irrational homogeneity. We are learning that it is *not* biorational for Phoenix and Denver to have bluegrass lawns, particularly when they commandeer water from remote water basins to support the lawns. Nor is it biorational to use adobe brick in northern Minnesota or to plant citrus trees in Illinois.

Burgeoning Bioregionalism

One dubious advantage to living in a squarish state like Colorado or New Mexico is that it fits so conveniently on the TV screen for statewide weather reports. Yet as any Colorado vacationer knows, Denver is simply not the same kind of place as Aspen or Grand Junction. The evolving discipline of bioregionalism acknowledges and celebrates these physical, biological, and cultural differences. At the same time, it acknowledges that because there is such great diversity on the planet, there should also be diversity in the designs and devices we use.

In *The Green Alternative*, Brian Tokar writes, "Within a bioregion, people can strive to create self-supporting ways of life that fully complement the flows and cycles of nature that already exist there. The sharing of goods and culture between bioregions then becomes a genuine expression of ecological diversity."[31]

Emphasizing the physical traits of a place, Ian McHarg writes,

> If you can identify what the land use is—whether it is a new town,
> an atomic reactor, a sewage plant, a highway, a single house or gar-
> den—you can identify what is most propitious for that thing or that
> person or community in terms of factors of climate, bedrock geology,
> surficial geology, physiography, hydrology and limnology, soils,
> plants, animals, and land use. If you can identify all these needs, you
> can find the most propitious location. It can be done in a handcraft
> way or we can ask the computer to find those places where all these
> factors exist.[32]

There are about 40 distinct types of places in this country, including roughly 700 soil regions, 17 major watersheds, and 97 water val-
leys.[33] When the climatic factors of longitude and latitude are
factored in, this makes for an incredibly diverse national landscape.
Bioregionalists maintain that we should *honor* and preserve that
diversity, because it is what gives our lives texture and meaning.

Certainly, Houston, Texas, and Boise, Idaho, offer different
options in terms of what will grow there, what the best architecture should be, what residents can do for recreation, and so forth.
Yet walking through the Boise airport is essentially the same visu-
ally as walking through the Houston airport, just as eating in a
restaurant in each place is pretty much the same experience.

Only by knowing what Boise *is* can we protect and maintain its
environment. Where does its water originate? Which way does the
wind blow? What industrial or agricultural activities are the *best fit* in
Boise, taking into account soil types, geographical location and
transportation, availability of resources, and other real-world characteristics? The activities that fit will be far more likely to operate
without creating polluting by-products. For example, apples seem
to fit growing conditions in Oregon, evidenced by a relative lack of
pests on the crop. But peaches are a different story—great volumes
of pesticide are required to protect the peach crop. In western Colorado, it's just the opposite: peaches are more self-reliant, while apple
orchards are plagued by pests. Clearly, each state needs to encourage its fruit growers to plant the crop best suited to that region.

A basic tenet of bioregionalism is that "any region that exploits
another region for its own profit is out of balance." Thus, Denver's
ongoing squabble over whether or not to build the Two Forks
Dam on the South Platte River is a moot point. From a biologic perspective, the dam would siphon water from another bioregion

(Colorado's Western Slope) to make the Front Range something it isn't and would have major downstream impacts on a third bioregion (the Great Plains region, where the South Platte flows through Nebraska).

Like all bioregions, the high plains zone in which Denver is located offers opportunities to put bioregionalism to work. The things that make Denver unique, such as the dry climate and high altitude, are the very things that can best be applied as ground rules for its environmental protection. For example, carbon monoxide (CO) is an especially troublesome pollutant in Denver because the air is comparatively thin and the lack of oxygen results in poor combustion. Problem-solvers in the area have applied bioregional types of solutions to help the problem. One is the mandatory use of oxygenated fuels during the high pollution winter season, a program that has achieved noteworthy reductions in carbon monoxide. These fuels consist of specified percentages of ethanol (made from corn) or MTBE (a petrochemical), both of which help the combustion problem caused by Denver's mile-high location.

Other carbon-monoxide-reducing strategies examine the overlap of climate, physical structure, and time. Don Barbarick, of the Colorado Health Department, is especially innovative in his approach. For several years, Barbarick has advocated that Denverites "outwit" air pollution by adjusting daylight savings time. By permitting sunset to take place at 6:00 rather than 5:00 in the dead of winter, carbon monoxide could be reduced substantially. Here's why: when the winter sun sets in Denver, the temperature can drop twenty degrees in a matter of minutes, trapping cold air down where people breathe it. A delayed sunset would permit commuters to get out of the city before that temperature drop.

Another of Barbarick's observations is that cold cars are polluting cars until their engines warm up. He proposes eliminating parking lots shaded by high-rise buildings. Under this plan, only cars with fuel injection or engine warmers (to be plugged in at the lot) could park in cold, shaded lots. All other vehicles would have to park in the sunny, well-ventilated areas that lie in the southern sector of the city.

The use of sand for traffic safety after a snowfall is another ingredient in Denver's soupy air, contributing as much as 15 percent to its "brown cloud"; the sand shatters into dust and gets kicked into the air by traffic, street sweepers, and wind. The city is investigating a biologic substitution of a harder grain of sand that won't shatter.

A bioregional group in Austin, Texas, wanted to make better use of a renewable resource, the mesquite tree. Although the wood is dense and durable, the tree grows shrublike and spindly, and does not lend itself to conventional lumber uses. Starting from a bioregional perspective, the group investigated two "sister" locations, the Argentinian and Uruguayan pampas, where they discovered that mesquite is extensively used in parquet floor tile. The group, known as the Center for Maximum Potential Building Systems, is looking into this use of mesquite and sharing techniques it developed for making wooden bricks out of mesquite sawdust.[34]

Bioregionalism is the game board on which biologic is played. Knowing the characteristics of a place is the first step in deciding *how* to live there. What devices are needed? What resources can be used on a sustainable basis? What does the history of a region tell us about its future? How many people can live there and at what level of consumption?

The Earth Is Shy:
It's Not Used to So Many People

Bioregionalism offers a conceptually concrete tool for dealing with the granddaddy of environmental problems, overpopulation. In *One Life At a Time, Please*, Edward Abbey rhapsodizes on the near-perfection of the Northern California bioregion, if only there were fewer humans in it:

> Imagine a Northern California where one-half of the human population suddenly, magically, painlessly disappears. Vanishes, like a bad dream. Imagine the results. Rents go down. The price of a house or condo drops through the floor. The cost of land goes down. Small farms and ranches again become available to the poor but enterprising. Food, clothing, wheels, gadgets go down in price. But at the same time there is an increased demand for labor, skilled and unskilled, in essential industries, such as the production of food and fiber; wages go up. And everywhere, in the towns, cities, and countryside, open space appears: the streets and roads are no longer jammed, the parks and forests and beaches no longer crowded. The decibel level goes down by half. The air becomes clear and clean again. Mountain streams, perhaps after a time even some rivers, become pure enough to drink from.[35]

Physicist Al Bartlett would agree with Abbey, but he is troubled by the prospects of *arriving* at a sizable reduction in population.

In lectures at the University of Colorado and elsewhere, he points out wryly that everything we regard as good (from the left-hand column below) makes our population problem worse, while many things that are regarded as socially undesirable (from the right-hand column) make it better:

Population

Peace	Abortion
Law and order	War
Scientific agriculture	Disease
Accident prevention	Murder
Medicine	Famine
Environmental protection	Pollution

Bartlett concludes that nature will choose from the right-hand column unless we choose some things not on the menu: birth control and voluntary limitations on growth.

Population is no longer just "something that happens to us." Either we control it, or we will be controlled by it. Interestingly, Paul Ehrlich has pointed out (in *New World, New Mind*) that the entire world population could fit within an area the size of the city of Los Angeles and we'd still be able to bow to our neighbor.[36] The major problem, then, isn't *density* but resource misuse.

The integration of bioregions into global environmentalism is well summarized by Peter Berg, founder of the bioregional group Planet Drum: "All the planetwide pollution problems originate in some bioregion. It's the responsibility of the people who live there to eliminate the source of them. If you strike a five-finger chord—by promoting more community gardens, more renewable energy, accessible public transportation, sustainable agriculture—rain forests will stop getting chopped down in direct proportion."

Gaia—A Beautiful Woman

In 1605, the noted astronomer Johannes Kepler wrote, "My aim is to show that the celestial machine is to be likened not to a divine organism but to clockwork." For several hundred years, the western world had been fascinated with the clock, conceived by Benedictine monks to keep rigorous track of prayer obligations. It was the symbol of a new arrogance just coming into vogue in Europe, which Kepler and his colleagues exemplified. Using precise scientific methods, nature could be subjugated, and humans could happily ever after occupy an engineered throne. This exaggerated estimate of human power and judgment has dominated Western thought ever since.

One very hopeful sign of the transition back to a more realistic humility is James Lovelock's Gaia Hypothesis. This stunning theory suggests that the earth is *not* a clockwork but an organism (called Gaia, after the Greek earth goddess) capable of regulating life-sustaining parameters just as the human body does. Temperature, salinity, and the cycling of gases and essential minerals may all be part of a self-regulated living system, according to Lovelock.[37]

Ecologists have long been aware that life forms react to perturbing crises, resisting the assaults and trying to "stay afloat" by maintaining favorable survival conditions. But until Lovelock's theory surfaced, scientists did not view the entire planet from this perspective.

It is comforting to imagine that various forms of life, such as plankton and bacteria, can regulate methane cycles and remove excess carbon dioxide from the atmosphere, since these are the kind of skills that may come in handy if humans are stubborn enough to insist on "business as usual." Responding to quizzical inquiries about global warming and how it disproves his hypothesis, Lovelock recently shrugged his shoulders and answered, "She has a fever."

Apart from its spiritual or at least "deep ecology" elements (deep ecology is the school of environmentalism that insists the value of life forms is exclusive of their relation to humans), the Gaia Hypothesis puts needed focus on the idea of feedback mechanisms. In ecological terms, negative feedback is good since it corrects a situation that would otherwise get out of control. The standard example of negative feedback is a thermostat, which tells the furnace to come on when a house becomes too cold and to go off when the house is sufficiently warm. Population dynamics in nature have negative feedbacks. When the pest population of a crop starts to get too large, the natural enemy's population expands to control it. When hazardous wastes are finally perceived as a genuine threat to living systems, a cultural feedback in the form of regulations begins.

Sometimes, however, things go berserk, like a cancer that keeps receiving instructions to grow. At a cocktail party, the talking becomes slightly louder, so the guests start speaking even more loudly. A highway becomes crowded, so the city council votes to build *more* highways, which will also become crowded. A certain pesticide doesn't seem to be working, so increasingly larger volumes are sprayed, resulting in pest resistance. Global warming will increase energy demands for air conditioning, which will in turn increase global warming.

These and other positive feedback loops now running wild throughout our world *seem* to call out for engineered solutions. But like increasing the dose of an ineffective pesticide, these solutions often just add to the problem. A central theme for our times is expressed by bioregionalist Peter Berg when he asks, "Should we try to bend nature to our will, or conversely, control ourselves instead?"

Obviously, we need to let our own negative feedback systems operate so that as the party gets cooking, we acknowledge the noise and lower our voices to normal levels. When a city becomes too frantic, we need to close off some of the streets to through traffic, as the city of Berkeley has done, or limit the amount of new residential construction, as Boulder has done.

Are we part of Gaia's self-regulating strategy? Is our evolving awareness of feedback loops coming about just in the nick of time? One of humanity's greatest strengths—its adaptability—could also be a weakness from the perspective of negative feedbacks. A French high school experiment provides an objective look at what might be happening in our culture. Students placed a frog in very hot water, and it immediately jumped out. When placed in lukewarm water, however, the frog adapted as the water's temperature increased and eventually became frog's legs.

We're not frogs, of course. We're just concerned people, emerging from an underground tunnel to discover that the terrain on the far side is familiar, in a déjà vu kind of way. Things work, we remember that part. If we let them, they work. That is the *bio* part of biologic.

In South America, a certain plant has "learned" to coat its seeds with a sweet substance of great interest to ants. The ants carry the seeds underground, eat the substance, and unintentionally plant the seeds. The unerring blindness of the system is fascinating. It works because it works.

The *logic* part of biologic involves the wise use of resources, and brains are up near the top of our list of resources. What is the most pressing thing for our brains to be doing as we head en masse into the next century? As a first, relatively painless priority, we need to focus on eliminating unnecessary junk from our "social diets." Economist Hazel Henderson has remarked that "the U.S., with the richest and most wasteful economy, is in the most advantageous position to cut out flab without cutting into muscle." While the Japanese recycle half their trash, we recycle a mere 10 percent. West Germany and Sweden use about half as much energy per capita as we do, and Great Britain uses only a fifth as much water per capita. We've got some flab to cut out, that's a fact.

In conjunction with our quest for technological fitness, we need to remember that life is a process, not a product. As Ghandi phrased it, "There's more to life than increasing its speed." As our technology-craving fingers continue to look for something to play with, our creativity-seeking, designer brains must remind the fingers that it's okay to use "all natural" materials and methods. To design technologies that run *counter* to natural laws is not only wasteful, it's futile.

These themes are explored in the chapters that follow as we trace the evolution of biologic from theoretical to pragmatic. We will progress from environmental awareness (*Knowing*) and individual action (*Choosing*) through social and technical experimentation (*Designing*) that bears fruit in the mainstream of American society (*Implementing*). The overall objective is solutions that are workable, affordable, and capable of being accepted by middle America (even if that means marketing a new mind-set to *achieve* the acceptance).

The first step is knowing. Our brains are far more than two and a half pounds of cargo—they are the evolutionary device by which we will succeed or fail. Unless we bring a clear understanding of the natural world into our brains, we will inevitably project chaos onto the "movie screen" of nature.

CHAPTER 2

KNOWING

Coming up the front walk, we hear laughter and music—the party's in full swing. As we ring the doorbell, we hope one last time that we've brought the right gift and worn the right combination of clothes.

A lot of Americans seem apprehensive about our collective party. They want to be told exactly what to do to help protect the environment. In my opinion, the very first step is to understand how that environment works and what it needs. We should know what kind of party we've been invited to *before* we show up. Many of our products and technologies are as inappropriate for their bioregion or their intended use as pumpkins would be at a Christmas party or Frosty the Snowman at a Fourth of July parade.

Too much is catching us by surprise. We've filled our heads with quiz-show facts and talk-show comebacks rather than useful, fundamental knowledge. Most of us are well intentioned enough— we just lack the information and the consensus to put our intentions to work.

"I Got Killed in Vietnam,
I Just Didn't Know It at the Time"

So said a veteran, now dead, of the Southeast Asian war. By the time the long-delayed, cancer-causing effects of the defoliant Agent Orange were known, it was too late for this individual. But his poignant words spotlight a fundamental link in the chain of nature-based design: Unless we know what's *causing* a certain problem, our first-aid attempts can only react to symptoms, not prevent them.

Basically, human-caused pollution and environmental damage are due to a lack of information. We don't know enough about eco-logical systems, and we don't know which of our problems war-rants priority treatment. Where should we focus our attention, and where should we spend our money? What needs redesign *first*?

Since we tend to become caught up in routine ways of know-ing—standard operating procedures—we often overlook opportu-nities to make designs compatible with our basic needs. Instead of designing a process that utilizes "smart inputs," we continue to blunder along with an outmoded process because "that's the way we've always done it." For example, a manufacturer of ozone-depleting chemicals for fire extinguishers continued to spray-test the devices even though the chemicals' harmful effects were well known—simply because it was routine. ("There's no reason for it—it's just our policy.")

In *Gaia: A New Look at Life on Earth*, James Lovelock writes, "The remarkable success of our species derives from its capacity to collect, compare, and establish the answers to environmental questions, thus accumulating what is sometimes called conven-tional or tribal wisdom."[1] Different societies accomplish this goal in different ways. The bushmen of southern Africa have an extremely verbal tribal wisdom, closely linked to direct observa-tion. A tribesman can recall exactly where a kill was made years earlier, weaving this recollection into a story-told stream of infor-mation that benefits his tribe members.

In our society, we wouldn't be able to trace the origin of our din-ner if our lives depended on it. Yet we *need* to know about the pathways and cycles of chemicals, resources, and waste products to be able to create and choose products and systems that make ecological sense.

Designing something without first knowing basic ecology is like getting on a train without the name of the town you're going to.

Good design eliminates this kind of confusion, coherently answering a question it seems like everybody's been meaning to ask. It fits a felt need precisely, like a puzzle piece.

Returning to the Fork in the Trail

Because of the abundance of fossil fuels, rich topsoil, and stored-up groundwater, we got into the habit of substituting resources for skill and genuine expertise. But in *The Next Economy*, Paul Hawken predicts some basic changes:

> The mass economy is being replaced by an economy based on the changing ratio between the mass and information contained in goods and services. Mass means the energy, materials, and embodied resources required to produce a product or perform a service. While the mass economy was characterized by economies of scale, by many goods being produced and consumed by many people, the informative economy is characterized by people producing and consuming smaller numbers of goods that contain more information.
>
> What is this information? It is design, utility, craft, durability and knowledge added to mass. It is the quality and intelligence that make a product more useful and functional, longer-lasting, easier to repair, lighter, stronger, and less consumptive of energy.[2]

A few examples of information-packed design will help illustrate Hawken's point. A California group, Solar Box Cookers International, has been promoting an "appropriate technology"—solar ovens—for many years. Built out of insulated cardboard boxes and aluminum, these devices could be of great value to fuel-scarce Third World countries, and in fact they are catching on in some locations such as Guatemala, despite the cultural barriers. What really promises to make them indispensable is an inexpensive add-on that makes the cookers "smart." Many Third World residents need to purify water by heating it, but until a small straw-like device was invented to go on the solar cookers, these people could not be sure if the water had reached high enough temperatures to be pasteurized. The small device can tell them that. If the sun shines while they are away from the cooker, a lump of waxy material melts and flows to the other end of the straw, giving a conclusive indication that the water is safe to use.[3] Another illustration of Hawken's principle is the design of wind turbine blades, which until recently have been modelled after aviation propellers. The new generation of airfoils is being expressly designed for wind turbines, not airplanes. According to Solar Energy Research Institute's director H.M. Hubbard, the new designs will cause less drag, last twice as long, require less maintenance and produce more power—all because they will have more relevant, nature-based information in them.[4]

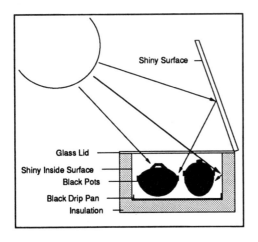

Solar box cookers are a good environmental design because they reduce deforestation, soil depletion, and air pollution. They can also be used to purify water, reducing intestinal diseases that kill millions of people every year. *Illustration courtesy of Solar Box Cookers International.*

A similar boost in design smartness is illustrated by the higher-strength construction materials now in use. A recent repair of the Eiffel Tower specified steel girders weighing only one-third as much as those used in the original construction a hundred years ago.[5] Another example is the emerging technology of evacuated vacuum windows, which achieve an insulating value nearly equivalent to that of a solid wall (more on these in Chapter 5). And the design of tires has radically improved since 1973, when radials came into popular use. The average life of a tire has doubled, dropping the annual contribution of tires to landfills by about a fourth.[6]

We're getting better! I still remember the first time a classmate hit a baseball over the centerfield playground fence. About a hundred of us had been playing baseball together for three or four years when suddenly Mark Mills broke the distance barrier in sixth grade. The two teams just stood there in disbelief, watching that ball sail over into that distant back yard. It was an undeniable sign that we were growing up. In the same way, our evolving regulations, designs, and attitudes are signs that as a culture *we* are growing up.

One of the biggest obstacles we face in putting intelligence back into our products and lives is the fencing-in of our own minds.

Water planners have been taught that the way to get water is to build dams and drill wells—in other words, increase supply. Power utilities have likewise seen their role as expansion in direct proportion to population increases and industrial growth. These frames of mind don't even acknowledge, let alone encourage, the possibility that we could save enormous amounts of water and power just by plugging leaks and upgrading appliances. There are ninety million households in America whose members need to be educated about efficient appliances and, ideally, given the right incentives to buy them. And there are somewhere between 100,000 and 200,000 contractors who need to change their habits about insulation, heating systems and glazings in buildings. Not only must individuals become enlightened about efficiency, but about the system as whole. Builders can make good choices only when when building codes, architectural specifications, departments of city governments, and schools of engineering *enable* those choices. So biologic is only as good as the education that brings it into the mainstream.

Recycling and "waste to energy" concepts are completely alien to many sanitary engineers, who have traditionally used bulldozers or smoldering fires to deal with trash. That's what they know how to do. In fact, this habit has extended into the realm of hazardous waste disposal, as Bruce Piasecki and Gary Davis explain:

> The evolution of hazardous waste management from garbage collection also helps explain America's long reliance on landfill disposal. Both the practitioners and regulators had long experience with landfill disposal; thus both parties were slow to address hazardous waste management as a chemical engineering problem instead of a dirt-moving one.[7]

The same oblivious mentality toward trash has resulted in syringes washing up on East Coast shores and hazardous pollution in the "limitless" space surrounding the earth. Thousands of objects left behind from previous space launchings are hurtling around the planet right at this moment at speeds of up to twenty-five miles per second. This space waste poses two major concerns to engineers and space scientists. "Debris the size of a marble can hit with the explosive power of a grenade," and radiation from cast-off reactors can cause false readings in scientific sensors.[8] The lesson that still needs to be learned is that you can't throw things away, because there *is* no "away."

Environmental protection by design will involve the recycling not only of products and worn-out hardware, but of companies, ideas, regulations, and institutions as well. From this recycling will emerge various types of "smart design" as well as many information brokers to keep these designs tuned up. We'll need reliable information about which biological strategies to use in agriculture; we'll need efficiency experts to audit and tune up our processes, from energy and water conservation through hazardous waste reduction; we'll need data bases and electronic bulletin boards to help form van pools, trade waste products, or exchange operating experience; we'll need environmental experts on our corporate staffs to keep track of regulatory compliance; and we'll need wide-angled professors in our colleges to build academic bridges between science, technology, art, engineering, and ethics.

In short, individuals like you and me can't be experts in everything, and the design upgrade that Hawken envisions will include many people who offer information rather than goods. At the same time, it appears that there is a trend toward more inter-disciplinary knowledge. Ecosystems are diverse, and human thinking must be broad-based to understand the social implications of a certain idea or design.

Knowing, then, is the first step in expanding America's narrow "tourniquet" approach to environmental protection. Fortunately, knowledge is an infinitely renewable resource. Resource, space, and ecological limitations may be lurking in the bushes, but there does not appear to be any limit to the ingenuity of the human mind.

Seeing Is Believing

Humans are exceptionally visual animals. We tend to believe what we can see, or at least sense. But many of our current environmental problems can't be perceived with the equipment we've been issued. We can't *see* ten parts per billion of Alar on an apple. And we can't directly sense the cause and effect of radiation exposure or of ozone depletion.

If something tastes "off" and we suspect it may be poisonous, we rely on evolution to have provided not only the recognition of that dangerous taste, but also quick enough reflexes to spit it out before it overcomes us. But what do we do about all those threats we can't sense?

We have to go far beyond what we can *see*. In New York State,

THE FAR SIDE By GARY LARSON

Early microbiologists

a 40 to 42 percent reduction in solid waste is mandated by 1997. The reason? Because there's no place to dump the trash. The Fresh Kills landfill site on New York's Staten Island is as massive as one of the Great Pyramids, with about two-thirds as many cubic feet in it as the Great Wall of China. It's now the second highest point on the Eastern seaboard, and rising. We react to tangible images like Fresh Kills and the "Garbage Barge" of 1988, but we need to take action much sooner. If we traced all the activities that led to the formation of the Fresh Kills mountain, we'd see clear-cut forests, streams filled with eroded soil, fish kills from industrial pollution, and on and on. Everything we do needs to have such tracers, linking up our activities with their unseen effects, like strings of causality.

In many cases, the technological extensions of ourselves (machines, chemicals, conduits) brought the environmental threats into our world, and it seems obvious that only by the use of *sensory* extensions of ourselves (air monitors, gas chromatographs, radioactive isotopes) will we perceive those threats. But can we really expect to solve all problems that we can perceive? And can we ever hope to perceive them all? We need elegant design that doesn't require vigilance, *not* ever-more sophisticated instruments.

What about problems that we are able to sense, but that take place over a long time period—such as soil erosion—and are therefore less likely to be perceived? How could we ever compare a good air quality day in Los Angeles with the memory of a good day back in the 1940s?

Having an automobile collision at thirty miles per hour has been likened to "diving head-first from a second story window," and the effect of smoking cigarettes has been graphically illustrated by showing an actual pair of human lungs with a quart of oil dumped over and inside them. We *know* there are risks involved in driving and smoking, but we are completely at sea when it comes to the thousands of other risks we encounter every day because we can't perceive them. The fact that our contact with them is involuntary makes us feel like things are out of our control, and we shout, "Not in my back yard!" when a waste treatment plant is proposed in our community. We're *against* the threat of involuntary risks, that's natural enough, but what are we *for*?

In *New World, New Mind: Moving Toward Conscious Evolution*, Robert Ornstein and Paul Ehrlich propose that our culture is moving faster than our evolved ability to understand it. "Our nervous systems are designed to make decisions based upon the presumption of a constant environmental framework," they write. Environmental planning and preventive problem-solving were not a priority in the evolution of humans, whose equipment instead has specialized in reacting to sudden, immediately perceivable threats: the snap of a twig in the forest or the sudden appearance of a bear silhouette in the shadowy entrance of a cave.[9]

As Tom Crum discusses in *The Magic of Conflict*, a lot of evolutionary effort has gone into our quick reflex.[10] In a stressful situation, we automatically receive the benefit of more than fourteen hundred physiochemical responses within seconds. Heartbeat increases to supply greater oxygen and glucose to every muscle in the body. Blood-clotting ability increases to handle potential wounds, eyes dilate for better visual ability, and the kidneys hold more water and sodium so blood volume can expand. All of these things happen when we are driving to work and someone swerves in front of us. Gastric juices, saliva, and adrenalin all start flowing immediately without our permission, and by the time we arrive at work, we're a mess. We can notice the difference when we start riding the bus, as I did three or four years ago. I no longer had to make fight-or-flight decisions, and I kept all my juices in the contemplative state. Yet even with my reflexes comfortably "tucked in," there was no way I could have known that the ozone layer was deteriorating over Antarctica.

The fact is, we can neither run from nor fist-fight ozone depletion: we've got to perceive cause and effect, and make constructive modifications up front. Because our biological evolution is much too slow to adapt us for the changes our culture is creating, Ornstein and Ehrlich call for the development of "slow reflexes," which will allow us to make long-term planning a possibility.

But we haven't yet gotten our technology in focus with our surroundings. The pictures we're taking are blurry ones, with pollution and stress in the foreground. We just don't know enough yet. We're still immature as a species, no matter how tall our high-rises are.

One thing is certain: what goes into our brains and what takes place in them will determine the future of the world as we know it. Already, our technologies and land uses have changed the world into a hive of human activity. As author Jerry Mander suggests, "We find ourselves living inside a kind of nationwide room.

Reprinted courtesy of the *Rocky Mountain News*.

Of all the species on the planet, we have become the first in history to live inside projections of our own minds."[11] If this is true, then we need to put pure wilderness back into our minds to keep our imaginations healthy. Not just for sentimentality's sake, but for survival. We're used to a mode of thinking that says, "I'll believe it when I see it." But as America moves into a less reactive, more anticipatory way of protecting the environment, we will increasingly acknowledge that we'll only "see it when we believe it." In other words, because we tend to see what we're looking for, we sometimes miss pieces of reality. When we finally concede that our rule book is outdated and constricts our creativity, we'll see all kinds of things we never realized were there—both good and bad.

Death and Disease:
Bricks of Environmental Awareness

Ignorance is pollution's best friend. Fortunately, mistakes generally make us smarter (and we *must* be getting pretty smart by now). Our biggest concern at this point should be over the social *acceptability* of remaining dumb. That is, will we continue to tolerate looking the other way? To do so may be profitable in the short run but suicidal in the long run. The examples offered in the pages to follow spotlight the behavior of a species caught fast in the currents of evolution. We're not always heroes, but we're not always villains, either.

Dying to Make a Living

According to documented corporate reports, the manufacturers of asbestos knew back in the 1930s that this naturally occurring mineral with incredible insulating and fireproofing properties was a significant health threat. But public awareness of this fact, and consequent regulatory action, did not begin to occur until much later, when suspicions turned into statistics and dead bodies. Asbestos workers at shipbuilding yards got lung disease in sufficient numbers to put the finger on asbestos, which had been treated with about as much caution as children give to snowflakes.

In 1958, a consulting chemist for Shell Oil found that Shell's pesticide DBCP represented a health hazard, particularly for the male reproductive system. But the research report was put away on a shelf and did not resurface until nearly twenty years later, when a group of workers at a DBCP production plant happened to compare notes about their coincidental inability to start families. It turned out that thirty-six out of thirty-eight of the men were sterile.[12]

The noted scientist Isaac Newton may have hit upon the force of gravity, but he didn't have a clue about the effects of heavy metals on humans. Suffering from severe insomnia, poor digestion, amnesia, depression, and paranoia, Newton in 1692 wrote a letter to colleague John Locke, blaming his maladies on "sleeping too often by my fire." Nearly three hundred years later, the cause of Newton's affliction may have surfaced after the analysis of several locks of surviving hair, passed down through the generations along with manuscripts and other relics:

> Over the years before his breakdown, Newton did many experiments in alchemy with a wide variety of metals, including lead, arsenic, antimony, and mercury. Most of the experiments involved heating the metals in large open vessels, in furnaces and over candles, undoubtedly exposing him continually to toxic vapors.
>
> Newton also had the early chemist's penchant for tasting the products of his experiments. On 108 separate occasions he recorded that he had tasted materials, whose flavors he described as ranging from "tastless," "sweetish," and "saltish," to "strong stiptic vitriolique tast."

Another source of toxic material may have been the dark red paint, with cinnabar (mercury sulfide) as its chief pigment, that had been freshly applied to the walls of his room in London at about the time of his breakdown.[13]

It's ironic that we can make 300-year-old deductions such as these but all too often overlook threats in our own lives. For example, even though lead has now been banned from most of its many prior uses, physicians continue to diagnose severe lead poisoning in children (especially inner-city children) who have eaten "sweetish" lead-based paint flakes from the peeling walls of tenement buildings.

Nobel Prize for Dumb DDT Design

The infamous pesticide DDT sat on a German laboratory shelf for sixty-five years before research chemist Paul Muller tried it out, hit-or-miss, as a possible bug killer. It killed bugs in true "Rambo" fashion, and humans didn't seem to be affected by it (that is, they didn't immediately keel over dead when exposed to it). So during World War II, DDT was widely used by Allied forces to control mosquitoes and lice to prevent malaria and typhus, getting an enthusiastic thumbs-up from everyone, including the Nobel committee, who awarded Muller its prize in 1948. Ten years later, this wonder compound was being used at the rate of eighty million pounds per year.

But there were many things we didn't know about DDT, such as its quirky biomagnification in the food chains of ecosystems. Because the compound is easily stored in fatty tissue, the predators at the top of the food chain can end up with dangerous concentrations of it from eating all the microbes and small animals that have stored DDT in *their* bodies. Eggshells of eagles, which had been preserved for other reasons, offered proof that DDT had long-term effects. In this case, the more DDT that was accumulated in eagles' bodies, the thinner their eggshells became, until survival of eagle chicks was becoming a rarity.

This unwanted persistence of DDT was first made public when robins were observed dying half a year *after* DDT application for the control of pests like gypsy moth. The birds exhibited the same tremors they had when DDT had poisoned them directly, and this visual clue was instrumental in the realization that DDT had outstayed its welcome by hitching a ride in the fatty tissues of soil microbes, worms, and then birds.

A classic story about the Dyak people of Borneo illustrates how one thing can lead to another when natural systems are not fully understood. DDT had been sprayed by villagers to control malaria-spreading mosquitoes. But other organisms also took in some of the spray, as the Dyaks would soon discover. The bodies of cockroaches living in the thatched huts absorbed enough DDT to kill their predators, the gecko lizards, when the roaches were eaten. Because the DDT became more concentrated at each level of the food chain, the bodies of these lizards then contained enough pesticide to kill the village's whole population of cats. When the cats were gone, woodland rats invaded the village at about the same time that the roofs on the village huts began mysteriously collapsing. The DDT had killed the parasites of caterpillars that liked to feed on the thatched roofs, and with no control on their population, the caterpillars took over. But the most serious threat was the rats that brought fleas and lice with them. To prevent an outbreak of the plague, hungry cats were parachuted into the area!

In sharp contrast to this tale of dark humor is a report from California about a tiny fish with a big appetite, which consumes mosquitoes by the millions. Since 1970, the use of pesticides for mosquito control has been reduced by more than 75 percent in that state, thanks to the massive introduction of the minnow-sized mosquito fish into sewage treatment ponds, roadside ditches, and animal watering troughs. The fish have "naturalized" into many additional habitats, such as abandoned swimming pools, rain barrels, stagnant rice fields, and tunnels. Recognizing a good thing, Disneyland uses the fish in aquatic exhibits and in storm drains.[14]

Which method of mosquito control has more high-quality information in it? Obviously, the second one. The natural control of mosquitoes is far more ingenious because it is tailor-made by evolution. As opposed to DDT, its focus is narrow and its purpose specific. DDT killed not only mosquitoes, but birds, fish, and mammals. It didn't fit in, and we can do better without it. (Some Third World countries, however, are still using DDT that the United States exported to them. Though DDT residues in humans and other organisms continue to decline, the problem has not yet disappeared.)

Foams, Explosions, and Smells

The chemists who stumbled onto the detergent properties of phosphates didn't realize that when waste washwater got into our streams and lakes, the nutrients would permit algae to have an orgy. They also didn't realize that detergents were "biologically stubborn"—until mounds of soapsuds started appearing in streams and, in some places, water drawn from taps foamed like beer. A similar connection was made between a leaking underground storage tank and gasoline-contaminated fish when a backyard barbecuer in South Dakota had the misfortune of watching fresh trout explode on the grill.

The full scope of the country's Dust Bowl in the 1930s was not politically perceived until red dust from the massive erosion blew past the windows of Congress in Washington. Citizens and tourists in the Caribbean were given the same alarming announcement in the 1980s when the sands of the African Sahel blew past—a recurring event that has been documented by astronauts orbiting the earth.

In 1348, the most prestigious medical institution of the day, the College of Physicians at the University of Paris, pronounced that the cause of the Black Plague was the conjunction of three higher planets in the sign of Aquarius. Jupiter, a warm and humid planet, had drawn up evil vapors from soil and water, and Mars, being very hot and dry, set fire to those vapors.[15] Another prevalent explanation was that the plague was caused by "foul odors," so many homes of the period burned juniper, rosemary, musk, and laurel. To walk through stricken areas of a town was treacherous unless one had a piece of burning amber along, smelling it constantly.[16]

A genuine environmental threat, sewage, was not perceived as a disease carrier until the nineteenth century, after Pasteur and his colleagues caught microbes in the act. Once sewage *was* given a bad name, toxic wastes, such as metal refinery discharges into rivers, were perceived by many to be a good thing since these wastes killed off the disease-spreading microbes and made the rivers "clean."

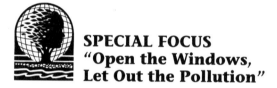

SPECIAL FOCUS
"Open the Windows,
Let Out the Pollution"

Like the people of the plague-ridden fourteenth century, our responses to many environmental threats are likely to be bound up in our current belief systems, fashions, and superstitions, no matter *what* data are available. We'll see threats when we believe they are there, but in many cases, not before.

For example, the data on indoor air quality say that our homes and other buildings—where we spend 80 to 90 percent of our time—are far more polluted than even the urban outdoor environment. Yet we continue to assume that city air—where the factories emit their waste products—is far worse. In fact, a survey of senior EPA officials ranked indoor air pollution as a greater health threat than both hazardous waste sites and outdoor air pollution. According to EPA indoor air expert Lance Wallace, "All our findings are showing that the small sources right under your nose—either the air freshener or the paint, even the hot shower, are causing high levels of exposure [to hazardous compounds]—much more than the manufacturing plant or the oil refinery down the street."

Where are these chemicals coming from? From combustion (gas stoves, water heaters, cigarettes), consumer products (paint, glue, cleaners, insecticides), and the building itself (sheetrock, particle-board, insulation). As a cross-section of America's "better living through chemistry," the American home has become an invisible showcase of molecular mischief.

Indoor air quality is the perfect example of humans battling unseen and unknown forces. In this case, the forces are micro-scopic bits of matter, such as asbestos from insulation and chloro-form from the tap water. A typical American home has far more going on in it than you or I would ever suspect. As sunlight begins to stream through the living room window, carpet fibers begin to undulate organically, as if sending some kind of signal to the many

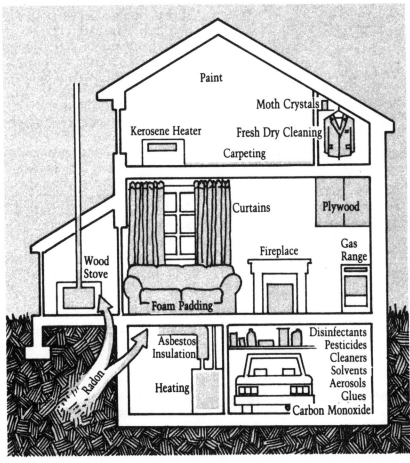

The best way to reduce indoor air pollution from various sources is to create and demand better design in our consumer products.

particles drifting in the airspace between floor and ceiling. Among those particles are tiny fragments of metals like shiny, toxic cadmium, iron, and manganese. Spots of radon explode tiny flashes of red as they radioactively decompose, and formaldehyde molecules begin to "off-gas" from the walls and furniture in direct proportion to rising temperatures and levels of humidity.

The quarter-million-pound house begins to expand, making barely audible cracking sounds in chorus with inaudible low-frequency groans from coat hangers, complaining about the weight of the clothes they must support. With the right instrument, the hissing of air escaping from the house can be heard, and close to two million dust mites can be observed cavorting in the typical cozy American bed, grazing on sloughed-off skin flakes.[17]

Analytical techniques have become so sophisticated in recent years that detection of parts-per-billion (ppb) is routine, with instruments such as the gas chromatograph/mass spectrometer. To put this sort of measurement in perspective, a single drop of coffee spilled into an Olympic-sized pool before a meet would still be detectable in ppb after the swimmers had thoroughly mixed the water up. A ppb is also equivalent to an inch in sixteen miles, or a minute in two years.

Because of the new analytical capabilities, researchers often become detectives, coming up with some very Holmesian deductions. By analyzing the contents of badge-like devices worn by volunteers, researchers can make educated guesses about the day's activities. For example, if heavy concentrations of benzene show up in the analysis, chances are good the volunteer either pumped his own gas while he was wearing the sampler or is a cigarette smoker. (Cigarette smoke also has more than two thousand other detectable substances in it, including arsenic and formaldehyde.)

Although indoor air pollution has always been a problem to some extent (thousand-year-old Eskimo mummies have black deposits on their lungs from breathing whale oil fumes), two recent developments have made the air in American homes less healthy. One is the proliferation of synthetic substances, and the other is the conscientious tightening and insulating of our homes, which prevents air exchange with the outdoors.

There are many troubling implications bottled up with the air quality in our buildings. One is that our immune systems are working overtime, trying to form antibodies to these domestic substances while we are supposedly relaxing in our living rooms. Another is that many of our immune systems are simply giving notice and quitting. A small but steadily increasing percentage of the U.S. population is developing "multiple chemical sensitivity" (MCS), an affliction that sometimes forces a complete turnaround in lifestyle because virtually all synthetic substances become sources of extreme discomfort. The National Academy of Sciences estimates that up to 15 percent of the U.S. population suffers from heightened—though not necessarily debilitating—sensitivity to chemicals.[18]

One Cincinnati couple, after having a carpet installed in their office, developed flu-like symptoms that would disappear when they left the office.

> As their health deteriorated, the Bs worried increasingly about the office. Suspect number one was the wall-to-wall carpeting. They sought help from the store that had supplied it, but it soon became clear that nothing would come of those efforts. They petitioned the Board of Health, then the city where they lived, and eventually the Accident Prevention Control Center.
>
> After several weeks of getting nowhere, they hired a private chemist to investigate. The consultant's measurements showed that over the months, the carpet had been releasing several dozen toxic chemicals, including ethylbenzene, formaldehyde, methacrylic acid, toluene, and xylene. The walls, ceilings, and floors of the annex were saturated with these poisons.[19]

Unfortunately, the story of the Bs does not have a happy ending. Like other refugees from the chemical cornucopia, they lead a comparatively austere life on the outskirts of the country's humming routine.

Twenty miles southeast of Denver, a 1,875-home community is being developed for chemically sensitive people, with $1.7 billion in financial backing from U.S., Japanese, Canadian, and Malaysian businesses. The developer's original impetus was that his wife had become "allergic to the twentieth century." The 716-acre community is located on high ground to eliminate possible toxic leaching; there are no overhead electromagnetic wires; the land has never been farmed and is thus free of fertilizers and pesticides; and the homes are built using far fewer potentially toxic building materials than conventional homes. For example, the homes are framed with all-metal studs since wooden studs often emit terpene gases.

Connecticut builder Paul Bierman-Lytle also specializes in low-toxic design, preferring such materials as silver plumbing solder and magnesium oxide wallboards imported from the Netherlands and Sweden. "The wonderful thing about these materials," says Bierman-Lytle, "is they have a long life, they are ecologically sound, they don't deplete fossil fuel resources, and they tend to not pollute the environment during their manufacture."[20] At the carefully designed new headquarters of the Natural Resources Defense Council, the carpet chosen is an 80/20 percent wool-nylon blend, with a natural jute carpet backing and a jute and hair carpet pad. Rather than being glued down, the carpet is a "stretch-in" type, minimizing toxic gases.[21]

The question is, what does the MCS feedback tell us about our world? Is each of us slightly affected but not yet diagnosed? Is our quality of life and our vigor unwittingly being diminished because of pollutants, such as formaldehyde? Are the particularly sensitive people in effect "scouts" reporting trouble ahead?

What about the more publicized victims of "sick building syndrome," which is apparently becoming an epidemic in our tightly sealed office and public buildings? Sometimes even the most sensitive instruments can't perceive what building occupants know to be true. In one occurrence in Idaho, a large percentage of a government work force complained of similar symptoms, and employees were transferred to another building—despite environmental surveys that showed no significant contaminants in the original building. According to inspector Dr. James Melius, "Our investigators later found that the air intake for the building had been covered with plastic one year earlier, to protect the air-handling system from airborne debris from the eruption of Mount St. Helens, and that this cover had never been removed. Removal restored intake of adequate outdoor air to the building and allowed reoccupancy without significant problems."[22]

Because of energy conservation considerations, many ventilation systems have been designed to shut off intake air when it is either very cold or very hot outside. To our previous inventory of invisible particles, add cold germs, circulating and recirculating throughout a sealed building, along with fungi from standing water in air conditioning and heating systems.

In another instance of sick building syndrome, an outbreak of coughing, dry throat, and headaches prompted employees to recall that symptoms had surfaced right after the office's carpet had been shampooed. The shampoo product had been improperly diluted, resulting in a toxic, concentrated solution. Interestingly, the areas with heavy walking traffic were shampooed more thoroughly, and in those particular areas, workers showed the most striking symptoms.

What can be done about this previously unknown hazard? How do you monitor and regulate eighty million separate buildings? How can you invade the privacy of America's families? Indoor air pollution represents a situation that is best handled preventively. Ideally, each of the 1.5 million housing units built in this country every year would reflect an awareness of indoor air quality measures, such as good ventilation, toxin-free building materials, and prevention of radon exposure. It seems inevitable that building for health will become as much of a design priority as has building for conservation.

A transitional solution is being investigated by the state of California. A 40 percent reduction in toxic gases was observed after an experimental three-day "bake out" period, during which hundred-degree temperatures forced furniture and building materials to release gases.[23]

Anticipating complaints from home buyers who may later discover radon in their new houses, some builders are adding preventive features into their designs. Subslab ventilation systems cost about $300 to $400 to install during construction but would run about $2,500 if added later on. These systems, consisting of perforated pipes under basement floors connected to exhaust pipes, not only intercept a potential problem in the design phase, but also offer a marketing option. Other builders take prevention one step further by not building in potential trouble spots at all.

Consultants with expertise in preventing indoor air pollution can also play a role. One company, ACVA Atlantic, offers a review of architectural and engineering plans during schematic design to ensure that the physical layout of a building will not contribute to poor air quality. At UCLA, a health and safety review is provided for all new buildings. "With millions of square feet in construction," writes architect George Rand, "modern campuses are a special concern because they tend to mix 'incompatible' uses in close proximity, for example, labs with classrooms."[24]

Prevention also plays the major role in consumer products that are polluting our homes. Books such as *The Nontoxic Home*, by Debra Lynn Dadd, discuss alternative products in depth.[25] In addition, an increased awareness of alternative products should be reflected in legislation that mandates higher standards for them.

To make our homes havens again, we need to gradually redesign not only the houses themselves, but their fixtures and furnishings as well.

It has been demonstrated, for example, that various plants, such as philodendrons and spider plants, have the ability to filter impure air, breaking the toxic compounds down into harmless by-products, such as carbon dioxide. Maybe one answer to cleaner indoor air in high-rise buildings is rooftop greenhouses through which circulated air would pass.

For some pollutants, such as tobacco smoke, control of indoor air quality can be accomplished only by the decisions of individuals. Cigarette smoke remains one of the biggest indoor-air villains. Referred to as the most lethal instrument ever devised by humans for peacetime use, cigarettes claim more than a quarter million American victims every year, as well as an unknown number of victims of side-stream smoke. Studies have indicated that awareness of tobacco's effects has dramatic results in reducing its use; on the other hand, the $25 billion tobacco industry is an important economic force, and it is peddling an addictive drug.

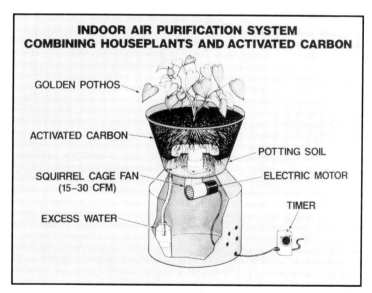

Philodendrons, spider plants, and aloe vera plants have been shown to remove three of the most hazardous air pollutants in the American home—formaldehyde, carbon monoxide, and benzene.

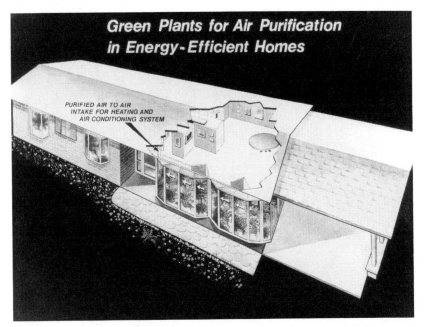

Green Plants for Air Purification in Energy-Efficient Homes

PURIFIED AIR TO AIR
INTAKE FOR HEATING AND
AIR CONDITIONING SYSTEM

Plant leaves absorb air pollutants through the same openings that take in carbon dioxide. Many pollutants are broken down into water vapor and oxygen by plants' life processes. Soil and charcoal act as filters to feed pollutants to microbes and plant root systems.

In the case of radon, a naturally occurring by-product of uranium decomposition, Americans have shown a tendency to not take action in their own homes while at the same time becoming very vocal about less hazardous environmental risks that are *not* naturally occurring. For example, in Montclair, New Jersey, a pile of mined uranium tailings was emitting radon gas, and the townspeople were furious. Yet a survey by the state health agency indicated that very few of them had bothered to have their own houses tested for radon and that concentrations in homes were typically higher than those coming from the mining wastes.

You Can't Tell the Players Without a Scorecard

How can we really be expected to know what's risky and what's not? The good news is that a steadily evolving discipline, risk assessment, is adding some degree of certainty to our everyday

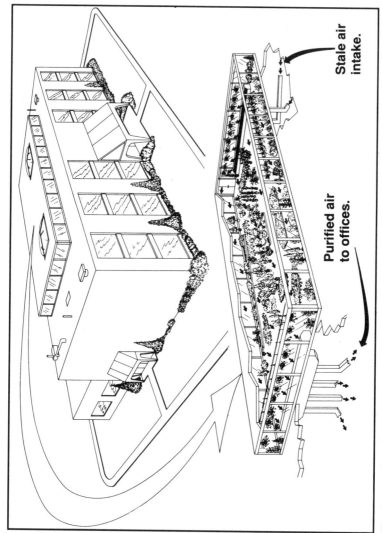

The integration of plants and building air conditioning systems can serve several functions at once, including air purification, aesthetics, and solar heating in the winter.

Stale air intake.

Purified air to offices.

decisions—in effect, giving us a "scorecard" for telling one player from another. The bad news is that quite a few of the numbers are wrong and that there are a helluva lot of players—for example, about seventy-five thousand different chemicals now in use in our world. So even the well-informed among us are left wondering who's on first. It's species depletion, isn't it, with global warming on second, hazardous wastes on third, and radon at the plate?

Which risk is worse? The scientists tell us that if we live for forty years within five hundred yards of a certain chemical plant, we'll increase our chances of getting cancer by seven in a million. But what does this mean? Should we be worried or not? Should we let our kids play in the back yard? If the factory has a minor release of chemicals through the stack, are we safer to stay put or get in our statistically lethal automobiles to drive away?

To give another example, how concerned should I be that my kids are changing schools and moving to a location that has high-voltage wires directly over the playground? Recent studies have linked such voltage with elevated cancer risks, but the school itself is a good one, with top-quality teachers and a wealth of school friends.

A 1987 survey of EPA experts ranked environmental problems as follows:

Overall High/Medium Risk
"Criteria" air pollution from mobile and stationary sources (includes acid rain)
Indoor radon
Other indoor air pollution
Drinking water from tap
Exposure to consumer products

High Health, Low Ecological Risk
Hazardous/toxic air pollutants
Stratospheric ozone depletion
Pesticide residues in or on foods
Runoff and air deposition
Worker exposures to chemicals of pesticides

Low Health, High Ecological Risk
Global warming
Surface water pollution
Physical alteration of aquatic habitat, such as estuaries and wetlands, and impact by mining wastes[26]

But what can we *do* with this kind of information? We need to use it to help us make design, regulatory, and personal decisions. By knowing what problems are the worst, we can create a strategy to reduce the more severe risks more quickly. In Benjamin Franklin's time, it wasn't hard to see that fire was causing a lot of death and destruction in cities. Franklin's efforts with lightning rods, building codes, and volunteer fire departments got a lot of mileage for the effort expended. But even locating the right risk to attack in our world would be a challenge for Ben.

What's the basis for the EPA's ranking system? The criteria air pollutants—those substances for which standards already exist—are listed at the top because a large overall population is exposed to them. Toxic wastes, on the other hand, are far more hazardous pound-for-pound, but a much smaller population actually faces risks from direct contact with them. Worker exposure risk is high because contact is direct and the chemicals are highly concentrated. But the overall ecological risk of hazardous wastes is relatively low now that regulations have helped confine those chemicals to industrial and waste disposal sites.

Worry Overload

Some scientists have characterized our country as being on "worry overload." In a world with so many risks, we don't know when to breathe and when to reach for a gas mask. Professor Bruce Ames of the University of California has continuously reminded us of the natural toxins in our food, such as cancer-causing aflatoxins in foods like spoiled wheat and peanut butter. Ames argues that our concern about human-made chemicals is overblown when the risks from these *natural* chemicals are considered.

At the same time, government agencies have volumes of data indicating that this particular chemical causes nerve damage, and that one, cancer. But companies typically hire their own scientists to assess the hazards of their products, and citizen groups sometimes get into the ring as well. Whose study do we believe in this wrestling match of scientists?

This is the question that gives environmental managers fits. Since the early 1970s, when radioactive tracer studies first found residues of the growth promoter DES in livestock, these managers have had to draw comparative distinctions between "significant" and "insignificant" levels of harmful substances. If the detection of *any* level of a cancer-causing compound were enough to ban a given product, our supermarket and drugstore shelves would be bare, concluded officials at the Food and Drug Administration, where the DES problem first surfaced. Quantitative risk assessment was brought into the ring to give a semblance of precision to a very complex situation.

But EPA toxicologist Suzanne Wuerthele summarizes her personal frustrations with the uncertainty of risk assessment: "The people who call me want yes/no answers—will substance X give me cancer or won't it? But it's not nearly that simple." She continues:

> To make a direct correlation between rats and humans, we'd feed the rats chemical X for fifty years, taking their body weight and potential surface area exposure into account. But there's a basic problem with that—the rat would have been dead for 48 years, since they only live to be two years old under laboratory conditions.
>
> So we feed megadoses of X to the rat and try to translate our results to humans. Then we try to determine how many of those humans will be exposed via which types of exposure pathways for how long. We also need to know are these humans male or female, child or adult, susceptible or non-susceptible, among a whole field of other variables like, "which other chemicals has the human been exposed to, during his or her life?"
>
> Is X going to kill you? Only God can give you that kind of zero or 100 percent probability. The best I can do is give the public something reasonable, somewhere in between.[27]

What role can risk assessment play in the intentional, informed creation of better products and better designs for our everyday lives? What kind of transportation do we want? What do we really need our household products to do? For one thing, all our data bases and alarming news reports have made us aware that there *is* a problem. As Chapter 5 will discuss further, companies have become extremely wary in recent years about the liabilities that bad design can bring. At last, they're learning to design their products to reduce those liabilities. So our environmental awareness is helping to stamp out sloppy design by threats of legal actions as well as bad product reputation. In addition, our concerns about risk have been built into some of our national laws, such as Superfund, Resource Conservation and Recovery Act, and the Clean Water Act. But the truth is, we're still operating in a twilight zone of uncertainty.

In Lewis Carroll's *Alice in Wonderland*, Alice tries in vain to play an improvised game of croquet with a curled-up hedgehog as the ball and a flamingo as the mallet. Neither device works, of course, because they are alive and therefore not predictable. Gathering data on the behavior of living systems and the pollutants within them often seems just as futile, as scientists working on Superfund-related problems will attest.

Each hazardous waste site is completely unique, due to varying geology, climate conditions, proximity to population centers, and so on. Jim Baker, then a scientist with the EPA, gave an example. "Two apparently identical mining waste piles in different towns may pose completely different risks, because heavy metals in one pile are in a soluble form, while those in the other are not. Or one of the piles may be located near a school or over a groundwater source."[28]

After an extensive study has concluded that one of the waste piles is indeed a hazard, the social element comes into play. Old-timers in the mining town have been exposed to the tailings for close to a century and it hasn't affected *them*, they say. Property owners are vocal about federal and state meddling in the town's affairs. By pronouncing the waste pile a genuine threat, these agencies are instantaneously chopping the value of residents' property in half. The citizens want to know how the data was collected and how it was analyzed. They don't want to be told that science is uncertain, not if it's going to mean that they're stuck with an unmarketable house.

It boils down to this: How can we expect to completely catalog and cross-reference something as intricate as the global biosphere? Data's great, but we've got to be realistic; numbers in a computer do not reflect the ever-changing reality of our environment. The map is *not* the territory itself. The truth is, many of our decisions will be based not on data, but on social criteria and intuition. Gut feelings sometimes annoy data-oriented scientists, but in certain cases they're all we've got. The federal Toxic Substances Control Act (TSCA) acknowledges the genuine value of "funny feelings" about chemical exposure by requiring that all complaints have to be kept on file and can be requested by state agencies and the EPA. The recent Community Right-to-Know amendment to the country's Superfund law is also very valuable as an attention-getter. It requires companies to report what chemicals are manufactured and used at a facility, helping prevent future Bhopals. The EPA has also compiled a computerized inventory of toxic air emissions, accessible to the public via a hotline: (800) 535-0202.

We do know a lot more now about ecological systems than we did even ten years ago through new techniques, such as gas chromatography, remote satellite sensing, computer modeling, and a more interdisciplinary approach that helps fit the pieces together.

But there are two problems. The first is that new technologies and products keep rolling off our production lines faster than we can develop an understanding about their effects. Second, we often fail to include people (and other natural wonders of the world) in our engineering formulae.

Knowing the Right Stuff

Are we drowning in data? Do we have too much information and no way to make sense of it? The data stream sometimes resembles a high-pressure fire hose from which we're trying to get a single gulp of water.

The central question here is, what do we *need* to know in order to design strategies and devices that will prevent environmental damage? In a nutshell, we need to know the requirements of living things. We need to avoid those self-defeating positive feedback loops. A simple illustration is the houseplant, mentioned earlier, that filters our indoor air. If the leaves of the plant are wilting, it may be that we've given it too much water. This is a positive feedback, since the plant had excess water in the root zone already, displacing oxygen and also inhibiting nutrient uptake. Many of us, however, seeing those droopy leaves, would reach for the watering can.

The less complexity we build into our world, the easier it will be to safeguard our environment. Likewise, the less we need to know, the better, because we do not have the capacity in our brains, our ecosystems, or our computers to make sense of a world that's getting more complex every second. Design is a key word, but if we're being honest, we realize that some of our naive design experiments—such as certain products of biotechnology—are a little like chickens trying to design a chicken coop.

We should welcome designs that are structurally simple and easy to comprehend, and discourage (even prohibit) those that are not. In the meantime, to deal with some very pressing problems—like Superfund sites that threaten water supplies—we have no choice but to deal with human-generated complexities, and learn the appropriate lesson from them. Of necessity, we must act on many environmental problems even though our understanding is incomplete. But at the same time, we need to keep learning, and we need to keep simplifying our designs.

Referring to the urgency of saving complex habitats like rain forests, ecologist Paul Ehrlich says, "We don't need to know more about the details of ecosystems' workings (although it would be useful) to know that we need to protect them." Ecologist Edward

Wilson addresses the social applications of knowledge when he says, "We are locked into a race. We must hurry to acquire the knowledge on which a wise policy of conservation and development can be based, before opportunities of unimaginable magnitude are lost forever."[29]

If species and habitat depletion is our number one priority, running close behind are the globally scaled greenhouse effect and ozone layer depletion. Yet these problems present a jigsaw puzzle the size of Manhattan Island. It's true the puzzle-solvers have computerized global modeling on their team, as well as an expanding base of experience, but even entering all the pertinent data into the model is an epic feat. (Recently, scientists admitted they hadn't included the ocean in their global warming model.) And in order to enter relevant data, we need to *have* it in the first place.

Reading Nature Like a Map: Biomonitoring

Several years ago, I was assigned by the EPA to write an article about a mysterious fish kill in one stretch of a Rocky Mountain stream named Chalk Creek. Something like fifty thousand baby fish had died virtually overnight. I got an early start one morning to meet EPA and Colorado Health Department scientists at the site. The scientists planned to use "biomonitoring" to try to track the pollutant back to its source. My article would focus on how tiny, shrimp-like organisms called ceriodaphnia could act as yes/no indicators of toxicity, sort of like the do-it-yourself tests that indicate pregnancy.

Usually, water samples are sent to a lab for complete analysis, but chemical and physical analyses can give only a blind report—they don't indicate synergistic effects, such as two chemicals becoming more deadly in combination than they are separately. Besides, lab tests take a long time and are very expensive. Biomonitoring seemed like a great way to eliminate some of the complexities in scientific analysis.

By the time I got to the site of the fish kill, the scientists had already pinpointed the toxic source. After taking water samples both upstream and downstream of the site, they had exposed the organisms, counted the tiny dead bodies, and discovered that an abandoned mining site was releasing pollutants. Contamination of the creek had occurred right after the snow melted during a warm spring week because a lot of water had washed over the mining wastes all at one time. (The same "pulsing" effect is observed in

EPA water quality specialist Loys Parrish is not panning for gold, but ecological information. Counting the number and variety of species in the streambed will enable Parrish to rate the quality of the stream.

alpine lakes when heavy snowmelt releases large quantities of stored-up acid snow.) Upstream from the old mine's tailing piles, there was a 100 percent survival rate; below the wastes, a 100 percent mortality. This thumbs-down indication enabled the scientists to focus their attention on the mine site, rather than try to guess if the fish kill was caused by pesticide spraying, septic tank runoff, midnight dumping, or one of many other possible sources.

The mission of ceriodaphnia "volunteers" is to survive if water samples are clean, and die if they are not—it's that simple. This method works so effectively that biomonitoring—with fish, algae, and other organisms as well as ceriodaphnia—has now been built into the Clean Water Act discharge permits of many wastewater plants and factories.

There are many other successful applications of biomonitoring, some of them occurring at the level of the backyard naturalist and some at the level of planetary geophysics.

Still-silent Spring

If a tree falls in Central America, all we hear in the United States is silence—in more ways than one. Many of our songbirds migrate

to such countries as Guatemala and El Salvador, and the destruction of their habitats is causing a drastic decline in bird populations. The seven million Americans who can recognize forty or
more species of birds haven't seen or heard certain species of war-
bler and vireo recently, and are beginning to suspect that the birds
have gone the way of the passenger pigeon, which at one time
formed breeding colonies forty miles long and several miles wide.
(John James Audubon once witnessed a passenger pigeon flock so
large that it took three days to pass overhead.)[30]

What is causing the disappearance of our songbirds, as well as
a decline in shorebirds, such as herons and turnstones? The loss of
trees, which reduces the protective cover for nesting birds, is just
one cause. Others are the damage and disappearance of wetlands
and estuaries that the birds rely on for migratory resting stops, and
the impacts from acid rain, oil spills, and metallic poisons. Birds
are among our best ecological indicators for several reasons:

• They are widely noticed by American hobbyists.
• They are small organisms with high metabolic rates, and therefore sensitive to toxins.
• They are often dependent on restricted sources of food so they
  quickly report the bad news about damaged habitats.

Birds indicate the vigor of American habitats, writes Paul
Ehrlich, and "they also bring news from areas remote from the
thinking of most North Americans, but crucial to our civilization.[31]

A recent survey of water bird eggs in the upper Great Lakes
region indicated a startling increase in bird deformities (as high as
thirty-one times more than normal) as a result of toxic chemicals
in food chains.[32] Such observations are far from unique—fishermen from Long Island Sound to Miami's Biscayne Bay have been
reporting ulcerated and hemorrhaging fish in their catches for several decades. These biological cues, along with our increasingly
sensitive instrumentation, provide us with critical feedback about
environmental quality. In fact, such observations often alert government agencies and environmental groups to become involved
in a specific issue.

Sometimes whole ecosystems can serve as indicators. For example, scientists rely on high-altitude western lakes as alarm systems
for acid rain damage. These lakes are highly sensitive and lack
"buffering capacity"—in some cases, the lakes resemble laboratory

beakers because of the relative lack of plant and animal life and soil in them. When acidity begins to build up, the lakes show signs of distress almost immediately. (The disappearance of a species of salamander from some of these lakes has been offered as evidence that damage is indeed starting to take place.) Another characteristic that makes the mountain lakes a good indicator is their location: pollution can come only from the sky.

Fingerprinting Air Pollution

Other indicators of environmental damage are saguaro cacti and lichens. The disappearing saguaro is being cited as evidence that automobile exhaust from Phoenix and Tucson is taking its toll on the familiar armed cacti, which are afflicted with "brown decline" (green cactus turning brown and dying) in increasing numbers. Lichens are excellent indicators of air pollution, also. Like mussels in the ocean, lichens just sit there and filter out what comes along, which may include such toxins as sulfur dioxide, lead, and copper. According to Dr. Clifford Wetmore, a University of Minnesota botanist, the appearance of lichens in urban areas is generally a sign of good air quality, while the loss of certain species is directly proportional to the degradation of air quality.[33]

Because they are widespread, relatively untouched over time, and easily damaged by airborne pollutants, marble tombstones can be used as chronological indicators of air pollution. University of Delaware researchers have discovered that rural tombstones deteriorate at a rate that is one-tenth the rate of urban tombstones. They have also found that rates of deterioration have slowed down since the Clean Air Act was passed in 1970.

One of the most important uses of indicators could potentially be the addition of intentional "fingerprint chemicals" to air emissions from a given plant. Radioactive carbon dating and analysis of chemicals that occur naturally in fuels is already being done to help pinpoint the source of air pollution. For example, fuel oil, which is burned mostly on the East Coast, contains the elements vanadium and nickel, while high-sulfur coal contains more selenium and arsenic. By analyzing rainwater samples, Vermont researchers were able to conclusively put the blame on distant midwestern coal-burning power plants for the high levels of sulfates they were finding.[34]

The addition of highly stable tracer chemicals to industrial emissions is still theoretical but could be a valuable tool in the regulatory toolbox. Pollution could be tracked from stack to monitoring station, thus eliminating that still-familiar industrial gesture, the shoulder shrug.

A Swedish scientist has proposed that glass in windows, doors, and picture frames could be used as an indicator of radon exposure, as decay products of the pollutant have been discovered to accumulate in the top layers of glass.[35]

The environmental group Clean Ocean Action uses plastic tampon applicators as rough indicators of water quality, in what they call the "tampon index." Writes Stephen Sautner, "If a beach is laced with enough tampon applicators, rest assured that the area has recently been exposed to raw or poorly treated sewage."[36]

Geophysical Messages

At the bottom of the world, planetary history is recorded in a frozen "data bank" almost two miles thick. Ninety percent of the earth's ice is in storage on the continent of Antarctica, and that ice is full of information. Scientists have recently tapped those files—in the form of ice cores—to find out how much carbon dioxide was in the atmosphere as long as twenty thousand years ago, when the island of Manhattan was almost as icy as Antarctica is now. The record is alarming: there are higher levels of the "greenhouse gases"—carbon dioxide, methane, CFCs, and nitrous oxide—in the 1980s layers of ice than in all previous decades within measurement. (How ironic that this warning of possible planetary overheating is documented in a "library" where the temperature routinely sinks to fifty degrees below zero!)

By examining the ice cores, informed scientists are able to pinpoint the beginning of the Industrial Revolution, the passage of the U.S. Clean Air Act, and the worldwide nuclear test ban in the 1960s. Ice cores can also chronicle toxic air pollutants, such as lead, which has increased two thousand percent since the eighteenth century. And tissue samples from Arctic animals, such as penguins, tell a similarly grim story: chemicals such as PCBs are now worldwide pollutants.

Satellite pictures of the earth reveal a million-square-mile, dense smoke cloud floating over the Amazon Basin, where forests are being burned to clear land. Composite shots of the North American continent at night remind us of all the oil and gas going down the drain to light up the Broadways and Lake Shore drives throughout the country, while streaks and splotches in some of our bays and estuaries remind us that too much of that oil is being carelessly slopped into the environment.

Yet the same series of pictures shows the Great Barrier Reef, eleven hundred miles long—a living system announcing that the planet is far from dead. They show greenish tinges extending farther into the Sahara than they have since 1965, when photographs were first being taken. And they show barely discernible features, such as the Great Wall of China, testimony to the enduring potential of human design. The news is not all bad.

By Knowing, We Can Design

The significance of these various indicators of environmental quality is in the sense of reality they confer. These symptoms are contained not just in a computer model, bureaucratic memo, or scientific journal, but in our lives. These real-world cues will help us demand realistic boundaries and restraints—socially and economically—and offer support in our inevitable quest for sensible design.

We have permitted emissions and discharges to be "innocent until proven guilty," by allowing untested substances to enter our air and water. But now the evidence is right in front of us and we can no longer hide behind a curtain of ignorance, insisting that pollution and environmental impacts came from somebody else's pipes.

We've always *suspected* that industrial dischargers were messing things up. Direct observation told us so: things don't grow in mining wastes, and there were never any fish where the paper company discharged. Now we even know why: because of such heavy metals as lead and zinc and because of the oxygen demand that pulpy wastes place on a river or stream.

In the last twenty years, we've become aware that we contribute to this mess as individuals through the things we use without demanding better. A bumper sticker in response to the Exxon Valdez oil spill was right on target: "It wasn't the *pilot's* driving that caused the Valdez spill, it was yours and mine."

The fact that we know makes us responsible. It's up to us to create and to insist upon smarter ways of getting a given job done. Once government officials realize that we *are* aware, and that a lot of us *want* pesticide-free apples and higher mileage cars, they won't have any choice but to pass laws and implement regulations that make better design the target. We need to tell them that we don't want planned obsolescence—we want durability. Throwing everything away isn't acceptable to us anymore. We don't want a product that "does everything," because it probably doesn't do anything well. We don't want the appearance of satisfaction, we want the satisfaction itself.

Ecological Impact Assessments

In most environmentally related areas, from birth control through waste reduction, a close scrutiny of *inputs* is a key theme in figuring out how we should proceed. Examining the interaction between what goes into a process and how efficiently the process *uses* the inputs—without anything being "dumped"—is a first step, but a comprehensive ecological strategy should be our ultimate target. We need to know if our products are equipped for the journey we are asking them to make. As Barry Commoner wrote in *The Closing Circle:*

> What is needed is a kind of "ecological impact inventory" for each productive activity, which will enable us to attach a sort of pollution price tag to each product.[37]

The design of environmentally sound products, processes, and regulations must somehow consider everything in the biosphere, including six hundred miles up and several miles down beneath the ocean. No small order, but some of the specifics we need to know more thoroughly include:

- The functioning of biological, geological, and chemical cycles, to be able to predict where a given chemical released into the environment will end up.
- The limits and capabilities of ecosystems, including the limits of sustainable resource extraction. Sensible, sustainable design mandates that "nothing lives at the expense of the source."
- Knowledge of immunology, to prevent the catastrophic collapse of our overworked maintenance systems.
- The capabilities of microbes, which process most of the earth's "waste products." We need to confer with them before we invent anything, to get their approval.
- The functioning of the planet's vast weather systems, to predict rainfall, wind, and the dispersion of pollutants.

- The requirements and eccentricities of each individual species, for use as biological "road signs."
- How specific materials behave under environmental conditions, such as moisture, pressure, heat, and so on.

Who's working on these things? And how do we make sure that the work gets synthesized into intelligible, useful chunks of understanding that we can build into our designs?

A Shift in Focus

Some of the most useful, biorational research is being carried on in this country's "new age" institutes, which are increasingly being recognized as an important tributary of the mainstream. A common starting point for many of these researchers is that nature already has most of the answers; we just have to ask the right questions. At the New Alchemy Institute, Land Institute, Worldwatch Institute, Rocky Mountain Institute, Institute for Local Self-Reliance, Farallones Institute, Solar Energy Research Institute, and others, America's excess baggage (including "junk" information) is turned away at the gate.

Accepting the reality that our society is in transition, these enclaves—a little like the monasteries of the Middle Ages—are helping to provide not only twenty-first-century kinds of ideas, but 1990s transition technologies as well. For example, building on the nation's heightened awareness of energy conservation, the Rocky Mountain Institute (RMI) is performing a much-needed analysis of where our energy (and water and agricultural inputs) is currently going, so that well-designed substitutes can be brought on line. The simple upgrading of home appliance standards, they have found, will result in far less pollution (something like thirty power plants' worth) without *any sacrifice in performance.* Another hundred or so power plants could be shut down if the nation's "drive-power" were upgraded to state of the art. Drivepower refers to electric-driven motor processes, which cumulatively consume more than half the country's electricity.

Many U.S. motors are only 60 percent efficient, leading Rocky Mountain Institute's Amory Lovins to characterize the many outmoded drivepower systems in the country as "a sort of financial tapeworm." He estimates that 28 to 60 percent of the electricity for motors could be saved, and recommends that we encourage legions of "torque teams"—specialists in drivepower systems—to economically tune up America's millions of motors. "If we could somehow put taxi meters on our motors," Lovins muses, "I imagine the motor users would start thinking about efficiency." Such practical, commonsense knowledge can play a major role in making the transition to the Ecological Age a smooth one.[38]

Long-term research also needs to be carried out if U.S. environmental strategy is going to shift from a focus on pollution/production/supply to prevention/design/demand. A recent proposal by the EPA's Science Advisory Board (SAB) calls for a doubling of the EPA research budget in order to pursue two major goals: First, to prevent pollutants from being generated rather than clean them up after their release, and second, to reach a better understanding of how ecosystems work and what processes should be monitored to distinguish a healthy system from one in trouble.

The 1988 report by the SAB, entitled "Future Risk: Research Strategies for the 1990s," emphasizes a "musical chairs" tendency in traditional methods of environmental protection: "End-of-pipe controls have tended to move pollution from one environmental medium to another, not eliminate it," says the report. "For example, air and water pollutants captured at the end of the pipe usually are disposed of on land. However, land disposal of hazardous pollutants is now being curtailed."[39]

Gravity, chemistry, weather, and creatures such as gophers combine to "liberate" toxic substances from even "secure landfills" with double and triple plastic liners. These substances are then free to seek out groundwater supplies, the root zones of plants, and the lungs of neighborhood kids. As a consequence, amendments to the nation's Resource Conservation and Recovery Act (RCRA) have prescribed a gradual phasing-out of certain hazardous chemicals into landfills, an initiative that has become very instrumental in pushing pollutants back up the pipeline. (In a few years, under the RCRA amendments, landfills will be able to accept wastes only when they meet stringent pretreatment rules. Some wastes will not be permitted in landfills at all.)

Recommendations such as those of the SAB recognize that the design phase of our economy is equally as important environmentally as the production and consumption phase, and that ecological knowledge is ultimately far more important than engineering knowledge. We need research of a visionary nature, as well—research that seeks to define the direction of the planet as an ecosystem. In southern Arizona, an attempt was made to fit various pieces of the global puzzle together. Though far from perfect, the project is at least a start.

 SPECIAL FOCUS
Biosphere II—A Millionaire's Hobby
or a Critical Piece of the Puzzle?

Remember the feeling of pedaling a bicycle for the first time without any help? That's similar to what the Biosphere II project is all about. Built on Arizona's desert floor (near Tuscson), the space-age structure housed eight Biospherians for a period of two years—in total isolation, physically, from our planet's life systems. Beneath the twenty-thousand-square-foot structure is a stainless steel platform that was designed to permit no exchange of gases or liquids. Likewise, a high-tech sealant was designed to prevent air exchange through the structure's glass. (Unfortunately, some of the seals leaked during the experiment, allowing some air exchange.) In effect, Biosphere II is "a world within a world."

The project is a for-profit venture that was given seed funding by Texas millionaire Edward Bass. Among many possible spin-offs of the research are the sale of Biosphere units and expertise to other research institutes, including government agencies that may be interested in applying some of the project's findings in space outposts on the moon, Mars, or a space station.

Inside the structure are seven biomes—a tropical rain forest, savannah, marsh, salt water ocean, desert, small farm, and human habitat. Built on a sloped site, the ecosystem mimics the cycles of Biosphere I, the Earth. Warm air rises from the south-facing desert biome, picks up moisture from the ocean biome, and continues rising into the rain forest's crown, where refrigerated coils cause the humid air to condense into rain. The cooled-off air falls into a "cold air return" to the desert, where it repeats the cycle.

The reason this project is important is that it offers a reality check on whether or not we know enough about natural systems to design a working model of one from scratch. Like the Earth itself, the only income the ecosystem receives is solar energy. As a closed system, Biosphere II regenerates its own atmosphere and nutrients. The concepts of "wastes" and "dumps" are not relevant

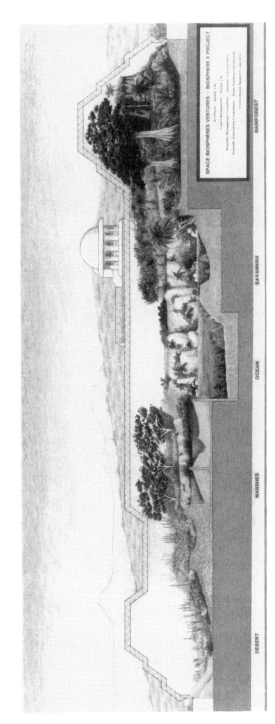

The first self-contained living unit ever constructed on earth, Biosphere II is a challenging experiment in ecological design. Eight biospherians lived in the human-designed ecosystem for two years, growing their own food, nurturing the environment, and re-cycling everything from air and water to wastes.

here since there is no extra space. Recycling is not just a good idea in this project, it's the only way the system can work on a sustainable basis. Human wastes, for example, are composted and steam-sterilized before reentering the loop, which includes goats, chickens, the African fish species tilapia, over two hundred species in the rain forest, and fifteen hundred in the ocean, and the familiar plant species of wheat, sorghum, rice, soybeans, beans, peas, potatoes, safflower and sunflower seeds, and citrus fruits.

The environmental "regulations" are quite definite, and the eight Biospherians did not have the option to disregard them. For example, the experiment permitted no combustion and no human-made pesticides were allowed, either. Says Kevin Fitzsimmons, one of the designers of the agricultural biome, "In a system of this scale, if we sprayed pesticides on the garden one day, they would show up in your drinking glass a week or so later."

The design of the biomes has been a highly interactive process. Each species was chosen not only for its own specialty but also for its ability to interact with other species and not interfere with *their* specialties. For example, the hummingbird was chosen because it is a highly effective pollinator, visiting three thousand flower blossoms a day for its nectar supply. The project's ecologists had to carefully match the hummingbird's beak length and shape with flower corollas to ensure a good "fit." They also had to include the bugs and flies that supplement the hummingbird's diet, along with the plants that those insects feed upon and the pollinators for those plants.

At the base of the designed ecosystem, as in our real world, are the microbes that recycle wastes. The scientists had to decide the best way to "seed" the system with the right microbes. Do you import them in the soils of existing ecosystems, such as in Brazilian rain forests, or do you culture them and add them to sterilized soils from local sources?

Research Director Carl Hodges, a scientist from the University of Arizona's Environmental Research Lab (ERL), has great respect for the microbial base of an ecosystem. Experimentation on air-purification systems has demonstrated that microbes can recycle even "bad actors," such as methane, ethylene, carbon monoxide, and methyl mercaptan. Gases like these were piped into microbe-populated soil columns, which converted the pollutants to carbon dioxide, water, and other harmless by-products. Because toxic gases such as these are given off in natural processes (for example, tomatoes exhale ethylene), a system for air purification was necessary in Biosphere II's closed system. Hodges speculates that "soil bed reactors" will soon become a standard item in office buildings, homes, and maybe even industrial processes. "Industry has been putting its dirt into the air when it should have been putting its dirty air into the dirt," he commented.[40]

Another ERL design that uses biologic is the "cool tower," a device that builds on the traditional Middle Eastern method of air conditioning, the wind tower. For centuries, wind has been used in Iran and neighboring countries to evaporate water at the base of a chimney, causing a cooling effect. But ERL's refinement of the concept permits cooling even when there are no breezes: excelsior pads at the top of the "solar chimney" are kept moist with a tiny pump. Air passing over the pads becomes heavy with water vapor and sinks into the building, effectively cooling even desert homes for less than ten cents a day.[41]

Still another innovation that Hodges has nurtured are saltwater tolerant crops, or halophytes. An especially promising species is salicornia, which produces high yields of vegetable oil, dried meal, and straw. "There are 22,000 miles of desert seacoast in the world," says Hodges. "If you develop even a small percentage of that, you feed an awful lot of people."

Hodges believes, with architect Paolo Soleri, that researchers and designers have to be "intentionally naive," using trial and error, intuition, and observation to bring new designs into play. At Biosphere II, observation was a central theme: because of the ambitious nature of the experiment, the world's scientific community carefully watched the interaction of biospherians with their artificial world. The eight experimenters may have lost quite a bit of weight, but overall, the project was an important one to undertake, and has paved the way for future refinements in the design of living systems.

Just Say Know

We've come a long way from intimate contact with our land. The hunt is reduced to an anonymous burger patty and a gas-powered barbecue grill, and our garden crops are mainly grass clippings. (How would you explain to an Arab or Eskimo why you carefully plant grass, water it, weed it, feed it, manicure it, and then *throw it away?*) The things we use, like soap, clothes, and toys, don't come from animals and plants anymore, which means that they may not *fit* in the world of plants and animals, either. In fact, in

University of Arizona's Cool Tower design is similar to the wind towers that have been used in the Middle East since antiquity, except they have a new twist: evaporative cooling pads are located at the top of the tower to allow cool air to fall into the structure. Rather than "hoping" for a breeze, these towers create their own breeze. *Photo courtesy of Environmental Research Laboratory of the University of Arizona.*

many cases, our products are designed *not* to fit. For example, the design strategy of many pesticides is that of a land mine—to persist in the environment and destroy whatever comes along. Plastics are designed *not* to decompose; disposable razors *can't* be used more than a few days.

But *knowing* can change all that, *if we build our new awareness into laws, subsidies, incentives, designs, demands, and taboos.* If the feedback our new knowledge provides can effectively adjust our behavior, then our cultural evolution is right on track, and with it, our odds for survival-in-style.

Certainly, human history is full of mistakes (learning opportunities?), but in general, we haven't been nearly as malicious as we have been stupid. For example, even after years of gathering data, we still don't completely understand the phenomenon of acid rain. Fishermen had observed for many years that their catches were decreasing, and some scientists had measured the drop in the pH of lakes and rivers. But virtually no one connected the cause with the effect. Monster smokestacks were prescribed as a method to disperse factory air pollutants in industrial areas, sending them far away to become "diluted." Ten years later, we discovered that this method had been bombing ecosystems in New England and Canada with pollutants originating in Ohio.

Recent research suggests the rather startling possibility that the acidity of precipitation may have been partially neutralized in the past by alkaline particles contained in the same emissions that are now being "scrubbed" by expensive add-on technology.[42] In other words, removing particulates may also be removing an antidote for acid rain.

Trying to use relevant pieces of that data base is a bit like trying to get a sip of water from a high-pressure fire hose or juggling weightless bowling pins in outer space. Our quest is for scientific certainty, but we may never get there. Four hundred years after our culture announced the infallibility of science, we may have to admit that knowledge is an ever-changing process and not a final product. And sometimes we may have to act without the reassurance of certainty.

Caring Capacity

We're grudgingly aware of *carrying capacity* because we can sense when it has been violated in our own back yards—when the city council frantically votes to import water from another county, or when the state park begins to look like a dump. But the capacity to care remains elusive. We seem to be waiting for instructions and guidelines for behavior. Like a child who stays out too late on a summer evening, we keep repeating, "But no one ever *told* me to come in."

Huge chemical companies such as Dow, DuPont, and Monsanto may suspect that their discharges don't "fit" in the environment, but until someone tells them to stop, they continue to discharge hazardous wastes, and they continue to manufacture products that don't fit. The tuning-up of regulations like the Clean Water Act, Superfund, and the Resource Conservation and Recovery Act (RCRA) includes a greater focus on making wastes stay within private boundaries. RCRA, for example, encourages the recycling or avoidance of hazardous wastes by prohibiting them from being dumped in landfills. The Clean Water Act recently required all dischargers of toxic substances to report which waterways were being impacted by their waste products. Slowly, industry is getting the message that times have changed, and we need to make sure that message continues to be delivered.

As Chapter 5 discusses, our challenge is to create new incentives that make profits dance to the tune of good design. By reducing the amount of water, power, and landfill space its citizens need (using more efficient fixtures and recycling), a city can come out way ahead. Along the same lines, a farmer can make just as much money by producing a *smaller yield*—if that yield does not require wasteful expenditures for pesticides and fertilizers that wash away right along with eroded soil. A company such as 3M can save hundreds of millions of dollars by eliminating hazardous wastes, which must be treated according to increasingly stringent rules.

The implementation of these efficient new measures is going to require some support from America's voters and consumers, and that support must ultimately be built on a firm, expanded environmental ethic. As Edward Wilson explains in *Biophilia*, this ethic will develop "inductively, in the manner of common law, with the aid of case histories, by feeling and consensus, through an expansion of knowledge and experience, during which well-meaning and responsible people sift the opportunities and come to agree upon norms and directions."[43]

In short, an environmental ethic resembles an evolutionary process—the development of a resilient ecosystem. It's fine to have emotionally charged feelings that nature should be protected, but until those feelings are woven into political reality, they constitute not a working ethic but an idealistic one. It can't be denied that one of the most effective tools for environmental change can be the grade-schooler challenging his/her corporate father/mother with ecological lessons learned in school, or in the neighborhood forest. At the next board meeting, a new idea is presented, with a passionate origin, but a newly devised, pragmatic justification: "We can save money by using rail rather than trucks, and it will reduce pollution and the threat of global warming. The public would respond favorably if the word 'somehow' got out . . ."

An energetic group of Salt Lake City elementary schoolchildren recently lobbied the Utah state legislature to establish a state-level Superfund that would indirectly clean up the waste site near their school. They received a Presidential Environmental Award for their efforts.

One of the most exciting aspects of our era is the collective convergence of the left and right sides of the brain. I can never remember which side is which, but I do sense that the rational side has been in charge for the last few centuries, resulting in far too many right angles in our world. On the fringes of ecological systems are areas called "ecotones"—transition zones between one community and the next that include features of each. Ecotones are fertile, diverse zones, teeming with life. I think it's fair to say that the United States is traversing a "sociotone" right now. Our culture is teeming with ideas as we make the transition from one era to the next.

Video vs. Values

In *New Rules*, social researcher Daniel Yankelovich characterizes the United States as a nation "hovering midway between an older postwar faith in expanding horizons and a growing sense of limits. We are in search for new rules, because the old rules don't work anymore."[44]

Futurist/economist Hazel Henderson refers to values as "essentially packages of social software which produce various mixes of behavioral output." She thinks of this software as a bank of resources, fully as tangible and useful as a newly discovered oil field.

And Henderson's colleague Marilyn Ferguson (author of *The Aquarian Conspiracy*) refers to our evolving value system as the

"New Common Sense, an acknowledgment that our brains were designed not merely to survive but to create." Ferguson strives to bring the "V" word into the mainstream when she writes, "Visionaries discover an empowering paradox. If you make peace with the unknown, it becomes your guide. They begin casting lines into the future. They seem to be remembering the future, moving toward some target that the culture has not yet articulated but that can be sensed by the sensitive."[45]

Does this sort of intuition offer the mainstream something it can sink its teeth into? Judging from the radical change in health patterns, diet choices, corporate seminars with "touchy/feely" themes, and polls indicating that many Americans want less stress in their lives—even if it means a lower salary—I'd say the answer is an unequivocal yes.

Yet there is still a silent majority in the United States that continues to be transfixed by the old value system, as symbolized by network television. This silent majority receives a watered-down version of environmental reality on the evening news. For example, one study of how the media shapes American environmental opinion concluded that "scientists and doctors were not major news sources for the Bhopal chemical disaster because reporters believed such experts would complicate the story." This lack of scientific input resulted in a collective belief that environmental catastrophes *can't be prevented*, the report stated.[46]

Other evidence of environmental fatalism is offered by 128 fisherman of the Tittabawassee River, in Midland, Michigan. These fishermen, who fished the badly polluted river an average of twenty-nine days annually, knew that their catches were contaminated, but many continued to eat the fish anyway. They voiced opinions such as "Everything you do will eventually kill you. I have eaten these fish for twenty years and I feel fine." Others admitted that "as soon as the fish were in the frying pan, they gave off a chemical smell," compliments of Dow Chemical discharges. The study's authors concluded that the fishermen for the most part felt they had lost the power to make choices in their lives and had become skeptical about all the bad news they had heard over the years: "The news told them that saccharin would cause cancer. They did not get cancer. Smoking was going to give them heart disease. They did not have heart attacks. Nuclear proliferation was going to end the world. The world was still here." So they continued to fish.[47]

Six hundred miles farther northward, Eskimos of the Northwest Territory sat in their traditional log houses watching satellite TV, with dog teams tied up outside and dried fish hanging on the lines. "They're watching a bunch of white people in Dallas drinking martinis around their swimming pools and plotting to destroy each other, steal from each other and get their friends' wives into bed." According to author Jerry Mander, one native lamented, "Our traditions have a lot to do with survival here. Cooperation and sharing and non-materialism are the only ways people can live here. TV presents values opposite to these."[48] Nature shows on public television warn us that our ecosystems are in grave danger and report the impacts of the Western lifestyle on our quality of life. But the awful truth is, it's not real. It's just another television show, telling a distant, unconnected story.

What's more, the shows rarely offer the viewer options. As a culture, we need to become aware of choices. We need to preserve and nurture our options as if they were a garden of prize-winning perennials.

Obviously, a good first choice would be to push the TVs "off" button and get outside to experience firsthand what the environment is about. More importantly, we need to be *evaluating* our options, just as if we were studying lifestyle menus. We need to be talking about those choices, and complaining when we don't see something that we want. We need to agree on "what's good here," using fundamental, nature-based criteria as a guide.

If we can't figure out how we'll ever pay the bill, we need to get creative and arrange ways we can pool our resources, make deals, and do dishes if we have to. We need our collective sense of power back. We need to *take* it back by making informed, inspired choices.

CHAPTER 3

CHOOSING

Picture this: we're sitting in a pleasant restaurant with lots of hanging plants, sunny windows, and some good background music. We made the right choice coming here. The most amazing thing is the menu. We can select not only what we want to eat, but what we want to use in our everyday lives as well, and even how we want to *live*.

The doors swing open from the kitchen, and a waiter with a huge platter hustles by. The platter is filled with familiar, brightly colored containers and boxes: soaps, paints, synthetic clothes, plastic items of all shapes, aerosol cans, charcoal briquettes, and a hundred other "necessities." Another waiter's platter is covered with a scale model of the city of Los Angeles, and a third platter contains computer chips, solar cells, high-efficiency light bulbs, the prospectus for a "socially responsible" mutual fund, and bowl of fruit salad labelled "grown locally and organically." The menu is a hundred pages long, concluding with the instructions, "If you don't see what you want, ask for it!" Talk about options!

How can we ever decide what we want? What criteria should we use to make our choices? Which technologies do we want to scrap, and which do we want to keep and perfect? What kinds of jobs and communities? If we are concerned about the environment and want to choose a product with very little ecological impact, how can we identify it?

Ordering à la Carte from a World-class Menu

This chapter is about ways that you and I can protect the common good at the individual and community level, using a more biologic way of thinking. The whole universe of effective grassroots action seems to come down to three critical types of choices: we can create and insist on nature-compatible design and designers, open new channels of information flow, and amplify our voices by joining ranks with others.

Many times, it's not what we *do* that will make the difference, it's what we *know* and insist upon. We don't directly formulate building codes, vehicle mileage efficiency, or the contents of a furniture-stripping product, but if we meekly accept everything we're offered, we are in effect saying we're satisfied—with the extinction of species, global warming, chronic allergies, and lifeless rivers. (The political leaders in Minneapolis, for example, were *not* satisfied with unrecyclable plastic packaging, and they voted to ban its sale in their city. As of mid-1990, only recyclable packaging is legal, and several plastic recyclers have moved into the area to take advantage of the new business opportunity.)

The point is, if enough people support certain design criteria, those criteria can be built right into the law, eliminating the need for consumers to know *everything* about their purchases. Choices take place by political consensus as well as consumer awareness.

"To be or not to be" has always sounded pretty dramatic, but for most of us, it's not really the question. We're committed to *being* here, but we don't seem excited about making "here" an excellent place to be. We keep thinking somebody else is going to take care of things and make the important choices.

But the fact is, we each choose whether to work where we want to live or live where we want to work. We *choose* whether or not to add to the population, and whether or not to insist on health rather than cosmetics. We *choose* whether to buy a new car or put a rebuilt engine in our weather-beaten but still dependable old one. As a town, we *choose* whether to develop a prime piece of nature or preserve it as open space. And as a species, we *choose* whether to change our own behavior or try, tragically, to bend nature to fit outdated assumptions.

The story of the village idiot is a good one to keep in mind as we make individual commitments to go against the current of American consumerism and move *toward* simplified, elegant lifestyles. Every time the village idiot was offered a choice between a nickel and a dime, he chose the nickel. When asked why, he explained in a crafty, confidential voice that if he chose the dime, the amused villagers would quit playing the game. Village-idiot choices we make as crafty individuals can raise our quality of life by giving us more time, less conflict and stress, and more flexibility. For the sake of our planet and our own individual sanity, we need to practice choosing the nickel: consuming less and knowing exactly why.

Frances Moore Lappe, author of the classic *Diet for a Small Planet*, suggests, "In our homes, classrooms, study groups, churches, synagogues, union halls, civic organizations, and through the media, we can explore our *public* values and how they help point toward solutions."[1]

Choosing the Nickel

There are two natural windows of opportunity for making wise choices at both the mega- and mini-level: when a product or process is first introduced and when it is replaced. As Langdon Winner points out in *The Whale and the Reactor:*

> Consciously or unconsciously, deliberately or inadvertently, societies choose structures for technologies that influence how people are going to work, communicate, travel, and consume over a long period of time. . . By far the greatest latitude of choice exists the very first time a particular instrument, system, or technique is introduced. Because choices tend to become strongly fixed in material equipment, economic investment, and social habit, the original flexibility vanishes. . .
>
> For that reason the same careful attention one would give to the rules, roles, and relationships of politics must also be given to such things as the building of highways, and the tailoring of seemingly insignificant features on new machines.[2]

Like natural succession, cultural evolution is a trial-and-error affair. Sometimes the challenge lies in recognizing an error and separating ourselves from it in order to try again. In nature, most mistakes don't survive, but in human society, they become bound up in profits, egos, and infrastructure. For example, many of our federal subsidies are stuck in the error mode, like dinosaurs in quicksand. Rather than bolster biologically sound ways of doing things, we're still trying to carve up nature as quickly as possible because that's the way the game is set up.

When a technology, product, or process starts to wear out, opportunity is knocking. The upgrades we choose can help conserve energy, prevent pollution, reduce stress, and save money over the long haul. Rather than mistake these opportunities for obstacles, we have to look at them from a fresh perspective. The Osram Company, for example, markets its high-efficiency light bulb as "the world's least expensive light bulb," even though it retails for more than $20. Over the course of its life, the bulb will save not only money but energy, resources, and pollution. By using these light bulbs, we choose the nickel over the dime, and come out way ahead.

The Chinese government recently made a less-than-optimum choice when it built one hundred refrigerator factories, all designed to produce conventional, inefficient refrigerators. The less developed countries have a great opportunity to bypass many of our mistakes, but they have to quit buying products and technologies that we've banned (like DDT) or consider obsolete (like the refrigerators).

A single 18-watt, electronically controlled "compact fluorescent" light bulb produces the same light as a 75-watt incandescent bulb and lasts thirteen times as long. *Photo courtesy of Osram Corporation.*

For each choice at both the mega- and mini-levels, we need to ask certain practical questions about *use*. What is it we are trying to accomplish? For example, what do we want transportation to *do* for us? We don't really want highways, cars, or mass transit; instead, we want access to jobs, stores, and activities. Maybe we wouldn't need to drive as much if our neighborhoods were designed to include these needs. In other words, if we choose a mixed-use, well-designed community as an *entree*, a richer, less frantic social life comes with it.

What's the *purpose* of a pesticide? To protect crops. But maybe those crops could be more effectively and ecologically protected if the farmer took the time to *know* his farm, using biologic rather than the weird molecular code that pesticides represent. (For example, the spray of pressurized water on the underside of leaves when pests are vulnerable can substitute for chemicals, washing insects and their eggs off a crop. Upward-spraying nozzles on hanging irrigation systems are being used this way in the High Plains.)

What's the *reason* for plastic containers? How long do we need a certain package to last? If all they're really doing is replacing a few minutes of our time, maybe we'd rather have reusable glass containers and not have to worry about toxic air emissions from incineration or contaminated drinking water from leaking landfills. What chemical reaction in a manufacturing process results in hazardous wastes? There must be a substitute reaction or chemical that works more efficiently; we just need to focus our attention on finding it. (One of the best places to look is in the diversified rain forests of the world, where evolution has already invented a multitude of nature-compatible molecules.)

How is our water being used? Aren't there smarter, cheaper ways of taking a shower (efficient showerheads) and watering the lawn (only when it needs it)? What's *in* the mountain of trash that is giving our community leaders fits? If we compost the yard wastes, recycle all the recyclables, and boycott products containing toxic substances, we've reduced a nightmarish dilemma into a mere routine.

Carbon Copies

It is probably fair to say that in this century, we really didn't choose "dinner," it chose *us*. Technologies and products kept popping up that roughly fit the American mold of convenience, fashion, and power, and one after another, they became standard fare on the menu. As Langdon Winner has written, "Any notion that ordinary people might want to have control over production or have a say in decisions beyond those of the immediate enjoyment of goods and services seemed out of the question . . . It did not matter how electricity was made or carried over a vast electric grid as long as you could flick a switch and have the lights go on."[3]

The microwave oven is a good illustration of our bumbling, mindless, so-called success in the realm of design. An engineer with Raytheon Company was doing research on magnetron tubes—used in radar equipment in World War II—and happened to have a chocolate bar in his pocket. After discovering how quickly the magnetron tubes melted the candy, he rushed out and got some popcorn, watching gleefully as it exploded all over the lab.[4] Forty-four years later, four out of five U.S. families have microwave ovens, cooking meals in minutes in engineered packaging that is far more expensive than its supermarket price alone reveals. For another few hundred years, that packaging will be hanging around like a delinquent teenager looking for trouble.

Plastic first got onto the menu more than a hundred years ago when ivory for billiard balls was in short supply because elephants were being pushed toward extinction. A contest sponsored by a New England billiard ball company offered ten thousand dollars for the best substitute, and a plant-derived plastic, cellulose, was the winner. There was no pause for reflection about whether or not we really wanted to open the door into the world of plastics.[5] Like the first plastics, the tin can was a contest-inspired innovation. Around the beginning of the nineteenth century, the French government offered 12,000 francs to the inventor who could find a way to keep meats and vegetables fresh. A few years later, Napoleon took the contest-winner on his invasion of Russia.[6] About the same time period, British soldiers were observed ripping into "tin cannisters" with bayonets, pocket knives, and even rifle fire, because no practical *opener* had yet been invented. A can found at the site of an 1824 Arctic expedition carried the instructions, "Cut round on the top with a chisel and hammer."[7] Perhaps the U.S. government should sponsor a few contests for super-high-mileage cars, economical fuel cells (a promising technology that cleanly converts fuel into electricity), and other nature-compatible designs. (What about computerized trash cans that beep obnoxiously when items that still have value are pitched?)

We take bright colors for granted in our world, but they too are a recent invention. A few years before plastic came on to the scene, the true birth of chemical "cuisine" had occurred when English chemist William Perkin was looking for a way to synthesize quinine, a natural compound used to fight malaria in Africa. Instead of quinine, he accidentally created the first synthetic color (purple) by using coal tar wastes (a carbonaceous by-product of the gas-lighting industry) as a feedstock. Until that time, colors had been derived from plants, shells, and minerals.

Within months, chemists all over the world were mixing a pinch of this with a pinch of that, trying to synthesize not only colors but fertilizers, fabrics, and other cheaply mass-producible "carbon copies" of natural compounds. The newly emerging science of molecular chemistry had coincided with the discovery of oil, a coincidence that quickly led to a hazardous alphabet soup of chemicals.

What about automobiles? Did we really intend to give them 10 percent of our arable land (2 percent of total U.S. land area) for paved "pasture," or were they essentially the only choice on the menu?[8] What role did the buy-out of the nation's trolley lines by GM, Firestone, and Standard Oil play in the car's takeover? After those companies had succeeded in eliminating much of the competition (one hundred separate transit systems nationwide), large sections of the menu were rewritten. Essentially, our transportation and many other lifestyle options were narrowed to a choice of condiments.

Everything on It?

Let's assume we want to "hold the mayo," or completely invent our own combination. How do we do it? How do we get precisely the sandwich we want? How do we even figure out what we *want?* Obviously, we'll choose something that tastes good to us, but if we're in tune with our own bodies, we'll go beyond that, ordering something that actually has some nutritional value and makes us feel good—something that we won't later regret.

It's exactly the same with social choices. In addition to short-term gratification, we want long-term satisfaction, and that means we've got to make a few decisions. But where do our guidelines come from? How do we know our biologic is sound? Before they are even considered, our consumer and design choices need to meet certain criteria.

Desirable	**Unacceptable**
Uses renewable resources	Energy, materials glutton
Little or no pollution in use or manufacture	Waste accompanies product use or manufacture
Reversible, recyclable materials and processes	One-time use, one-way processes
Diverse solutions to technical and social problems	Singular, inflexible solutions
Increases access to nature	Isolates from nature
Leaves natural systems intact and functional	Disrupts natural balance, causes ecosystem collapse
Increases social options, doesn't require extra protection	Decreases social options, requires guards, monitoring, protective equipment
Easily understandable	Understandable only by experts
Emphasis on quality, durability, specificity	Emphasis on quantity, appearance, brute force
Empowers indigenous cultures	Eradicates indigenous cultures

The characteristics in the right-hand column are all too common in our world. They are based on four fundamentally incorrect assumptions: that resources are unlimited, that nature exists for the sole purpose of catering to humans, that happiness can be achieved only with material goods, and that complexity is preferable to simplicity.

We need choices characterized by the left-hand column. Whether we're choosing cars, houses, manufacturing processes, consumer goods, or city designs, we need to apply these basic criteria—and similar ones—to make sure our choices don't result in a bellyache.

In our world, the choices seem overwhelming, and we often throw our hands up in desperation, saying, "There aren't enough hours in a day to make informed decisions, and they cost too much anyway!" What we're really saying is, "Our world is poorly designed. We live too far from our jobs; we're paying too much for clean-up taxes, liability insurance, and unnecessary packaging; and we don't know how to demand better!"

Mega-Choices/Mini-Choices

A deliberate social choice was made by the Japanese during the period 1543–1879, when the rulers of Japan outlawed the use of firearms. It was a conscious, purposeful decision, documenting that cultures can opt not to deploy a given technology even if it's new and powerful. The decision was based on a kind of biologic, as Robert Ornstein and Paul Ehrlich observe in *New World, New Mind:* "No longer was there much room for the heroism of individual combat; the skilled and armored samurai knight, carrying a blade never surpassed in the technology of cutting weapons, could be potted like a partridge at two hundred yards by a crude peasant." The authors continue:

> Subsequently, the Japanese advanced in agriculture, mathematics, hydrological engineering, marketing, and other fields. It was not a stagnant society that forgot how to make and use guns; it was a sophisticated society focused on quality of life. It did not take up guns again until intrusions by modern navies began to persuade the Japanese that their national security demanded firearms.[9]

Another example of deliberate social choice is a real-world enactment of "you take the high road and I'll take the low road" that occurred in Scotland. In a 1989 paper, Amory Lovins cited Frank Fraser Darling's *West Highland Survey,* in which he described two Scottish villages, one with a road and the other with a dirt track:

> In the former village, soil and fisheries were being depleted; people ate little of their own produce, substituting canned porridge and all sorts of packaged goods; productivity, morale, health, and culture were in decline. In the latter village, however, fisheries were sustained, the land was in good heart, the people's diet and health were excellent—and at first they too wanted a road, but only until they observed that roads merely tied their economy into the commercial web of the South and East without so reshaping their habitat as to enable them to pay for the expanded trade's transaction costs and middlemen out of increased exports. On further reflection, they chose to keep their dirt track, and with it, their ability to trade only when they wanted to, not because they had to.[10]

There are many American examples of mega-choices as well, in areas as diverse as chewing tobacco and nuclear power. During the eighteenth and nineteenth centuries, the use of chewing tobacco was so common that the floors of public places were "slippery with tobacco juice." Historian J.C. Furnas wrote, "Though folklore made range and accuracy in spitting matters of humorous pride, care to hit the sandbox or cuspidor was considered unnecessary, even rather unmanly."[11] Unfortunately, the social megachoice America made in the twentieth century was to chew less and smoke more. Yet even smoking is now being weeded out of public places as restaurants, airlines, and government agencies continue to exile it to isolated areas or ban it altogether. A survey taken by the Centers for Disease Control revealed that 42 percent of polled workplaces restrict smoking, and 3 percent have banned it. The point is, we can change sloppy habits—we do it all the time. Kicking the toxic chemical habit is fundamentally the same thing as giving up tobacco.

Nuclear energy, being touted by some as a possible solution to global warming, has a major problem with public acceptance. Since the near-meltdown at Three Mile Island, no new plants have been constructed in the United States. Americans have made their choice clear.

Other collective decisions involving the use of land are still on the menu. Should we permit a hazardous waste treatment facility to move into town? Should we preserve certain pieces of land to encourage the survival of endangered species (a "condos or condors" choice as Langdon Winner has phrased it)? Should we support a mass-transit referendum, even though population density along proposed routes doesn't appear to justify such a system?

If menu choices such as these are "entrees," thousands of other everyday choices are garnishes, appetizers, and beverages. The supermarket clerk wants to know, "paper or plastic bag?" The car salesman wants you to choose the model with air conditioning, even though it reduces mileage substantially and uses ozone-depleting CFCs. You're uncertain about the environmental trade-offs of *driving* to a recycling drop-off station or burning wood to eliminate the need for coal-powered electrical heat. You want to choose a detergent with fewer phosphates, a breakfast cereal boxed in recycled cardboard, or a garden pesticide with the fastest decomposition rate, but there are uncertainties here, too—gaps in knowledge and prices that favor the "wrong" choice.

Fortunately, help is on the way in the form of certifiers, information brokers, and analyzers. By using criteria such as those mentioned earlier, many agencies, citizen groups, and companies are

beginning to fill the gaps in the public's quest for knowledge. In coming years, "label-looking" is destined to become second nature to consumers. (When enough consumers agree on the qualities of a given product, they can support legislation that does the label-looking for them.) Just as health-conscious consumers have learned to watch for key words, such as "preservatives," "polyunsaturated," and "artificial flavors," environmentally sensitive citizens will observe an exponential increase in environmental cues.

Environmentally Friendly Products: It's Easy Being Green

Until environmental sensitivity becomes an ingrained habit, we're going to need constant reminders to help guide our behavior, in the same way that the odor intentionally added to natural gas reminds us to turn the stove burner off. For example, at the

University of Colorado, neatly typed file cards are posted above elevator call buttons. "Elevators use energy," they remind us. "Please take the stairs." California's ground-breaking Proposition 65, which requires that any item containing toxic chemicals be labeled, has resulted in many such reminders. "WARNING: Paint products in this department may contain a chemical known to the State of California to cause cancer or other reproductive harm," reads one such reminder. But above and beyond passive warnings, Proposition 65 also is forcing the redesign of products. The Gillette Company, for example, recently opted to change the formulation of Liquid Paper, which contains the cancer-risk trichloroethylene, rather than duke it out in the courts with the Environmental Defense Fund. EDF and several other environmental groups filed a complaint that Gillette had not issued adequate warnings. EDF's David Roe commented, "Here's one less risk for everybody to have to worry about."[12]

"This magazine is printed on recycled paper," "This packaging contains no CFCs." In a sense, these increasingly familiar cues represent invisible threads, weaving environmental consensus into our culture. We need to insist on them, letting the business world know that there are profits to be reaped from biologic-type thinking. The fact that environmental groups are now able to suggest alternative products rather than merely call for product boycotts is an indication of the developing market. The inventors and designers *know* that we know, and they have no choice but to respond with designs that will gain our approval.

Europeans and Canadians seem to be pacing Americans when it comes to "green" consumer choices. (The Greens are an environmentally conscious political force in several European countries, and their ranks are also increasing in America.) "Any company that ignores public opinion in Europe today does so at its own risk," says European Commission environmental specialist Michael Berendt.[13] European consumers are choosing greater volumes of nature-compatible products every year. In Sweden, concern over the bleach used in paper-making has resulted in an off-white paper product acceptable to consumers. (The bleach resulted in water pollution and traces of the hazardous compound dioxin in paper products.) This change was extremely significant, requiring a $600 million investment by Sweden's huge pulp-and-paper industry, which contributes almost half of the country's export earnings.[14] In Sweden and Norway, a deposit is required on new automobile purchases. It is refundable along with a bonus when the car is returned for recycling.

In Britain, when surveys revealed that a third of the shoppers were intentionally avoiding products containing CFCs, companies such as Gillette, Unilever, and Beecham were forced to switch propellants. Britain's Body Shop, a retailer of natural cosmetics, watched its annual sales increase in the last four years at the rate of 92 percent per year and has extended its "partnership of profits with principles" to about four hundred worldwide locations from "the Arctic to Australia." In France, Wonder, a mercury-free battery, has reached annual sales of over ten million batteries.

Author John Elkington, whose 1988 book, *The Green Consumer Guide,* sold a quarter of a million copies its first year, refers to acid rain and global warming as "unparalleled new business opportunities." Elkington, who is trying to sell the idea of a pan-European labeling system for environmentally friendly products, says, "The main message is that up until now environmentalists have gone for regulations. But now companies are getting the signal from the marketplace to adapt and that has an impact on manufacturers. Changes which might have taken three to five years are now taking place within three to five months."[15]

In *Changing Course* (MIT Press, 1992) author Stephan Schmidheiny's major observation is that the only human institution with enough power to turn the tides of environmental destruction is the corporate world. According to Schmidheiny, the choices made by corporate giants (and their suppliers and customers) will determine the fate of our environment.

Following the lead of West Germany's Environmental "Blue Angel" program, which gives an environmental seal of approval to consumer products, the Canadian government has implemented an Environmental Choice program, in which a logo identifies products that are less harmful to the environment than the standard fare. Surveys have repeatedly indicated that Canadians are willing to pay up to 10 percent more for benign products, creating a business opportunity that companies are eager to grasp. The program requires each company seeking certification to apply to a fourteen-member panel of consumer advocates and representatives from such areas as business, science, and environmental law. If products measure up to the panel's guidelines, companies can license the EcoLogo endorsement for a three-year period, subject to annual verification. Because product testing costs are covered by company applicants, the program will be largely self-supporting. Consideration is given to physical, chemical, and ecological effects of production, consumption, and disposal. Products should conserve energy, be recyclable or made from recycled material, or be free of ozone-depleting substances or other contaminants. The first three product categories the program assigned the logo to were recycled motor oil, insulation made from recycled paper, and products, such as flower pots and outdoor furniture, that are made from recycled plastic.

When the program is well under way, the Canadian government will encourage federal procurement of products that bear the logo—a maple leaf formed from three intertwining doves symbolizing the interdependence of consumers, industry, and government.

The West German Blue Angel program, now in its fifteenth year, has approved more than 3,000 products in fifty-seven categories, and has achieved household recognition by four out of five con-

Product labeling programs like those of West Germany and Canada help direct consumers toward good-sense purchases. Momentum is now building in the U.S. Congress for such a program.

sumers. Sometimes a careful review of a product's full life cycle results in both pros and cons, the West Germans have found. For example, a cloth diaper service may dramatically reduce the impact of disposable diapers going to landfills, but the strong detergents used by the service routinely result in water pollution.

Some of the products bearing the West German Blue Angel:
Retreaded tires
Low-formaldehyde products
Returnable bottles
Composted soil
Aerosol cans without CFCs
Low-emission burners and furnaces

Sanitary recycled paper
Zinc-air batteries
Paint low in lead and cadmium
Durable, low-noise car mufflers
Benign drain cleaners

The Blue Angel Program defines clean products as those which "when compared with other products fulfilling the same function and when considered in their entirety, taking into account all aspects of environmental protection (including the economical use of raw materials), are, as a whole, characterized by a particularly high degree of environmental soundness without hereby significantly reducing their practical value and impairing their safety."[16]

Norway, Japan, and Australia have also announced environmental labeling programs, and almost every state in the United States has expressed interest in Canada's program by requesting information.

 **SPECIAL FOCUS
Organic by Choice**

Americans in the age group of 25 to 45, the so-called Baby Boomers, represent this country's most environmentally conscious sector. They are also the group with the fastest growth in disposable income. One of the most dramatic indications of the boomers' economic punch occurred right after heavy media coverage about pesticide-contaminated apples in the summer of 1989.

A Natural Resources Defense Council (NRDC) study on the "intolerable risks" of pesticide residues was heatedly discussed on *60 Minutes*. Alar, a pesticide used on apples to regulate growth, promote firmness, and enhance color, was singled out by the NRDC as a particularly dangerous substance because of its potentially severe effects on children, who consume more apples and applesauce per pound of body weight than adults. Within a few days, according to newspaper headlines all over the country, consumers were stampeding health food stores and isolated organic produce counters in supermarkets, looking for pesticide-free fruits and vegetables. The same week, the National Academy of Sciences released a report advising Americans to eat more produce to reduce risks from chronic diseases. Which way to go? Obviously, if you want to have your fruit and eat it too—and if you're genuinely concerned about pesticide residues—you go organic.

All of a sudden, wholesalers reported that retail grocery customers who once carried out a few bushels of organic produce were now requesting full truckloads. Major supermarket chains, such as Safeway, Kroger, and Lucky, began test-marketing organics in more than two hundred stores. Consumer experts at the Center for Science in the Public Interest claimed that "there isn't a single supermarket chain in the country that isn't looking into alternatives."

Food industry experts nationwide agreed on two things about the new trend. As out-of-place as "organic" signs might appear under the bright supermarket lights, they probably are there to stay, and ultimately will assume a 10 to 20 percent share of the market. The explosion of interest in large-scale organic food marketing was not the result of calculated market research or investment analysis, but was a genuine example of a consumer-driven, grassroots change.

A March 1989 Harris poll documented that an overwhelming majority of Americans (84 percent) would buy organically grown food if it cost the same as pesticide-treated produce. About half responded they would *pay more* (typically about a fifth more) for organic food because it tastes better and is more nutritious.

According to NRDC's Janet Hathaway, "The USDA should give growers incentives for using safe farming practices and get rid of legal impediments that force them to use pesticides, such as grading standards which emphasize appearance." USDA grading standards, which help a grower receive top prices, are based on engineering-type considerations (diameter, length, and color) rather than such biologic factors as taste, nutrition, or lack of pesticide residues. To receive an "Extra Fancy" ranking, a given fruit or vegetable basically just has to be big and unblemished.

There's been a small-scale but devoted demand for organic produce for the past forty years or so. For example, Walnut Acres in Pennsylvania has had continued success since the 1940s, relying on health food stores and mail order customers. In recent years operations such as Organic Farms, Inc. of Washington, D.C., have been able to get their foot into America's refrigerator door. Joseph Dunsmoore, founder of the $20 million business, says, "I look at organic agriculture to be the equivalent of Star Wars space technology. It's a whole new concept of agriculture and prevention."[17]

Whole Foods Market of Austin, Texas, with annual sales of over $40 million, is currently the largest retailer of organic food in the United States. Much of its pesticide-free produce comes from "transition" acreage—cropland that has in past years been conventionally farmed but is now organic on a trial basis. According to Dan Kelly of the Texas Department of Agriculture, one of the largest cantaloupe farms in the state has just converted three or four hundred acres to transitional organic. In the past year, the Texas office has had more than a thousand inquiries from conventional farmers wanting more information about organic farming.

Texas is one of a handful of states (along with Washington, Oregon, and Minnesota) with official organic certification programs. But California, which grows about one-half of the country's fresh produce, is the capital of organic produce, on a volume basis. A flurry of consumer demand in the state has kept the industry group, California Certified Organic Farmers (CCOF), busy in the past few years. The group has helped set the standard for determining whether a farm rates an "organic" certification or not. In order to be certified by the association, farmers must document alternative means not only of pest control, but also of fertilization. This means demonstrating that soil fertility is being improved through biologic techniques, such as recycling of crop residues, animal and "green" manures, composts, and rotational cropping.

In addition to "Integrated Pest Management," a decision-making tool that enables conventional farmers to move closer to organic techniques, many farmers have increased their use of various standard soil tests, to determine if the soil already has enough fertility for the intended crop. One field at a time, America's billion acres are becoming more like nature and less like factories.

Farmers, food retailers, and consumers are responding to various food certification programs across the country.

Mail Order Menu:
Here Come the Boomers

A nagging, recurring question about environmentally friendly products is, "Where can you get them?" (See Appendix.) Although things like recycled-paper stationery are starting to appear in stores and supermarkets, it's a slow process, and one with a built-in "Catch 22." The prices of these products are typically a little higher because the market for them hasn't encouraged cost-reducing manufacturing and distribution systems. In effect, American consumers are being called upon to "put our money where our mouths are" and demonstrate our convictions by a willingness to pay a little extra for quality.

The payoffs are there, but they come *after* the consumer choice. And they expand and link up with other people's choices, like pond ripples in a rock-throwing contest. First comes the satisfaction of doing something right as well as having a durable, solid product. Next comes a gradual, steady reduction in environmental impacts from the collective decisions. As impacts decrease, so do taxes, insurance, lawsuits, stress, and time spent battling poor design. As more time is available, we begin to use it in quality kinds of ways—doing things we had quit doing because we didn't have the time. We begin to garden again, re-establishing physical contact with an extension of ourselves, the soil. We get to know our neighbors, trusting them enough to leave our children with them while we go on that backpacking trip we never had time for. In short, options increase, costs decrease, life is more fun.

And all we have to do is start buying compact fluorescent bulbs and recycled toilet paper? No, but it's a start. If you can't find the right place to buy the right products, there are some catalogs out there that make it easy. Followers of Stewart Brand's evolving *Whole Earth Catalog* (which has now sold more than 2.5 million copies "in its various permutations" over the past fifteen or twenty years) are aware that the catalog has a new form: "compact digital ROM" (read only memory), which combines an ability to be read *and* heard. Some of the recordings mentioned in the catalog can be previewed by a link-up with a compact disk player. The company also publishes a quarterly periodical, *The Whole Earth Review* (originally called *Co-Evolution Quarterly*). Both publications provide access to hardware and software for a more sensible century.

The *Seventh Generation* catalog does not contain sexy swimsuits, cellular phones, or computerized exercise equipment—but it does have some high-tech kinds of hardware, from solar fans and battery chargers to test kits for carbon monoxide, formaldehyde, radon, and seventy-three water contaminants. Efficient water fixtures are also included: low-flow toilets, showerheads and faucet aerators that will reduce both water use and electrical bills. Environmentally friendly soaps, light bulbs, and recycled paper products are also in the catalog. Alan Newman, owner of the business, believes that the key words for the 1990s will be renewable, biodegradable, and recyclable—not just because they "feel good," but because the market will demand them. Like organic produce, many of these products carry a slightly higher price tag than their petrochemical cousins, which doesn't seem to deter a steady stream of customers. Newman's staff receives 100 to 200 requests a day for the small catalog, and he hopes to distribute up to half a million copies this year—a fivefold increase over last year.

Co-op America has a variety of tools to help create an "alternative marketplace," including an alternative product catalog; a quarterly magazine (*Building Economic Alternatives*), investment and insurance services, and *Eco News*, a newsletter about the activities of socially responsible companies.

Several pocket-type guides for environmentally responsible shopping have been put together. The nonprofit Council on Economic Priorities' *Shopping for a Better World* is a well-researched "quick and easy guide to socially responsible supermarket shopping." The guide lists hundreds of products and companies and ranks them according to environmental concerns, women's and minorities' advancement, animal testing, nuclear power, community outreach, and four or five other categories.

Nontoxic Home Products

In the 1990s, consumers in search of nature-compatible products will be able to find them, if they make the effort to look.

Another shopping guide put out by the Pennsylvania Resources Council helps supermarket shoppers understand the recycling implications of the products they choose. The guide counsels us to "vote for the environment by buying items packaged in recycled or recyclable materials or in reusable containers." It also reminds us:

- Impulse buying often responds to bright, excessive packaging—stick to your list.
- To identify recycled packaging, look for "recycled" symbol, or gray interior in cereal, detergent, and cake mix boxes.
- Buy in bulk; bring your own container.
- Avoid "mixed packaging" containers like square juice boxes and squeezable ketchup bottles—they're difficult to recycle.
- Use consumer hotlines; make suggestions to store owners.

A forty-year-old "beautification" and anti-litter organization, the Pennsylvania Resources Council has effectively tracked litter back to its sources in both the corporate world and the American household. Its newsletter is filled with practical, biologic suggestions, such as alternatives for hazardous household chemicals:

Pesticides	Spray plants with soapy water, pyrethrum, *Bacillus thuringiensis.*
Mothballs	Use cedar chips or cedar chest.
Ceramic tile	Mix 1/4 cup baking soda, 1/2 cup cleaner white vinegar, and 1 cup ammonia; mix 1 gallon warm water.
Furniture polish	Olive oil, 100% lemon oil, beeswax.
Toilet bowl cleaner	Liquid chlorine bleach—soak 30 minutes and scrub.

The truth is, Americans may not use homespun products such as these until companies *sell* them to us because we've been taught not to trust our own instincts. We put our trust in multinationals like Procter and Gamble and DuPont because it's too much effort not to. (They wouldn't come out with an oven cleaner that was *bad* for you, would they?)

Why *shouldn't* we try homemade pantry-shelf chemicals? (Nobody's looking.) There are many "formula books" out there now with recipes for simple concoctions like windshield spray (for which we pay good money to get alcohol and water). John

Seymour's and Herbert Girardet's *Blueprint for a Green Planet* is an excellent "practical guide to restoring the world's environment," that takes the lay reader behind the curtains of everyday products and processes.[18] A few quotes from the book illustrate its direction:

> Many household products are highly reactive substances. Their advertising emphasizes this by describing them as "extra strong," "powerful," "high speed," and "super-concentrated."
>
> What is needed instead are chemicals that are created from natural substances. Timber treatment liquids, paints, glues, and cleaning fluids can be made from plant substances such as turpentine, pitch, latex, beeswax, natural oils, and dyes.
>
> Instead of carpets containing manmade fibers, they can be made of wool, coconut fiber, or sisal (or at least recycled plastci). Furniture can be made of wood that is joined together in the traditional manner, rather than glued together.

Windstar publication *Everyday Chemicals: 101 Practical Tips for Home and Work*, one of a series of booklets for sustainable choices, is a great resource for alternative methods and products, and includes resource lists for the reader who wants to try out some of the ideas.[19]

The 1989 book, *50 Simple Things You Can Do to Save the Earth* from the Earthworks Group, is another sourcebook for changes at the individual level. The book became an immediate best seller in America, selling more than 170,000 copies in two months. Says author John Javna, "It's remarkably simple to make the right environmental choices. All it takes is the right information."

The magazine *Alternative Sources of Energy* has been a persistent, reliable voice for information on new developments in renewable energy. The same people also publish a catalog of products, from solar cells to high-efficiency fixtures. Jade Mountain, a Boulder, Colorado, supplier of biologic-type products, stocks a variety of alternatives in appliances, housing accessories, and renewable energy supplies. For a comprehensive, cross-sectional look at the field of alternative energy products, Solaplexus of Fish Kill, New York, is a good bet, while the voluminous *Thomas Register of American Manufacturers*, available in many libraries, lists everything from soup to nuts and bolts by product type.

The number of newsletters and journals that center around the idea of a "sustainable world" has mushroomed in recent years. A few of the better ones, in my opinion, are the previously mentioned *Whole Earth Review, Harrowsmith,* Sierra Club's *Sierra, Garbage, E, Environmental Action,* the NRDC's *Amicus Journal,* the eclectic *Utne Reader, Environment,* and *World Watch.*

Several other publications are worth mentioning here as indicators of the rapid transition in environmental awareness. The *Guide to Eating Ontario Sport Fish,* which appeared several years ago, focuses not on lures, flies, or favorite fishing spots but on levels of contaminants, such as PCBs, mercury, and pesticides in fish. The Ontario Ministry of the Environment distributed 200,000 copies to fishermen, whose reaction was largely one of gratitude.

Another environmental shopper's tool, *The Good Wood Guide,* lists furniture and other products that are not made from wood harvested in tropical rain forests.[20] For guidance on where to buy recycled products, Robert Boulanger's *National Recycled Product Directory* will appear quarterly, giving subscribers access to a telephone hotline.

"The Consumer Doesn't Want High Efficiency"

Don't you get tired of being "the consumer"? The phone rings right at dinnertime and it's some fast-talking guy doing a market survey of your preferences as the consumer. I usually skew their data by responding with Flintstones-like answers: sawdust on our floors instead of carpet, wringer washers, wool clothes, grow and hunt all our food.

I made a phone call to the corporate headquarters of a certain Japanese car company whose name has become an American household word. I'd heard about a 98-mile-per-gallon prototype car the company had been working on, and I wanted to include a picture of it in this book. But I was told that the project had been shelved because there was *no interest* in high-mileage cars and that the company was not interested in promoting the prototype.

They were right, of course. As long as the price of gasoline remains low, there is little incentive to pay extra for a high-mileage car. (What our country needs is a good stiff gas tax, like all the other oil-importing countries already have.) But the car company's attitude demonstrates what it will take to get the sort of car that is already technically possible: amplified demand.

I had the same sort of conversation with an executive at one of the world's best-known fast-food restaurants. "We're responding to what our customer wants," he said, defending the restaurant's method of packaging everything up one instant and collecting the waste paper and plastic the next. "Why can't you use silverware for orders that are not 'to go'?" I asked him. "Because it's not what our customer expects," he replied.

Come on, do we really go to fast food places just for the privilege of throwing away packaging? I'll admit it sometimes seems like it—we use about 600 pounds of paper per year per person, compared to 325 in Japan and 65 in Brazil. Obviously, we can get by with far less if we decide to. How many requests will it take before fast food places start reducing packaging and increasing recycling?

Many U.S. grocery chains replaced styrofoam egg cartons, which contained ozone-depleting CFCs, with cardboard cartons, largely because of consumer requests. A Maryland housewife recently caught the ear of General Electric when she discovered that the company was routinely venting CFCs when it performed repair work on an estimated one million recalled refrigerators. She correctly perceived that "every little bit counts," and in her quest to find a solution, she called not only GE but state and federal agencies, environmental groups, and politicians. Her persistence paid off: she arranged a meeting with then-Senator Albert Gore and GE executives, who agreed to offset the ventings through future recycling.[21]

At the University of Colorado's student-funded Environmental Center, the importance of individual action is emphasized through letter-writing campaigns, which help students learn about the issues and their political implications and teach students that their opinions can be amplified and heard. A Denver solutions-oriented discussion group (called Results) takes the same approach. The group informs itself on an issue, and *before the meeting is adjourned,* each person writes a letter expressing his or her convictions on the issue. Companies and political representatives simply cannot ignore an outpouring of public opinion; their survival depends on our support. They've become aware that each letter actually written and mailed represents the sentiments of another thousand or more who didn't take the effort to write. According to analyses by the Technical Assistance Research Programs Institute, a firm that advises corporations on customer relations, the magic number for consumer complaints is one hundred (if they are not related as part of a single campaign). At that level, "whether the product is an expensive car or a bottle of shampoo," chief executive officers become personally involved.[22]

In a 1989 *New York Times* poll, 80 percent of the respondents agreed with the statement, "Protecting the environment is so important that requirements and standards cannot be too high, and continuing environmental improvements must be made regardless of cost." Seventy-five percent responded that pollution laws are "too weak" in a 1989 Media General/Associated Press poll.

The environmental movement has matured in the past twenty years, progressing from a fringe minority right into the mainstream of America.

Cutting Wastes Rather Than Trees

When a wise environmental choice overlaps with a convenient method of *implementing* the choice, then choice becomes reality. Curbside recycling is a good example. If a city provides recycling containers, operates a standard, well-publicized pick-up service, and gives bonus incentives to good recyclers, chances are good that there will be some results.

What about the pinnacle of consumption, the American Christmas tradition? How much glossy paper in the form of mail-order catalogs is pitched as we shuffle through our pre-holiday mail? Rather than being passive consumers, drowning in junk mail, we need to have our names removed from mailing lists by contacting the Direct Marketing Association and other mailing list firms. The Office of Technology Assessment reports that in West Germany, it is illegal to deliver mail that is anonymous (not individually addressed) if a household puts a certain sticker on the mailbox. The growing medium of Cable TV "catalog shopping" seems to make more sense than ripping up forests to make difficult-to-recycle catalogs. And what about Christmas trees? How can we use fewer of them—and less wrapping paper—and still have the kind of Christmas we'll never forget? Rather than slice eighty million trees off at ground level, why can't we dig them up roots and all and invite them inside for the holidays? There's something radically out of sync when tree growers spend eight years growing a six-foot tree for two weeks of use.

What if each of us pre-dug a hole in the fall, and bought a living tree to plant in that grove, right after Christmas? Nurserymen report a survival rate very close to that of spring-planted trees if care is taken to do the job right. (Living trees should only remain inside for a week, and also need a week in a garage or other intermediate temperature location, both before and after playing the role of Tannenbaum.) As an alternative, some communities have developed innovative ways of recycling leftover Christmas trees, grinding them up for mulch, or even bundling them together with concrete blocks and sinking them in reservoirs to provide fish habitats.

Can individuals living in North America help save distant rain forests in South America or Asia? You bet. "Debt-for-nature" swaps, by which portions of Third World debts are absolved in return for preservation of forest land, is one way. These arrangements can be partly financed by citizen contributions to such groups as the Nature Conservancy. The careful purchase of products is another way. The avoidance of tropical woods such as mahogany and teak is becoming a well-known consumer option, but the preferential choice of products from uncut forests is less widely known. A human rights group called Cultural Survival has been studying and promoting rain forest resources, such as Brazil nuts, rubber, chicle (used in gum), and allspice, with the goal of increasing the value of standing forests. A joint three-year study by Missouri Botanical Garden, New York Botanical Garden, and Yale University concluded that revenues from edible fruits, rubber, oils, and cocoa from 2.5 acres of tropical rain forest are nearly two times greater than the return on timber or the value of the land if used for grazing cattle.[23]

The Greening of the GNP

The message is clear: we American consumers have to make pests of ourselves, as representatives of America's most powerful organization—purchasers. "Where did this come from?" we have to ask. "Does this battery contain mercury?" If store clerks respond, "I don't know," we then request that they relay our question to the store owners. Or we pick up the phone and call them ourselves.

Just as we became extremely materials-conscious during the World War II years, we must learn to consider it patriotic to buy products in sixteen-ounce containers rather than eight-ounce because the former take less plastic per unit of product. We have to start sharing lawn mowers, post-hole diggers, and even second cars. We have lots to learn from the Europeans, whose Green Party movement has brought environmentalism into the political and economic mainstream.

In general, Europeans are more willing to take reusable grocery sacks to the supermarket, wear sweaters in the winter rather than pad around artificially tropical living rooms, and educate themselves about environmental causes and effects than we young and "fuelish" Americans.

A graphic example of this is a Procter and Gamble product that passed a test marketing in Europe but flunked it here. The product is a concentrated fabric softener that comes in a large container the first time you buy it. From then on, you buy concentrated refill pouches. According to company spokesman Ed Fox, this can save 80 percent of the usual packaging required for such a product. But although Europeans can handle the concept of home-mixing, Americans kept using the product at higher concentrations than the directions called for, or they avoided the product to begin with.

The point is, America finally is starting to turn the faintest shades of green, a full decade after areas like Scandinavia. Given the business opportunities that biologic presents, don't count America out of the "Green Race" yet. The Rocky Mountain chapter of the Greens printed a list of "101 Things You Can Do to Promote Green Values," which can cumulatively elevate our quality of life. The suggestions include:

• Buy energy-efficient appliances.
• Put a catalytic converter on your wood stove.
• Use rechargeable batteries.
• Research socially responsible investments.
• Learn how your senators and representatives vote.
• Use cloth diapers, and rags instead of paper towels.
• Put in a water-conserving showerhead.
• Avoid using styrofoam—it can't be recycled.

- Recycle newspaper, aluminum, glass, tin, and motor oil.
- Avoid disposable plates, cups, and utensils.
- Use the back of discardable paper for scratch paper.
- Buy bulk and unpackaged rather than packaged goods.
- Grow your own food (even small kitchen gardens).
- Compost your food scraps.
- Acknowledge someone who provides quality service.
- Teach your children ecological wisdom.
- Discover your watershed and work to protect it.
- Buy locally grown produce and other foods.
- Invest in well-made, functional clothing.
- Shop by phone first, then pick up your purchase.
- Learn about the medications you put into your body.
- Practice responsible family planning.
- Decrease TV watching and increase creative learning.
- Take time to play, relax, and go into nature.

Commonsense suggestions? Absolutely, but if it takes a checklist fastened to our refrigerator doors to remind us to *use* common sense, let's get out the magnets. The Bonneville Power Authority, which supplies 3 percent of the nation's electricity, launched a massive conservation program that included a magnetized energy-efficiency label, "The Blue Clue," to put on the refrigerator with the shopping lists, pictures of and by the kids, *and* the environmental commonsense reminder list.

Thanks to federal legislation passed in 1987, twelve appliance categories must become "smarter" between 1990 and 1993. Collectively, this upgrade is projected to displace twenty-two power plants' worth of electricity since the appliances consume roughly 25 percent of America's juice. Covered by the law are refrigerators, freezers, window air conditioners, central heating systems, central cooling systems, water heaters, dishwashers, kitchen ranges, clothes dryers, furnaces, and pool heaters. In this case, the choice seems to have been made *for* consumers, but a closer look shows that the appliance industry negotiated with consumer and environmental groups to set the standards because of growing confusion over state regulations. It was more attractive for companies to encourage standards at the federal level than to have to comply with a dozen different efficiency levels mandated by the states. Of course, some appliance models will surpass the standards, so there is still plenty of room for consumer discretion.

DC–Powered Yin Yang

In *The Next Economy*, Paul Hawken offers a conceptual explanation of the "consumer tune-up" that is taking place:

> In an informative economy, we change from an affluent to an influ-
> ent society. If you are affluent, goods and services flow toward you;
> if you are influent, the information contained within goods flows into
> you. An affluent society may possess an opulent and abundant
> amount of goods, but that does not mean it will be able to utilize,
> appreciate, and maintain them . . . In other words, an affluent society
> amasses goods, while the influent society processes the information
> within goods.[24]

Although living green does not necessarily involve choosing
between A or B (we have a whole alphabet of choices available),
there is one underlying A/B theme in most of our choices. It might
be described as centralism/decentralism. Lewis Mumford observed
in his classic series, *Technics and Civilization*, that throughout history, two technologies have continuously existed side by side, "one
authoritarian, the other democratic, the first system-centered,
immensely powerful but inherently unstable, the other human-cen-
tered, relatively weak, but resourceful and durable." An interesting
example of the resourceful contingent are the DC-powered homes
scattered on the fringes of America's mainstream. They're the veteran *Mother Earth News* crowd, whose direct current appliances are
powered by wind generators, small hydroelectric turbines in
creeks, solar cells, and basement diesel generators. Think of the
glories of not paying a monthly utility bill! Of being able to live out
beyond the furthest reaches of the high-voltage lines! When George
Westinghouse's alternating current beat out the direct current of
Edison, it was because AC would travel farther and permit more
centralization. But DC never died, and may have a future yet.

Mumford's term for a diverse mix of technologies was "polytech-
nics." An advocate of "best use" for each resource, Mumford
believed that by distributing our eggs among many baskets, we
can maintain our resiliency, just as an ecosystem does.

The Western society has both technology types in it—both sys-
tem-dependent and self-sufficient, both consumer and producer.
At many of our jobs, we are components of a machine programmed strictly for profit-making, while at home we strive to be
nurturing parents, loving spouses, and good neighbors. Our challenge is to balance the two tendencies. The most realistic menu

choice for us, it seems, is neither "vegetarian" nor "carnivore" but "meat-eater in moderation." And as we begin to unite the opposites within ourselves, we will help bring about the same merger in the world of business.

Planting Seeds at Corporate Headquarters

The choice of where to invest our money (assuming we have some to invest after taxes and insurance premiums) is potentially one of the greatest allies of nature-compatible design. Vermonter Susan Meeker-Lowry has compiled an instructive, even inspiring, guide to "socially conscious investing," in which she suggests that "we can use money as a tool to make things happen." *Economics As If the Earth Really Mattered* provides both moral and economic proof of how ethical investment choices can pay off. The *moral* bottom line of the book is that "if we do not choose our own values, then we subscribe by default to the values of the prevalent system. Such acquiescence is always dangerous, but these days it's also suicidal. Business as usual is killing the Earth."[25]

Clearly, what business needs is money that is *greener* than green. For the discerning investor who doesn't want to support companies with bad environmental and social records, there are now about a dozen socially responsible mutual funds with combined holdings of about $800 million.

Ethical investing first became popular as a church-related statement against "sin stocks" like tobacco, alcohol, and gambling. It also came into vogue in pacifist and anti-apartheid circles. But recently the focus has shifted from companies and countries to *avoid,* to companies and practices to *support.* The New Alternatives Fund, for example, which invests in conservation, alternative energy, and recycling, has watched its assets grow in the last six years to $7.1 million. (These funds are not "sacrifice" investments, either, judging by their recent performance. The Dreyfus Third Century Fund grew 23 percent, and the Parnassus and Ariel Growth funds both placed in the top five of all mutual funds.)

Perhaps the most stringent fund from an environmental perspective is the Calvert Social Investment Fund, which avoids industries involved in toxic pesticides and CFCs, as well as documented violators of environmental regulations. During the five-year period ending December 31, 1988, the fund boasts a solid return of 13.2 percent to go along with its crystal-clear conscience.

Offering "creative tools for practical idealists," Working Assets is a company whose plastic is environmentally friendly: the company markets VISA and MasterCard accounts, with a certain percentage of the profits going to peace and environmental groups.

For down-to-earth investing, commodities and consumer products might be the best place to start. For example, two compact fluorescent bulbs, two faucet aerators, and a low-flow showerhead—approximately a $70 investment—will save $80 to $140 a year (depending on local utility rates, whether your hot water heater is gas or electric, and your level of water and electric consumption). "So if you have $70 or $80 in the bank drawing a paltry 6 percent interest," the newsletter advises, "you might consider investing in energy efficiency and reaping a 100 to 200 percent annual return on your money—while improving the environment."

In My Back Yard!

I stopped at the convenience store the other day to fill the gas tank and rent a video so I could "spud out" on the couch that night. But the only interesting movie I saw on the shelf had the rented tag on it, so rather than waste a couple hours on something stupid, I went home and worked in the garden. "I'm *learning*," I told myself, because I might have chosen a dumb movie just out of habit or to fulfill the original purpose of the stop.

We've got minds, and we can change them. You have to admit that's refreshing to think about. In the 1970s and 1980s, a familiar acronym was NIMBY!—"Not in My Back Yard!" (The even more strident slogan was NOPE!—"Not on Planet Earth!") As neighborhoods and communities, we exercised our rights not to have things like hazardous waste treatment facilities near us. In the 1990s, we have an opportunity to play the flip side of NIMBY and NOPE and choose what it is we *do* want in our back yards (the IMBY phenomenon). One of the best seedbeds for the germination of biologic is the community, town, or small city.

Protecting the Home Turf

Rene Dubos' classic advice to "think globally, act locally" has gone far beyond the slogan stage, as local governments all over the country exercise their option to make their own choices. In local toolboxes are control of zoning, permitting, building codes, open space acquisition, transportation planning, and the most valuable tool of all: protection of the "home territory." Environmental action makes more sense when you can see a factory's stacks, or when the water coming from your tap is under your own feet. The town of Brookings, South Dakota, for example, has developed a land use plan that will help protect its groundwater supplies. The first stage was learning about the hydrology and geology of the wellhead protection area. Then land uses and industry practices were matched with the physical characteristics. Through enlightened zoning regulations, certain activities—such as electronic manufacturers, fertilizer warehouses and other industries that sell or store hazardous materials—are not allowed in the aquifer impact zone.

The American tradition of burning wood, perceived as almost a God-given right, has come under the control of various city halls—especially in the Rockies, where thin, oxygen-poor air causes inefficient combustion. The tiny, storybook town of Crested Butte, Colorado, passed an ordinance requiring all woodburning stoves to be new, highly efficient models, or else the woodburner must pay a $30-per-month fee. To help facilitate this transition, the town arranged a Stove Fair to sell various models of stoves to the residents. In nearby Telluride, a mandated system of tradable permits ensures that the total number of woodburning devices does not exceed a certain number. Permits go for a steep $1,000 or more on the open market, but the initiative has resulted in air that is two-thirds cleaner.[26]

The biologic of local environmentalism is obvious: solutions are geared toward the specific conditions of a given place. When communities diversify to meet local needs, they provide not only fitting solutions, but "genetic material" that can be useful in other localities, as well. Two areas in which local decision-making works especially well are transportation and trash recycling, where land use and municipal equipment are critical.

One of the greatest strengths of local initiatives is that towns and cities can effectively tinker with the daily affairs of their citizens—something that is very difficult for federal legislation to do. Certainly, citizens can play a more active role at city council meetings than at senate hearings. As E.B. White said, "It is easier for a man to be loyal to his club than to his planet; the by-laws are shorter, and he is personally acquainted with the members."

SPECIAL FOCUS
Doing What's Right with What's Left

Recycling is slowly becoming a standard part of our behavior, just as it is at the core of all living systems. Think about it—if nutrient-recycling microbes had not helped us out by helping themselves, we'd all be shoulder-deep in dead dinosaurs. What if our circulatory systems didn't route blood through our lungs to drop off carbon dioxide and pick up oxygen? At a less vital level, what if we tossed our dirty socks into the laundry pile but they never came back to our dresser drawers? Of course, our lifestyles are only one small step away from throwaway socks—after all, we've had disposable gloves, diapers, and razors for just long enough to get used to the idea, and we'd be willing to throw away our socks too if somebody could convince us it's a good idea.

Throwing everything away may be convenient, but it's just not sustainable. We Americans want our trash faithfully picked up, but we're finally realizing that there's no good place to put it down. Material things are subject to unchangeable natural laws that rule that we *can't* really throw anything away—we can only change its form. If our town chooses to incinerate its solid waste, we can transform paper, plastic, and food scraps into ashes and smoke, but we haven't gotten *rid* of all the trash. The remaining ashes, which typically weigh about a third as much as the trash itself, will contain toxic metals from such items as batteries, lighting fixtures, and pigments. Unless special precautions are taken, the incinerator emissions will contain dioxin compounds formed during and after combustion from the chlorine in table salt, plastic, and bleached paper.

The biologic design goal of not throwing anything away comes down to one simple strategy: *Design things that can go through our social and industrial loops endlessly and never become trash.* "Pollution is just resources out of place" is a standard slogan of the 1970s and 1980s that reflects an infinitely higher understanding of ecology than a previous slogan, "The solution to pollution is dilution."

Biologic implies that the solution to pollution is cognition. Knowing that we have new design goals and that we even have a market for them, our inventors need to do some rethinking. Just as some house plants need to be root-bound in order to come into flower, our country's industrial and social designers now have well-defined boundaries in which to blossom.

The Transition to Clean Trash

As Worldwatch researcher Cynthia Shea has phrased it, most of our consumer goods are destined for a one-night stand. We're discreet enough to keep our trash out of sight (after twenty years of litter campaigns), but we aren't sticking to our overall goal: a faithful marriage of culture with nature. We need to extend our taboo against litter into a taboo against trash itself. We need to keep the things we use from becoming contaminated during and after first use. Conceptually, we've got to prevent the structural information in goods and resources from becoming incoherent and garbled like a load of recyclable paper when it contains unrecyclable, glossy magazines.

An excellent example of the evolution toward clean trash is the successful campaign against the plastic soft drink can that took place a few years ago. Because of their physical resemblance to aluminum cans, these containers mistakenly made their way toward aluminum recycling furnaces, where they fouled up the smelters. Environmentalists were also concerned about the polyvinyl chloride in the cans because of both worker safety and potential dioxin formation if disposed cans were incinerated. The same group that battled the plastic can, the Coalition for Recyclable Waste, is now opposing the use of polyvinyl chloride (PVC) as a food-packaging material. The coalition's main concerns are increases in plastic wastes and toxic air emissions.

Every product we use has a life history, from its birth in the mines and forests through its disposal in the landfills or reincarnation at the recycling plant. We are right in the middle of those billions of life cycles, and if *we* don't make key decisions about the integrity of our products and resources, nobody will.

Throwaways: As American As Apple Pie and Disposable Cameras

We know by now that there is a lot of trash out there. Journalists tell us how many times a convoy of garbage trucks could motor to the moon and back. They give us "ballpark estimates" on how many times Yankee Stadium could be filled with this country's annual eighteen billion dirty diapers. Pie charts from the EPA show us graphically that paperboard is a 41 percent piece of pie, and food wastes and glass are each about 8 percent. And we're told that a single tire has the equivalent of two gallons of oil in it. What I find amusing about these illustrations is how *American* they are: as American as space travel, baseball, and apple pie charts. What does this say about the nature of the country itself? All our standard Americanisms are becoming filled with trash.

The eight million televisions we throw away annually (because repair costs exceed the cost of a new set) could stretch case-to-case from New York to Los Angeles and back. Sadly, these illustrations, like TV nature shows, come into our minds but not our hearts. In order to generate a real integration of ethics and action, we need to become even more intimate with our trash. We need to *meditate* on it, if necessary, to genuinely understand what trash is: stuff that passes through our society exactly as nutrients pass through ecosystems. (In some cases, the wastes *don't* pass through, as when the endangered leatherback turtle mistakes floating plastic bags for jellyfish.)

Our children need to understand that in the past year their school threw away a forest just like the one they camped in during last summer's vacation. They need to grow up with the idea of product reincarnation. Concepts like "If you're not *buying* recycled materials, you're not recycling" need to become second nature to them. Recycling is kind of like a bucket brigade or a telephone tree—if one point in the loop fails, the whole system fails.

A student activist group at the University of Colorado takes "Eco-Shows" to elementary and junior high schools to try to instill these kinds of thoughts. Football players dress up as shell-shocked American housewives, throwing containers all over the stage and driving half a block to get more. Students are taught the subject of "garbology," which includes rooting through garbage bags on the gym floor to find out exactly what *is* in them.

The stuff we *use* is how we pollute—both directly and indirectly. We sometimes feel powerless concerning invisible toxic particles in our air, soil and water, but recycling is a different story: When we've made the decision to recycle our food wastes into our gardens and yesterday's news into today's, we're in the driver's seat because making good choices gives us power.

Gucci Garbage

A letter to the editor of the *Denver Post* congratulated the company for printing its paper on 75-percent recycled stock. The writer
felt that the most pressing thing about recycling is building it into
the mainstream by finding markets for recycled goods. But an article in the same day's paper reported that the market for recycled
paper and cardboard was collapsing because of too much supply.
Trish Ferrand, a solid waste expert whose creative mind is continually focused on garbage, believes these temporary gluts have to
be overcome with government subsidy if necessary. "We have a
bigger oversupply problem at the landfills," she commented. "The
real law of supply and demand is that when the public finally
demands that a problem be solved, industries often don't supply
the answers until government intervenes." Although this sentiment
contradicts free-marketers who are confident that solutions will
appear when the economy demands them, it also acknowledges
the bottlenecks and fluctuations of the market. The paper industry
is "influenced by everything from rising literacy rates in Third World
countries to office computerization, to new de-inking technologies,
to emergence of faster growing tree stocks, to new tree diseases in
foreign forests," Ferrand explains.[27]

The editor of *Garbage Magazine* made an informed choice
when she decided to print the magazine on recycled paper. "The
editor in me wanted recycled paper," she said. "The publisher in
me didn't." Because of a slightly higher cost as well as the shaky
reputation which recycled paper had in the past among printers,
she considered using standard paper. "Recycled paper generally
looks like whole wheat and has gooky things in it," she said. But
when her art director and managing editor confronted her with the
word "hypocrite," she looked around and found a way to go with
the recycled paper after all. She found a type of recycled
paper—Cross Pointe Troy book paper—that is very white, film-
coated, and easily recyclable itself.[28]

Printer Bill Hayes of Boulder, Colorado, who has had fifteen
years of experience with recycled paper, was not satisfied with it
at first. "It never ran well or dried well, and it created a lot of paper
dust," he said. But he emphasized that those problems have been
eliminated—the quality is good and the color selection is, too.

Since federal, state, and local governments collectively purchase
about 21 percent of the gross national product, it seems reasonable

Half the battle in changing over to more sensible designs is overcoming the fear of looking foolish. But if the rest of the world is willing to use vehicles such as the Dumptrike, why can't Americans loosen up a little? *Photos courtesy of George Bliss.*

to expect many of these purchases to bolster a young recycling market. Certainly, local governments are seizing a newly perceived opportunity to avoid the costs of disposal by recycling. Hundreds of innovative community programs are demonstrating that American ingenuity is far from dead. One small town runs a "take it or leave it" recycling facility complete with picnic tables. Residents drop off their own separated materials, stop to visit with friends if they want, and then take home anything they see that they need, ranging from half-used cans of paint to fixable TV sets.

In a few other towns, residents' recycled bags of goods are randomly inspected for correct recycling practices. Prizes are awarded if residents are doing it right. A trash lottery! A little town in Iowa combined its small power plant with a trash incinerator. The combined unit, now in operation for fifteen years, generates electricity and steam for heating, while reducing trash and utility bills all at the same time. Numerous other rural areas are pooling their trash resources to make recycling worthwhile, and some are becoming recycling centers for nearby urban areas.

Where's the money in recycling? That's the American question. If you can make a buck or avoid paying one, someone will figure out a way to do it. In many areas, scavengers and street people are delighted about curbside recycling, routinely beating municipal collectors to pick up the easily marketed aluminum cans and plastic soft drink bottles. Meanwhile, inside the houses of the Baby Boomers, the market is ripe for recycling gadgets to put alongside the juicers, salad dryers, popcorn poppers, woks, and ice cream makers. Writes Trish Ferrand, "I believe that we could have a virtually limitless market for more containers, bundlers, balers, racks, stacks, bins, smashers, smushers, grinders, binders, densifiers, and cradles for recyclables. And if we could get them in changing designer colors every year, we would find plenty of space for them in our homes." (For more on designer recycling, see Chapter 4, Designing.)

The alternative to connectedness with our trash is far less appealing. One notorious landfill site, Fresh Kills on Staten Island, has become the second highest point on the Eastern seaboard—the seagulls love it, but New Yorkers don't.

SPECIAL FOCUS
Driving Ourselves Crazy?

Most Americans believe that we've completely lost our options when it comes to transportation, that our choices are limited to buying an old car or buying a new one. But I disagree. Transportation is really about land, which, in the United States, is owned by the people. It's up to us to devise efficient, mutually agreeable

Americans want convenience and style. We'll be a lot more likely to recycle our wastes if our kitchens include designer recycle bins made from recycled plastic. *Photo courtesy of Rehrig Pacific Company.*

ways of using it. In half a generation, cars and trucks have gobbled up 60,000 square miles of America's land, which is more than 2 percent of the total surface area of the country, and up to 50 percent of many urban areas (the typical urban car commands 4,000 square feet just for home, office, and shopping parking spaces). Primarily because of the gasoline that trucks guzzle, we routinely use the equivalent of two thousand calories to transport a fifty-calorie head of lettuce across the continent, a calorie being the amount of heat energy it takes to heat a gram of water one degree centigrade. Over 40 percent of all commuter trips are now made from one suburb to another on congested freeways, while 40 percent of all *urban* commuters drive less than four miles. The development of our private vehicle transportation system has created an environment made up of dispersed communities, workplaces, and commercial centers that only perpetuates our dependence on automobiles.

The average speed cars now travel in urban areas is steadily *decreasing* in many U.S. cities. It is now down to an estimated eight miles an hour in gridlocked cities like New York. What are we trading for this decrease in overall efficiency? The privilege of listening to mocking helicopter reports on morning chat radio?

What about the "life-cycle" speed of cars? How much time do we spend working to make our car payments or directly pampering the cars themselves—filling them with gas, pleading for mercy at the repair shop, and searching for them in endless parking lots? Social commentator Ivan Illich has estimated that by dividing total car-hours spent into total distance traveled, we are going *less than five miles an hour*, in an overall sense. Four of our sixteen waking hours are spent either in the car or working to pay for it. The newsletter *New Options* reports that as much as half a year of our lives may be spent waiting at traffic lights. Really, we might as well be walking, and if we're going to walk, why not design a pleasant world to walk in?

Rather than cross a crowded "strip avenue" on foot, we invariably climb into the car and drive across the street, going from one huge parking lot to another. And who can blame us? There's nothing that refreshing about facing a lineup of growling, impatient cars at the stoplight while we hurry across the street, is there?

We need more surprises designed into our world to lure us out of our cars—what some designers call "aha's!" We need to be constantly discovering new sights and ideas on our walks; otherwise, we'll continue to substitute wheels for feet. I was walking along the bike and pedestrian path in Boulder, Colorado, recently and happened upon an aha! design feature that made my day. There was a dip in the creekside trail and, all of a sudden, I was looking through several glass portholes at a cross-sectional view of life under the creek's surface! For a quarter you can even feed the trout, which hang around the feed dispenser looking out at the people-world.

I remember walking beside my grandfather when I was a kid to his office near the courthouse square, six or seven blocks from his home: waving to everybody and going home for lunch. In our world today, we are forced to drive our cars across the metro area because our use of them has chased the jobs and stores out of our neighborhoods.

Psychologist James Hillman asks, "If we cannot walk around town, where will the mind go?" He believes that humans are *designed* to walk and that we *need* to walk to feel right, but we haven't left ourselves many creative opportunities. Says Hillman,

"Our modern urban landscapes—the malls, streets, building complexes—seem built for the eye only. The foot is forced to travel over what the eye has already done."[29] The view out of our car windows is filled with junk. One burger strip or gas station is the same as another—fixtures designed to serve automobiles, not people.

Front-row Seats at the Fossil Fuel Follies

Cars cause air pollution, acid rain, habitat destruction, water pollution from runoff and oil slicks, global warming, mining impacts, and fifty thousand fatalities a year in the United States. We rolled out the red carpet for cars a full generation ago, but we are just now figuring what the festivities will cost.

In addition to the inflating sticker price and insurance costs of a car, there are multitudes of hidden costs, such as highway construction and maintenance, police and paramedic services, and lost property taxes when land is converted to highways. According to Sierra Club transportation expert Stanley Hart, local, state, and federal governments subsidize each car and truck in the United States with more than $2,000 in taxpayer money—some $400 billion annually.[30] In addition, there is auto-related stress (which is impossible to quantify), plus wildlife losses from both pollution and land-grabbing.

It is becoming clear that our love affair with the car is reaching the "I can't see you as often stage." We need realistic, high-quality alternatives. For starters, we need to quit indulging our car/highway system by continually adding new lanes and parking lots. We need to let traffic congestion serve as a feedback mechanism for positive change. Employers should not offer employees free parking spaces, but rather a free van pool service or free mass-transit tokens. (Even a highly fuel-efficient car is inefficient if it carries only one passenger. Right now, in cities such as Denver, eleven people arrive at work in ten cars.)

What's the most efficient way to get around? The same as it has been the last hundred years—the bicycle. According to Lester Brown, "Investing in 28 pounds of carefully designed metal and rubber can triple one's transport efficiency. Walking one mile burns roughly 100 calories; pedaling on a bicycle reduces this to 35 calories. Covering the distance by either bus or train takes 900 calories of fossil fuel energy; doing so by automobile uses 1,900 calories."[31]

The American Dream: Tossing and Turning

The post-World War II American dream is built on two assumptions: that we will live in a single-family dwelling on a quarter-acre of land and that each family will get to these homes in a private automobile. In the years following World War II, the United States completely rewrote the land/transportation script. Trains and mass transit had been heavily used during the war but were not maintained when the war was over. Instead, the U.S. government became a legion of car salesmen. Veterans were given low-interest loans to buy housing, but only if the housing was *new*. Most of the new housing, of course, was in the suburbs, which required the purchase of a car. The tax on gasoline began to be perceived as a funding mechanism for building and maintaining roads rather than financing alternative transportation. In 1956, the 44,000-mile interstate highway system was signed into law, framing out America's transportation future. (The Netherlands had a different strategy—mass transit and bicycles. The Dutch now have 9,000 miles of bike paths in 13,000 square miles of space.)

As we approach our new century, we're using planning assumptions at least half a century old. As architect Peter Calthorpe has observed:

> Our household makeup has changed dramatically, the workplace and workforce have been transformed, real wealth is shrinking, and serious environmental concerns have surfaced. But we are still building World War II suburbs as if families were large and had only one breadwinner, as if the jobs were all downtown, as if land and energy were endless, and as if another lane on the freeway would end traffic congestion.[32]

In the excellent book, *Sustainable Communities,* Calthorpe describes modern suburbs as:

> truly "pioneer" urban ecologies where little time or thought has been given to the subtleties of place, shared amenities, a sense of community, permanence, long-term costs, or sustainability. The emphasis is on speed, short-run profits, standardized products, mobility, and mass.
>
> From the point of resource use and sociability, the suburban density of six to eight houses to the acre, or about fifteen to twenty people per acre, means a high per-capita cost of building and maintaining services such as roads, utilities, and any form of transportation. From the point of view of sociability, it is a density that is too low to support corner stores, cafes, and all the kinds of places we associate with conviviality.[33]

Nearly 70 percent of U.S. housing was designed for the "typical family" of four to six people, including a breadwinner and a breadbaker. Yet only a quarter of the country's population now lives in such households. Families with two working parents predominate, and nearly a quarter of all Americans live alone.

The country needs to rethink housing, incorporating new ideas based on biologic principles. In Denmark, the concept of "living communities," or "co-housing," is flourishing. Rather than fit people into standardized housing, the question becomes, "What do people want and need?" Typically, each household has a private residence, complete with its own kitchen, while sharing common facilities with the larger group, such as a kitchen and dining hall, day-care area, guest housing, workshops, and laundry. Why duplicate everything? For example, instead of everyone in the entire neighborhood hurrying home after work to cook twenty or thirty different meals, why not enjoy a little relaxation and then eat in the common dining area?

Ideas such as co-housing and similar concepts increase rather than limit options by opening up lifestyle opportunities that we have unintentionally closed the front door on. To have quality lives, we need time for recreation, reflection, and interaction, but the way we've designed our towns and cities, it would appear that the goals were isolation, congestion, and consumption.

What Calthorpe proposes instead of conventional sprawling suburbs are "pedestrian pockets," or clusters of housing, retail space, and offices within a quarter-mile walking radius of a light-rail system. These living/working spaces are modeled after a concept that has thrived over the millennia: the village. By choosing to live in such an area, residents could have their cake and eat it too. While the villages would not use cars as the focus of the design, multilevel parking lots would accommodate them as a complement to walking, bicycling, and mass transit. Calthorpe admits this concept is utopian in the sense that it is a conscious choice of an ideal rather than the result of laissez-faire planning. But why not stretch for utopia? Isn't that what developers tried to convince us that suburbs were?[34]

Which reminds me: Close scrutiny of city government rosters will reveal large percentages of developers. The way to make money in the building industry has been to have a say in the planning of a community. When city council members who also happen to be developers urge "no offices or retail businesses in

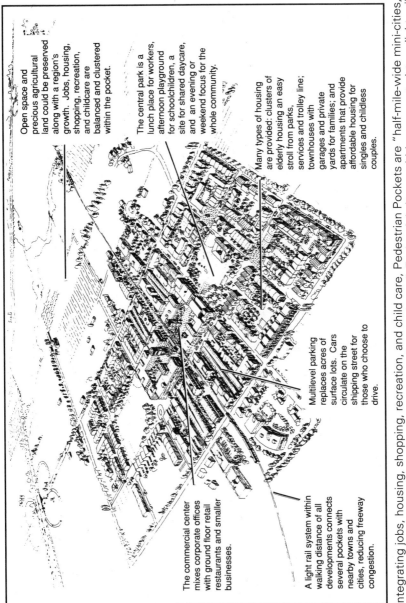

Open space and precious agricultural land could be preserved along with a region's growth. Jobs, housing, shopping, recreation, and childcare are balanced and clustered within the pocket.

The central park is a lunch place for workers, afternoon playground for schoolchildren, a site for shared daycare, and an evening or weekend focus for the whole community.

Many types of housing are provided: clusters of elderly housing an easy stroll from parks, services and trolley line; townhouses with garages and private yards for families; and apartments that provide affordable housing for singles and childless couples.

Multilevel parking replaces acres of surface lots. Cars circulate on the shipping street for those who choose to drive.

The commercial center mixes corporate offices with ground floor retail restaurants and smaller businesses.

A light rail system within walking distance of all developments connects several pockets with nearby towns and cities, reducing freeway congestion.

Integrating jobs, housing, shopping, recreation, and child care, Pedestrian Pockets are "half-mile-wide mini-cities, islands of 5,000 or so residents in a surrounding rural sea." Each mini-city would be connected to a light rail system, making travel from one Pocket to another effortless. *Illustration courtesy of Peter Calthorpe.*

residential areas," what they really mean is, "don't lower the selling potential of my properties." When a developer stands up in a council meeting and says, "we need growth," what he or she really means is, "*I* need growth." Recognizing the potential mismatch between quality of life and developer/politicians, such cities as Davis, California, have an informal policy of keeping the two categories separate.

Like many other things in the United States, suburbs are a fad. Because of their wastefulness, inability to support sensible transportation, and lack of inspiration (they've aptly been described as monocultures) many planners and architects now argue that suburbs will have to go. Calthorpe's colleague, Sim Van der Ryn, has even devised a semi-whimsical technology to help take them apart: an "asphalt-eater." This huge dragon of a machine rips asphalt like sod, converts it into fuel to power itself, recycles gravel, and plants trees in one monstrously benign swipe.

A few U.S. communities are already starting to convert this fantasy into reality. Architect Jon Jerde has successfully re-created bazaar or plaza atmospheres by tearing the roofs off existing shopping malls and letting the sunlight in. In Berkeley, California, the concept of "slow streets" has progressively gained speed (or is that *lost* speed?) as a result of neighborhood political activism. A city-approved pilot project will reshape seven city blocks with the installation of humps, islands, landscaping features, undulating lanes, and reconfigured curbs. The idea is to reduce traffic speed to fifteen miles per hour, and encourage bicycles and pedestrians.

In nearby Davis, a city with twice as many bicycles as cars, human needs likewise take precedence over auto needs. Like Boulder, Colorado, Davis has restrictions on its growth and a limitation on building permits for new houses. In each community, a point system rewards design diversity, energy conservation, and minimization of environmental damage.

Davis also limits the size of its shopping centers to eight acres to encourage smaller shopping areas in each neighborhood, each readily accessible by foot or bicycle. A sixty-two-acre model development called Village Homes illustrates a new, biologic orientation in community design, somewhat reminiscent of Calthorpe's pedestrian pocket concept. Homes are clustered in close proximity, and each home has a small private yard in addition to access to large public areas that encourage neighbors to become friends. Streets

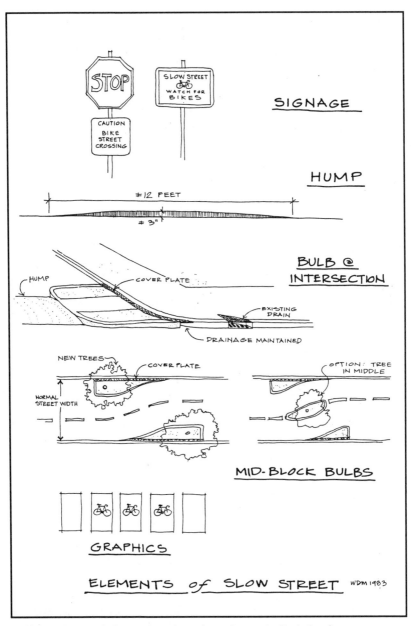

Traffic barriers and obstructions have been in use in Berkeley for many years, but the "Slow Street" design shown here has features that can be built into a street to encourage walkers and bicycle riders. *Illustration courtesy of Urban Ecology, Inc.*

through the development are very narrow, permitting extra space to be used for orchards, gardens, small parks, and paths. One very clear pronouncement that "life is different here" is that the houses are not just display boxes. They face shared countryside areas rather than roads, and they incorporate solar features that help make them living units in more ways than one. By almost any measurement, the community is wildly successful: less crime, higher selling price per square foot, less resident turnover, one-third the water usage and one-half the energy bill. What if the country was covered with thousands of these little communities?

Access by Proximity

What's our best design strategy for transportation? What do we want it to *do*? What role can design play in the reduction of environmental impacts?

It's not really cars, highways, and stoplights we need, but access to jobs, friends, and services. Why can't we live near these things? Our overall social goal should not be going there, but *being* there. According to transportation expert Richard Register, "If you start having mixed-use zoning, if you have the little compact European-style towns and cities, instead of these sprawled, scattered ones, *then* you'd have a context in which you could start talking about really good transportation policies."[35]

Rather than going to the world, we can bring it to us, with better design. Many of our industries and workplaces are now information-based and would make good neighbors, but we've banished them with zoning laws. These laws typically also prohibit mixed-income neighborhoods and retail establishments. Yet by having shopping opportunities right in the neighborhood, as well as housing for the employees who work there, transportation (and stress) can be radically reduced. It seems obvious that our goal should be satisfied people, not faster speeds or bigger houses.

Like a maturing ecosystem, our society needs to investigate and expand its options in transportation. Sometimes, a combination of bicycle and mass transit will be a perfect match. If enough bikes arrive at the transit station, why can't an attendant be hired to guard them? According to Worldwatch researcher Marcia Lowe, "So many Japanese commuters ride their bikes to public transit that train stations need parking towers. The city of Kasukabe now has a twelve-story structure that uses cranes to park over 1,500 bicycles." Many European cities also have bike racks on buses and trains, so the bicycle can be used at both ends of the commute.[36]

In some cases the answer might be special lanes for buses, as in Houston, where buses float past gridlocked single-passenger cars during rush hour. Houston's forty-plus miles of "high occupancy vehicle lanes" are located in the median of the freeway. In the morning, the lanes operate from the suburbs into downtown Houston; in the afternoon, the lanes reverse. Life in the fast lanes has encouraged commuters to find auto partners, vanpools, and buses, while "single-headed vehicles" get lots of brake and clutch use in the slow lanes.

In cases where density permits (generally an average exceeding six housing units per acre), mass transit may be the perfect answer. San Diego and Portland residents are delighted with their light-rail systems. Portland's "MAX," which debuted in 1987, includes cobblestone waiting areas, tree-lined rights-of-way, and a quiet, low-impact demeanor, all of which contribute to a higher quality of life. San Diego's system has for eight years consistently paid 90 percent of its own operational costs as commuters give up second cars and climb on the trolley.[37]

Various cities throughout the world are being intentionally rude to automobiles. For example, in Singapore, all rush-hour vehicles must pay a $30-per-month sticker fee. In the central sectors of Rome and Florence, incoming cars are banned altogether between the hours of 7:30 AM and 7:30 PM Tokyo's residents must show evidence that they have a permanent parking space for their cars, a regulation that has brought about a new design in residential garages—the double decker.

It shouldn't be any secret by now that I'm not overly polite when it comes to cars, either. A fifteen-year-old pickup truck takes me a mile or so up the highway to a park-and-ride bus stop, and I'd ride a bicycle to it instead if there were somewhere to lock it up. I find the irony in an article in an 1899 issue of *Scientific American* especially amusing: "The improvements in city conditions by the general adoption of the motor car can hardly be overestimated. Streets clean, dustless, and odorless, with light rubber-tired vehicles moving swiftly and noiselessly over their smooth expanse, would eliminate a greater part of the nervousness, distraction, and strain of modern metropolitan life." No doubt, the 140 million motor cars in the United States are sharing a good laugh over that one; just look at the grins on those bumpers.

Brewing a Better Cup of Coffee

A classic children's book, entitled *The Peterkin Papers*, offers the perfect metaphor for our current environmental follies. In it, Mrs. Peterkin pours herself a delicious, aromatic cup of coffee but mistakenly puts salt rather than sugar in it. A family conference is held, and a consulting chemist is summoned. His concoctions fail, however, to neutralize the tainted cup of coffee. The herbalist doesn't fare any better. Finally, Mrs. Peterkin takes the problem to the Lady from Philadelphia, who asks an alarmingly simple question: "Why don't you brew a fresh pot of coffee?"

Like Mrs. Peterkin, we persistently overlook the obvious: many of our environmental problems can't be "fixed up"—they have to be rebrewed. We need new approaches to recycling and transportation, starting in the design phase. If we design packaging with recycling in mind, we can save ourselves a lot of trouble. Likewise, if our zoning laws, taxes, and collective awareness encourage a shift in the way we integrate land with buildings, we can not only reduce vehicle miles traveled, but also pollution, stress, and many of the hidden expenses of transportation.

Our real goal is peace of mind, isn't it? When Thomas Jefferson penned the phrase, "pursuit of happiness," surely he didn't mean we should chase after it in Ferraris, 4x4s, speedboats, ATVs, and snowmobiles. I think he meant we should safeguard the right to make informed choices in our own behalf—choices that are based on something genuine, like biological and social well-being.

Our forum for decision-making is a good one. We debate issues in the press, over the back fence, in Congress, in classrooms, and in board rooms. In general, our common level of understanding determines the complexity of our society; however in recent years, our attitude has been, "as long as *somebody* understands how this works, we're all right because we trust each other, right?" In that respect, we're like Mrs. Einstein, who, when asked if she understood the theory of relativity responded, "No, but I know Albert, and I know he can be trusted."

But good intentions can sometimes yield bad results, as in the case of an apparently good thing like DDT. We need to move toward the convergence of popular understanding of designs and their widespread use. In other words, our products should not stray so far from comprehensibility that they can't be controlled if they turn out to be "misfits." The major problem with biotechnol-

Portland's light rail system, MAX, was chosen as the best solution to relieve highway congestion and increase transportation options in the city. *Photos courtesy of Tri-Met.*

ogy or nuclear energy is that not enough of us understand the implications, let alone the physics and chemistry.

A college-aged environmental activist I know observed that the environmental movement in the United States resembles a garden. Citizens and consumers soften the seedbed and choose the seeds with the help of environmental and consumer groups that do the planting, and government agencies make sure the crops are taken care of. The recurring question of our times, "What can the *individual* do on behalf of the environment?" needs input from all three groups to be adequately answered. But the correct response certainly would include making nature-compatible choices, getting involved in information-magnifying coalitions, and demanding well-conceived designs. Instead of surrendering one's power to the country's monoculture, a concerned citizen can be a holdout, sowing and nurturing diverse seeds of uniqueness.

CHAPTER 4

DESIGNING

When things work, it feels good. There's a little thrill of satisfaction, isn't there, as you twist the lid off a pressure-sealed jar of coffee and get that "thwup" sound as a reward, along with the aroma of hand-picked beans from the Colombian highlands. It's the same when you first sit in the driver's seat of a well-designed car, with dashboard accessories that are understandably labeled and logically arranged. A favorite hand-knit sweater can do it for you, too, or a brightly colored backpacking tent, sliding out of its nylon sack and just about self-constructing into a dome right before your eyes.

Design begins at a very basic level. Whether or not we choose to acknowledge it, human design has achieved its heights only by balancing on the steady shoulders of sun and soil. From this earthy, essential foundation, we skipped merrily up the inclined plane, beyond the cathedrals and steam locomotives, into the designed world of the twentieth century: the space shuttle, Froot Loops, and designer genes. Where to from here?

When things *don't* work, living things (including humans) are the losers. Victor Papanek, author of several highly useful books on real-world design, can't resist poking fun at certain items in the American marketplace in the book, *How Things Don't Work*.

Beneath a photograph of two cheese graters, he and co-author James Hennessey write, "On the left, the inexpensive, efficient, and nearly indestructible one which will work left- or right-handed. On the right, the 'improved' model, which is right-handed only and, after some months of use, grinds its own plastic coating into the food."[1]

In *Design for the Real World*, Papanek has some fun with the prototypical ballpoint pen, which emerged with much fanfare right after World War II: "With a Reynolds pen you could write under water but practically nowhere else. They skipped, they blotted, they leaked in your pockets, and there were no replacement cartridges because the pens were one-shot affairs. You threw them away as soon as they ran dry, if not sooner."[2]

Millions of similar episodes are occurring at any moment all over the planet. People are wrestling with devices and designs that simply *don't* belong in our world. A cardboard manufacturing company, for example, was polluting a river with salty discharges and was under the gun from the regulatory agencies. A company engineer came up with what seemed like a good idea: put the salt back into the cardboard boxes and send it out into the world *in the product*. This actually made the cardboard denser and stronger. But then the company started getting calls from a confused customer who used the boxes to ship steel parts. The parts were rusting in the boxes because the salt crystals stored up water and transferred it to the parts. Exit salty boxes.

When on Earth, Do As the Earth Does

As this chapter discusses, there are more alarming things than salt in many of our products. From the cadmium coating on bolts to the radioactive element in smoke alarms and the lead in bottle caps, the performance of many of our consumer goods (and manufacturing processes) currently relies on the presence of contaminants that need to be designed *out* of the products.

A device designed to conserve energy by automatically turning lights off when the room is empty is an example of a good design concept that hasn't yet been perfected. The device has a motion sensor to detect the presence of people in the room; after a certain period in which no motion is detected, the lights turn off. According to a friend who wears a hearing aid, one version of this design sends out a high-frequency impulse that interferes with the operation of hearing devices. Company designers are now working to overcome this problem with a switch to disable the signal when people with impaired hearing are present. This design, then, is a great idea that is being modified to address problems in real-world applications.

Sometimes, for the sake of profit, we've intentionally pursued sloppy design, as the inventor of the disposable razor blade did back in the 1890s. To this man, King Gillette, goes my honorary award as "Pioneer of the Throwaway Society." Humans have been shaving for twenty thousand years or so, using flint, clam shell, bronze, iron, and steel razors. And, undoubtedly, many of these razors were thrown away when they no longer functioned just right. But Gillette's dubious contribution to the twentieth century is that he deliberately searched for some item that could be profitably thrown away. Gillette's first attempt at fame and fortune was a poor-selling book, *The Human Drift*, which *was* thrown away all right, but without making him any money.

According to historian Charles Panati, Gillette "turned elsewhere for his fortune. A friend, William Painter, inventor of the throwaway bottle cap, suggested that the failed author devise an item that, like the bottle cap, was used once, then discarded. The idea intrigued Gillette. For a year, he repeatedly ran through the alphabet, listing household and business items in frequent use."[3] In 1895, while shaving with a dull razor, inspiration hit home in the form of a minor neck wound—blades that could be simply thrown away when they got dull.

How many blow-dryers, remote-control toy cars, and cheaply constructed garden tools has *your* family replaced? Such items are midway between excellence and stupidity—they're designed to do the job, but for a limited time only. Every time we send one of these partly broken items off to an overcrowded landfill, two more seem to spring up in its place, made in polluting factories from finite resources.

Minute Maid's Premium Choice orange juice is a good example of how mismatched our designs have become with our natural world. Marketed on TV as "mankind's perfect package" (the orange is conceded to be "nature's perfect package"), Premium Choice offers a shelf life that is weeks longer than competing brands, but at nature's expense:

> This new bottle is blow molded with sterile air and filled with cold juice in an ultrasanitary environment. A petrochemical smorgasbord of

layers that block oxygen and do not react with the acidic juice inside, the container is exactly the kind of bulky package that eats up space in landfills, never decomposes, and is tough, practically and economically, to recycle.[4]

Says designer Richard Gerstman of the packaging design firm of Gerstman and Meyers, "The most appropriate material is not just one that holds the product better but one that functions better in society." Papanek defines design as a "conscious and intuitive effort to impose meaningful order." He also writes, "Any attempt to separate design, to make it a thing-by-itself, works counter to the fact that design is the underlying matrix of life." If we define pollution as the lack of order and coherence, then good design appears to be our very best way of dealing with it.

Genetic Gin Rummy

Culture and nature evolve in precisely the same way. It's a perfecting process, like a game of gin rummy: the useful cards are kept and linked with other good cards, while the losers and misfits are rejected. Worthwhile information is extracted from the deck and stored (as structure and sequence) in one's hand.

The natural elegance of a butterfly wing is without a doubt a winner. The light, colorful wings of butterflies have just the right information encoded in them to perform several critical functions at once. Butterflies are energy-intensive, requiring high-yield nectar to fuel their flight. But before they even get off the ground, their bodies need to warm up, and the wings serve as solar energy panels to conduct and reflect heat to the thorax. The information-rich wings also serve as message boards. In the case of the monarch butterfly, the brightly colored message reads, "Predators beware! I've stored toxic alkaloids in my body. Eat me and you die!" If the message is successful, the butterfly is free to use those same wings to explore meadows and flower gardens.

In product and process design, we play the role of God. In effect, we build genetic instructions into our designs, and then we get to see how smart we were by having to live with those creations. The design decisions we make not only determine what sort of world we'll have, but also what sort of organisms we'll be. We are physiologically adapting to our own designs.

What kind of "genetic" strategies should we shoot for in our products and technologies in order to ensure natural compatibility?

How well do our creations *fit?* Is there a frugality of information in them, as in the wings of a butterfly? Can our designs perform their intended tasks while at the same time supporting/being supported by neighboring designs? Can they find their way back to the beginning of the cycle, to go on nature's "ride" yet another time?

These are some of the main themes of this chapter. We will look at some specific examples of designing *with* nature: ecological wastewater treatment; products custom-made for recycling and "source reduction"; designs that make the homes, appliances, and cars a better environmental fit; and strategies for redesigning institutions. The overall message is that *good* design is woven into the latticework of living systems and becomes part of the structure and coherence of those systems.

The Germination of Products

In *Building for Tomorrow,* Martin Pawley compares natural and industrial products. (Although in a sense, even industrial products are "natural," just like daisies and dinosaurs. Conversely, the ingredients in many naturally occurring products are reminiscent of something made from petrochemicals. What's in an orange? Why, it's 3-keto-1-gulonolactone, propanetricarboxylic acid, methanol formaldehyde, and synephrine, among many other unpronounceables.) Pawley suggests:

> The mechanism by which an automated drawing and ironing machine in a canning plant turns out 1,200 beverage cans every minute is actually very similar to that which enables a tree to produce a superfluity of seeds or a frog an immensely redundant number of eggs. In fact, the actual rate of recycling achieved with the aid of bottle laws is very close to the survival rate achieved by frog eggs and considerably better than the reproduction rate of trees.[5]

What design strategies permit products and processes to germinate (by being recycled) and come into flower (in a second incarnation)? Obviously, both the seed and the seedbed (the product and consumer) need to be full of design savvy. In the case of aluminum cans, process and structure combine with inherent value to bring about a relatively reliable "germination rate." Of the more than three hundred billion aluminum cans sold in this decade, well over half have germinated by being remelted, reformed, and refilled within about six weeks of use. This design process offers incredible environmental benefits: the energy equivalent of half a can of gasoline is saved when an aluminum can is recycled, and nine-tenths of the air and water pollution that the manufacture of a new can would cause is avoided. So "highly evolved" has aluminum become that the same container function is now provided by a much lighter design than in previous generations of cans.

How can we duplicate our success with aluminum? Should we ensure recycling by using *gold* in our packaging? Should our newspapers be spiked with nontoxic precious metals that can be retrieved at the recycling plant? (Remember, a four-foot stack of recycled newspapers spares the life of a forty-foot tree, and the recovery of an entire print run of one issue of the Sunday *New York Times* would leave 75,000 trees standing.)[6]

If germination can't realistically be assured in the structure of the newspapers themselves, then obviously we need to cultivate and fertilize the seedbed (with stringent recycling laws) or substitute another "crop" that accomplishes the same function. Perhaps a large percentage of our newspapers, for example, could be replaced with a "news table," a subscription service that would electronically display the news on a coffee table, angled like a drafting table. You could adjust the height, highlight articles for electronic clipping, and page through the "newspaper" by pushing a button (ultimately, just telling it "next page"). You could eat breakfast without having to *hold* the news in your hands! Instead of buying newspapers every day, you just buy the table and the actual subscription is free. If you go on vacation, tell the machine to store up the week's papers until you get back. Think of the energy and resources saved, and the pollution avoided in manufacturing, distribution, and recovery!

France has already implemented a similar system for telephone books. The "Minitel," a mini-computer terminal, is offered free of charge to telephone subscribers as an alternative to hard-copy directories.[7]

Nature-compatible Design Strategies

Biologic requires that we follow the leader, and the leader is nature itself. Successful natural systems invariably move toward the principle of least effort. Humans are not the only component of nature that craves convenience; through evolution, all living things try to achieve basic needs with a minimum of biological effort.

American society is not yet effortless or genuinely convenient, however, because what masquerades as convenience is in many cases just postponement. We're still in our adolescent years in terms of design. We make abrupt shifts from motionless stupefaction to high-stress deadline busting, but rarely achieve real convenience.

We've just snowplowed inconvenience aside because we had surplus land and power. The apparent convenience we gain by throwing everything away comes back and bites us in the behind in the form of higher taxes, negative health effects, and a degraded, impoverished landscape.

Our environmental strategy during the past thirty years or so has been nothing more than "pollution chasing." We take contaminants out of the air with scrubbers and precipitators, but then we're stuck with the collected wastes. And we often chase pollutants out of the water into the air, as when our wastewater plants release volatile industrial chemicals in the direction of our lungs.

In reality, we not only chase pollution, but are chased *by* it. When the city water supply becomes suspicious, we retreat to drinking bottled water (15 percent of U.S. households connected to municipal water supplies already have done so). When quality of life degenerates because of air pollution, we start looking for a job somewhere else.

So what do we need to do to get things back on track? I propose that we incorporate the following list of twelve "tributary" design strategies into our cultural mainstream and invent legal and social strategies to make sure they stay there! But before we even look at the list, we need to admit that we have a problem. We're trashaholics. From this point on, like participants in addiction programs, we have to agree not to tolerate design that perpetuates our addiction to cheap resources and energy or we'll never kick the habit. If our designs demand energy and endless cleanup, we'll be locked into maintaining our habit, even though we realize it's a trap. Like heroin addicts, we'll resort to anything to get the fix—tear up the environment, go to war, you name it.

Our economy and our society are defined by the designs we choose to implement. We're fenced within our own design strategies. Therefore, we can't design things as if humans were incapable of walking, lifting, or reading instructions. One of the greatest human pleasures is to have the brain and hands work as a team. But we've just about designed that pleasure out of our generic lifestyle. Our investment choices of the last fifty or sixty years resemble a very steep cliff:

don't look down, because we've just poured trillions of dollars into an infrastructure of homes, shopping centers, workplaces, and highway systems that is frighteningly dependent on the availability of cheap oil and the assumption of convenience.

1. The Strategy of the Backpacker (Unity of Mind and Nature)

The backpacker fits into his/her environment as neatly and efficiently as equipment fits into the backpack. Key words for this strategy are vigor, resourcefulness and efficiency. Backpackers use natural resources but they don't *use* them up. They bring precisely what they need, and no more.

Why pamper ourselves with unnecessary junk we'll just have to carry? And why not make good use of what we already have, like legs, and health?

The backpacker cleans up as he/she goes, leaving a campsite in just as good a condition as when he/she arrived. He or she packs out everything that was packed in, minus the food consumed. If our culture cleaned things up as *we* progressed, we wouldn't have to resort to "extra-strength" technologies in our manufacturing processes and Superfund sites.

To demonstrate the volume of trash used by a single consumer, Dartmouth professors volunteered to carry their trash *with* them for a week. Their habits began to change by midweek: reusables replaced items that would have to be stowed in their trash bags, and the need for many of our standard items was challenged.

The full costs of a product or process have to be understood. The backpacker knows where the stream originates and where it joins the river by following its course. We have to do the same with the things we buy and use. How much water pollution resulted from the manufacture of the office paper we scribble one mistaken sentence on and toss in the basket? There are subtle contractual agreements on everything in our material world, but we absentmindedly sign without reading them.

In the long run, what we're doing is *buying* pollution with peace of mind as currency. We pawn the territory both upstream and down for quick shots of gratification and then wonder what happened to our once-pristine forest. Because it seems convenient, we settle for linear thinking rather than permit ourselves to wander off the wilderness path for well-deserved picnics. By contrast, lateral thinking gets us into the sunny meadows, where we discover that it may not be A or B we need to be doing or buying, but C, D, E, or F (or parts of each). For example, we're trying so hard to decide between a paper or plastic bag at the supermarket that the correct answer doesn't occur to us: neither. We should be using reusable cloth or nylon bags that last for years. How many chain-sawed trees and how much petroleum-based pollution could be avoided if we just kept a compact bagful of permanent shopping bags in our cars? One of them could be an insulated ice cream bag, maybe, while another is the "master bag" with Velcro-flapped pockets.

Incineration of trash, or land disposal? Neither—it's got to be source reduction and recycling (including composting) for many reasons. Incineration can generate energy, but like the addition of another freeway lane, it encourages more of the same. If you build an incinerator, you need to feed it, so you don't think about the "D" alternative, which is cutting back to begin with on the unnec-

Paper or plastic? The correct answer is neither. Like many other commonly used devices, grocery bags should be durable and re-usable. *Photo by Doug Franklin courtesy of Windstar Foundation.*

essary junk we use. The incineration of trash demands that we go back into our forests and our mines to get more resource/fuel—causing major, chronic impacts. (For this reason, even abundant resources like iron, aluminum, silicon, and calcium should be used and reused efficiently.) By incinerating our products, we are prostituting their value and structure when we should be remaining faithful to our virgin resources (pun only partly intended), as well as our products, by designing our creations to have durable, multiple cycles.

A recent heavy autumn snowfall caused a power failure in our town. As darkness descended inside our house, we were forced to go into the backpacker mode. We cooked our dinner on a Coleman stove and watched the fire in the wood stove instead of the TV. We had a ball! It occurred to us that we don't need gadgetry and trash-to-be nearly as much as it needs us.

The strategy of the backpacker interacts with each of the following strategies. Just as the species in an ecosystem are continually bartering and negotiating, the twelve strategies contained in our backpack trade information and nutrients as they continue to evolve.

2. The Strategy of Steel (Recycling)

A fascinating example of resource reincarnation is presented in Martin Pawley's *Building for Tomorrow*. The steel in Civil War cannonballs moved from one life into the next:

> Large numbers of the cannonballs were sold as scrap after the conflict and broken up by the old method of pouring water into their handling holes and waiting for the winter frost to crack them into fragments. These fragments in turn were fed into furnaces to make steel and rolled into rails for the nation's expanding railroad network. After up to fifty years of such service, the worn-out rails were again sold as scrap, hundreds of tons of them being shipped to Europe for use as tank barriers before World War II.
>
> With the German occupation of the Continent, these tank traps were cut off at ground level with acetylene torches and shipped to German steel mills for the rolling and casting of alloy steel tank hulls and turrets; then they made their way into Russia with the invading German armies. By the end of the war virtually all this steel had been absorbed again by the Russian steel industry to be formed into beams, girders, truck frames, and yet more tanks—some of which found their way eventually to the Middle East, ending up in Israel after the Arab wars.[8]

Whether or not we believe in reincarnation, it appears to be happening all around us, at least on a material level. The carbon molecule in your tooth may have come out of the depths of the earth in a volcanic eruption, passed through the skeletal structure of a dodo bird, and drifted for eons in the atmosphere before becoming part of the soil that sustained the apple tree that lived near the house that Jack built. Things are in continuous rebirth, and good designs need to reflect that fact by being flexible, adaptable, and durable.

About thirty years ago, Heineken Breweries came up with an innovative idea for resource reincarnation that is a great example of lateral thinking—choosing D rather than being limited to A or B. "A brick that holds beer" was the synthesis of two observations made by a company executive as he toured a Heineken plant in the Caribbean. He noted a lack of affordable housing and a surplus of beer bottles with no economic means of getting back to the bottling plants. Returning to the Netherlands, he hired a designer to create a new kind of building material, the bottle-brick.

Research indicated that bottle production exceeds brick and building-block production in all of the world's developed countries and in many Third World countries as well. In addition, the processes of pasteurizing and capping the bottles require strength that greatly exceeds that needed for most simple types of construction.

As long as the bottle-bricks were used in the same area as the beer, distribution costs would be virtually nothing. But the company's designers were unable to settle on a truly workable prototype:

> Some effective building bottles were too heavy and slow-forming to be economical in production, for fractions of a second in forming time can greatly affect production costs. Other bottles were rejected by Heineken's marketing people because they were too "ugly" or too "feminine" in appearance. In the end, the bottle's appearance was squat and "masculine," but it could not be used vertically for building purposes (by far the strongest orientation for a bottle), and it required cement mortar bonding with a silicon additive in order to make a wall.[9]

Maybe one answer to the bottle-recycling question is neither glass nor plastic, but reinforced ceramic or even lightweight, glass-lined cement. (New techniques in cement-making incorporate fibers into the material, prompting predictions that it will be used in everything from speaker cabinets to telephones.)

Our asphalt-hungry roads offer another opportunity for the rebirth of materials. Since 1971, the city of Baltimore has used a recipe that includes 40 percent crushed, melted glass in its asphalt. The reason? To "make our streets sparkle."[10] Many cities are now thinking about using the strategy of steel to reduce their dead tire mountains. Public works engineers are seeing the advantages of using melted tires as a sealant for highway pavement; 1,250 tires per mile of road is the standard recipe there. A company in Minnesota converts used tires into doormats, athletic mats, grocery cart wheels, and liners for the beds of pickup trucks with their "TireCycle" process. Recycling tires eliminates potential rat colonies, mosquito breeding grounds, and tire fires, which have been known to burn out of control for months.

We *want* our products to evolve so that they have a crafty symbiosis with other natural and human-made designs. Ideally, the "genetic" instructions we put into our products will include self-propagation—just like cow manure in a pasture happens to be in precisely the right place to become cow manure again. The point is, we need long-distance runners in our designs. To bring those kinds of designs into our world, we'll have to make some cognitive leaps of faith, just as track athletes did when they broke the four-minute mile.

Taos architect Michael Reynolds uses aluminum cans and used tires as building materials. The basic structure is then plastered over to resemble adobe. Reynolds first got the idea twenty years ago, after watching two news programs—a Charles Kuralt report showing littered landscapes, and a Walter Cronkite piece on the high price of housing. *Photo courtesy of Michael Reynolds.*

3. The Goldilocks Strategy (The Right Fit)

Another strategy we need to keep in mind is the Goldilocks strategy—finding just the right size and just the right fit for each of our creations, or not creating them to begin with.

Until recently, underground storage tanks (to store gasoline and other liquid products) were a poor fit in many locations and soils. A naturally occurring electric current passed from the soil into the tanks, corroding their steel and leaking the tanks' contents into the ground (over half a million tanks are now thought to be leaking in the United States as you read this). When the problem was understood, a small "counter-current" device was developed, and it solved the corrosion problem. Another design flaw continues to plague many of the old model tanks, however. The level of liquid in the tanks is routinely measured with a long dipstick, since varying temperatures and pressures make electronic devices unreliable. When the leaks in many tanks were investigated, engineers discovered that the tanks had been punctured right where the dipsticks made contact. Many new tanks are now made of fiberglass, with reinforced strike plates where the dipstick touches the bottom of the tank. The point is, finding the right design for the job is not as simple as we sometimes assume.

The Goldilocks design strategy should be reflected in everything we make and do. Just as our houses need to be built to fit human needs, chemicals have to be designed to fit *microbial* capabilities. Institutions need to fit into—and enhance—our social fabric, and technologies need to be scaled to provide a match between what's needed and what's supplied. One down-to-earth example is a roll of toilet paper a friend brought back from resource-conscious Switzerland. Made from high-quality recycled paper, the width of the roll is a full inch narrower than standard U.S. rolls—and chances are that inch will never be missed for anatomical reasons beyond the scope of this discussion. Yet cumulatively, that inch will save thousands of trees. There *are* a few American brands of toilet paper that are more "environmentally friendly" than the competition because they are made from recycled paper, packaged in paper rather than plastic, and contain neither formaldehyde nor bleach (see Appendix).

With its central theme of the right tool for the right job, the field of "appropriate" or "intermediate" technology pioneered by E.F. Schumacher incorporates the Goldilocks strategy. According to this approach, no one energy source should be expected to pick up the tab for the whole meal. Instead, a region needs to use resources that are abundant in its own area.

For example, have you ever driven across (or lived in) Kansas? Did the wind ever stop blowing? The power of that incessant wind should be tapped with small, low-maintenance wind generators mounted on high-voltage power lines from one end of the state to the other. There's enough electricity in that prairie wind to send Dorothy and Toto back to get the Straw Man (we can use his brains to help us design things better).

Each region has its own kind of wealth. Even the so-called "wastes" of a given area have great potential. For example, in Texas, we should use cotton gin trash as a raw material; in California, walnut shells, rice straw, and spoiled grain are in abundance; and in the southeastern states, there's a wealth of peach pits, logging leftovers, and citrus peels. In Virginia alone, enough sawdust and other logging residues are produced to replace 42 percent of the oil and gas consumed in the state's commercial and industrial sectors.[11] We need to make adjustments in our ways of doing business to fit resources like these into the mainstream.

4. The Strategy of Compost (Microbial Wisdom)

The strategy of a tin can's contents is to be microbe-hating. You get rid of yeasts, molds, viruses, and bacteria with the help of pasteurization, and then you smugly kick back inside your fortress and make a bid for immortality. We need this kind of strategy for certain things besides food preservation—like antibiotics, for example, that can save lives. But the tin-can strategy has become an obsession. In our agriculture, housekeeping, and lives in general, we try for complete eradication of everything smaller than a hamster, when only a few of the millions of creatures "down there" are actually bad actors.

We've even adopted a tin-can orientation in the design of our landfills, which we intentionally keep dry and oxygen-free to prevent decomposition. We need to progress forward to a balanced, respectful relationship with microbes that can be exemplified by the diverse, can-do strategy of compost: "Just let me work." We need to recognize that most bugs are allies. For example, the active cultures that yogurt contains help our stomaches do what they're supposed to do, just as the right kind of microbes know how to convert overripe fruit into fine wine.

Moldy soybean curd was the first documented antibiotic, used by the Chinese as early as 500 B.C. to treat infections. Moldy bread and cobwebs soon found their ways into physicians' bags, too, but it was another two thousand years before the fungus penicillium was discovered, by accident, to be a potential ally of humans.[12]

Once we accept an inevitable alliance with microbes, we might be able to accept certain other things, such as the color off-white. For at least the past five hundred years, white has been a symbol of purity, indicating the absence of germs and disease. We bleach our clothes and paper snow-white, and we remove the bran from flour and refine sugar to make them as white as possible. But bleach contains chlorine, which has complex environmental impacts (see the section "Technologic vs. Biologic," later in this chapter), and we need to be eating *whole* grains, not grain remains.

The strategy of compost counsels, "Off-white's all right." In the same spirit, it reminds us that it's okay if the fruit has a slight visual flaw; taste buds and stomaches don't have eyes anyway. And that dent in your car just gives it character. "Relax," it tells us, "you belong here."

5. The Strategy of the Cactus (Efficiency)

Glancing through nature's inventory of design schemes, one would think that the planet's organisms had collectively received uncountable quadrillions in R&D dollars. Yet the actual cost for the cactus species to develop a water conservation strategy was zero, other than evolutionary patience. The strategy of the cactus demonstrates what can be done to get more mileage out of a limited resource.

Unlike cacti, leafy plants depend on water to maintain their structure. Since plant cells need water anyway, this is a pretty decent strategy, but it doesn't work in a low-humidity desert. As leafy plants open their "guard cells" to breathe in carbon dioxide, they can't help but lose water through those same cells by evaporation. Cacti "invented" a rigid structure that doesn't rely on water to maintain its shape, so they lose very little water to the dry air when they breathe. A similar human-designed strategy is the intentional storage of water underground in aquifers, where it can't evaporate. And in a wider sense, the computer is an analog of the cactus, since it stores information effectively, rather than letting it "evaporate" away or get jumbled up in our twentieth-century brains.

Cacti, aquifers, and computers are efficient because they store resources. Obviously, efficiency is a prerequisite for inclusion in our backpack of design solutions, but what exactly does the term mean? Until recently, efficiency has had a meaning roughly opposite to the one exemplified by the cactus and the computer. In the worlds of manufacturing, logging, fishing, farming, and most other American business activities, efficiency has in past years been synonymous with the quickest method of dicing up resources and converting them into profits. In other words, never mind how much stuff we use, just keep it coming.

The definition of efficiency that serves us best for optimum design involves "no *wasted* effort or resources." Currently, close to half of the gross energy outputs in the United States are devoted to the mining and processing of raw materials, according to the Institute for Local Self Reliance. In a world threatened by the greenhouse effect, species depletion, and chemical strangulation, this is unacceptable.

Many of our standard operating procedures, from electrical generation and use through package design, do not use the strategy of the cactus. They permit waste to move along with the product at each stage of production, consumption, and afterlife. In the typical power plant, for example, coal or uranium is used as fuel to boil water to produce steam to run turbines to make electricity for consumers at the other end of an energy-wasting distribution system. At each step in the process, energy gets away in the form of heat and pollution. Only one-third of the original energy in the fuel source is used as electricity. The rest is wasted. (Instead of space-heating, it gets away to heat outer space.)

One of our most pressing needs is to use the strategy of the cactus in the design of our automobiles, a species that guzzles gas like a thirsty weeping willow guzzles water. To allow the concept of waste to hitchhike along with our design strategies is to risk the highway robbery of environmental pollution.

6. The Strategy of the Lover (Essence before Appearance)

Since lovers are humanity's ultimate "product," human designs need to reflect a few of their uninhibited, essential qualities. Remarkable things happen when lovers are on the loose. Appearances become secondary to *essence*. The lover is a fool, but doesn't care. The important thing is the quality *within* a person or object. When love is the primary fuel, the future and past are also secondary. The present becomes very clear and is all that really matters. Trivialities are suddenly revealed as sham. Because there's no doubt that their instincts are correct, lovers find a way to get past the obstacles. They bypass the world's conventions—elope—if they must.

My own weather-beaten instincts tell me that our designs are uninspired because *we* are uninspired. Lacking the passion and connectedness of the lover, we settle for a calculated appearance of good design. Desert cities get made over with lush midwestern-type landscapes the same way a vain woman's face gets "lifted" to disguise what her life has written on it. Monocultural suburban homes are cosmetically identical, just like Miss America contestants.

We know at the gut level that we need better cars and transit systems, but we don't have the passion and commitment to remove the obstacles. We see life not as a wondrous unfolding process, but rather a series of mediocre products. Rather than flowing effortlessly with the stream, we winch ourselves along against the current from one shiny product to the next.

Just like the rest of the world, lovers get older, but they do so gracefully and without pretense. As Victor Papanek points out, our modern designs don't know *how* to go with the flow of time: "Throughout most of human history materials, being organic, have aged gracefully. Thatched roofs, wooden furniture, copper kettles, leather aprons, ceramic bowls, for example, would acquire small nicks, scratches, and dents, gently discolor, and acquire a thin patina as part of the natural process of oxidation."[13] But Americans are instructed that aging is a disgrace. The lovers and well-designed products in our world have a sustaining inner glow, but they are surrounded by toupeed heads, waxy apples, and colors never seen in any flower garden.

Taking a more passionate, grounded approach, poet Wendell Berry voices the strategy of the lover when he urges us to "love the board before it becomes a table, love the tree before it yields the board, and love the forest before it gives up the tree."

7. The Strategy of the Apples (Quality Control)

The strategy of the apples warns, "Watch out for the one bad apple in our midst!" When apples begin to get overripe, they give off ethylene gas that causes other apples to jump on the bandwagon headed for decomposition.

A lot of the throwing away we do is because a tiny amount of *bad* stuff has contaminated a large amount of perfectly *good* stuff.

Add a glass of vintage wine to a vat of hazardous wastes, and you get hazardous wastes. Add a drop of hazardous wastes to a vat of wine, and you still get hazardous wastes.

It's like the one bad fact in a newspaper article that casts shadows on the rest of the article, or the glossy-paged magazine whose contaminating chemicals make a stack of newspapers far less viable for recycling. If the neglect of a community permits a troubled teenager to become a criminal, the whole community suffers. Little impurities can spell huge problems. The toxic metals in sewage sludge spoil the sludge for safe use on crops. The chlorine compounds in plastics, table salt, and paper recombine into highly toxic emissions during combustion. The sodium azide in automobile air bags, the mercury and lead in batteries, and the herbicides in grass clippings become flies in the soup of our trash. Perfectly useful garbage becomes something we have to destroy or else put into permanent, precarious storage.

What's the common thread in all this spoilage? In each case, if an ounce of prevention had been used, great volumes of waste would have been avoided. The strategy of the apples demands that we fine-tune our systems, knowing what conditions will turn wine to vinegar. Sloppy designs and processes don't bother to take into account how things work. They don't use biologic. They assume there's room for wastes. The use of good design is far less tolerant of wastes, insisting that they remain useful resources.

Is America ready for the idea of "clean wastes?" Ready or not, here they come, because dirty wastes are becoming too expensive and too damaging in a world that's already filled up with them. We shrink back from being "inconvenienced," but on the other hand we are repulsed at the gut level by the idea of contaminated convenience. Sooner or later, it's got to go.

8. The Strategy of the Rice Paddy (The Systems Approach)

Ten thousand years ago, a family's nutritional needs required twenty-five hundred acres for hunting range. A thousand years ago, a medieval peasant family could eke out a living on one-and-a-half acres. Twentieth-century Japanese rice growers can provide the staples of their family's diet with a quarter of an acre or less.[14] This increase in efficiency is directly proportional to an evolved increase in human understanding of nature. Without sacrificing continued success or sustainability, rice farmers have mimicked the dynamics of nature's most productive unit, the marsh ecosystem.

As previously mentioned, young ecosystems are highly productive, while mature systems are highly *protective*. By alternately flooding and draining their fields, rice farmers do not allow them to mature as ecosystems, yet unlike intentionally immature systems, such as corn fields, rice paddies are *conservative*. This interrupted system provides a compromise between youth and maturity, permitting high yields on a continuous basis without excessive inputs of fertilizers, pesticides, and petroleum-fueled equipment.

The key to the success of the rice paddy is intentional diversity. The players in a typical rice field's cast have been carefully chosen over the millennia for their natural abilities to work as a team. Fish are cultured in the paddies during the flooded period. When the paddy is drained, the fish are herded into troughs or tanks in the corners of the field for harvesting. Each of the fish species is a specialist in different areas: some are surface feeders specializing in bugs and larvae, some are grass eaters, and some are algae eaters. Pesticides are unnecessary because pigs, chickens, ducks, and frogs play the role of scavengers, keeping pests under control (and later becoming part of the harvest themselves). The farmers also exchange rice seed with their neighbors to reduce pest problems (they have observed that any one variety begins to gain a following of pests after repeated use).

Nothing is wasted in the rice paddy, and everything has a purpose. One strain of blue-green algae has the ability to bring nitrogen out of the air and into the system, while the wastes of animal species, as well as nutrients in the floodwater, provide the remainder of the nutrients. The water "mulch" of the rice paddy protects the plants from high temperatures, high-impact rain, and winds, reducing soil erosion and thus keeping nutrients from getting away.

Like the cactus, the rice paddy is extremely efficient. One strategy is distinguished from the other by orchestration and dimensionality. The cactus is a solo virtuoso, while the rice paddy is an integrated, diverse system.

If our designs are to succeed in an ultimate sense, they'll have to fit in not only with nature but with each other. More than mere products, we need *systems* of products, capable of germination, adaptation, and reincarnation that can mesh with the cultural fabric of humans and all other living things. My conviction is that any species that can come up with computer chips and Rubik's cubes is smart enough to employ the strategy of the rice paddy in its everyday activities. But first we have to spread the word that such an ingenious strategy even exists.

9. The Strategy of Right Now (Marketing a New Mindset)

Our most pressing goal is to be alive in the present, not the future or the past; to acknowledge the importance of the journey, and not be so obsessed with the destination. We dream about how good things will be when we are rich, when we are retired, when we are on vacation—but we need to experience how good things can be, *right now*. Our inability to be fully in the present is a primary obstacle to having a coherent, well-designed environment. We fret about where we're going to put all our trash at the end of its useful life, but we neglect a far more important concept: that our resources are being wasted by taking the shape of trash right from the beginning. Similarly, we feel guilty about not getting enough exercise or eating the right foods—but for the wrong reasons. It's not death at the end of our lives that we should be fighting, but the death in our everyday lives. By living well in the present, we can be vital, energetic individuals, capable of experiencing joy and accomplishing just about anything. We sometimes spend time with our kids because we think we *should*, or to enrich their futures. A better reason is because it's fun. Emotions such as guilt and dread sap our energy, letting it leak out of the present like hazardous wastes from a drum.

We have reached the point where we actually have to *market* the present. We have to be sold on the idea that better design is possible right now. Even good designs need to be actively marketed, to overcome the momentum that bad design has achieved during our century of resource-gobbling. What kind of marketing will Americans respond to? Something that's upbeat and socially negotiable. Taking care of the environment has to be popularly perceived as admirable. The inherent slogan needs to be, "It's cool to care."

Insurance advertisements sell insurance by showing a happy family that dodged the bullet by having a benign umbrella of insurance over their heads. Communities that are successful with voluntary recycling programs do it with happy talk, slogans, brightly colored posters, and support from top leadership.

To buy and sell good design, America has to perceive the genuine benefits in satisfaction, cost savings, stress reduction, and better health. We're not going backwards, we're enriching *right now* by incorporating the best we have come up with so far (from *all* historical eras) into our present.

10. The Strategy of the Rat (Technological Discretion)

Even though they aren't our favorite animal, rats are highly successful and, believe it or not, we can learn a lot from them. One of the crafty techniques they use is a "go slow" method of testing food. After giving a new food source a thorough sniffing, a rat will take a single bite and then not touch it again for twenty-four hours. His comrades observe the tester's behavior during that period, noting any ill effects as he gradually adds the food to his diet.

Writes Paul Ehrlich, "This 'one-trial' learning makes rats extremely hard to poison with anything that gives prompt symptoms. That is why warfarin, which works by slowly destroying the ability of the blood to clot, is the most successful rat poison."[15]

The strategy of the rat is relevant in many areas of our high-tech research, such as biotechnology. In that field, it might end up being okay to splice a certain gene onto a certain embryo, but it might also be catastrophic. We need to proceed with the research, but cautiously. As National Wildlife Federation researcher Margaret Mellon has phrased it, "Genetic alchemy does not necessarily produce environmental gold." If our overall goal is species longevity, then what's our hurry?

11. The Strategy of the Athlete (Precision within Constraints)

A champion Olympic athlete doesn't try to overpower nature, but rather goes with the flow of it. The pole vaulter, gymnast, and figure skater each work within given physical conditions, such as gravity, anatomy, and the shape of the equipment. The difference between a gold medal dive and a belly flop is measurable in the size of the splash. In roughly the same way, the difference between a good design and a bad one is measurable in pollution.

The strategy of the athlete is a highly conditioned and attuned one. The athlete makes careful note of the magnitude of the error, measuring opportunities for improvement. Similarly, wherever there is excess heat, friction, erosion, pollution, or congestion, there are design opportunities, and an expert designer capitalizes on them.

In the area of hazardous waste minimization, waste audits are performed to trace pollutants back to their origins and substitute better designs to eliminate those pollutants. A wind generator uses the strategy of the athlete because it doesn't fight the wind but *performs* in it. In the same way, good architects use shape as an ally in their quest to optimize natural daylighting and minimize energy needs. Famed architect I.M. Pei was once asked if constraints such as building codes, lot and space requirements, budgetary limitations, and physical conditions of the terrain inhibited his creativity. He replied that his worst nightmare would be to have instructions to do anything he wanted, because constraints *stimulate* creativity. Far from being obstacles, they are opportunities for expression and excellence.

12. The Strategy of the Butterfly: (A New Design Ethic)

One of our culture's most vital distinctions is between having and being. I believe we are currently on a journey from one concept to the other—we're emerging from a cocoon of clumsy capitalism into a world of interdependence by design.

What we are beginning to insist upon are "smart artifacts" that know enough to become enmeshed in our living processes rather than become just throwaways. Those products and technologies that can augment our progress toward *being* will be winners in the next century. Whichever devices and processes can answer "yes" to the following types of questions will be hired on. (The others need more education.)

- Can humans understand the product, maintain it, and feel satisfied with it?

- Does the product increase rather than limit our choices and options?

- Does the product enhance self-reliance and self-worth, as opposed to creating dependency and insecurity?

- Does it make maximum use of existing infrastructure and recyclable resources?

- Is it safe to make, use, reuse, and recycle, not requiring barriers and gas masks during and after use?

- If and when it needs to be discarded, will it fit into natural processes like decomposition and nutrient cycles?

- Does it leave room for imagination and creativity? (Can these qualities be a human "output" rather than a pre-molded "input"?)

Criteria such as these are the foundations of the new design ethic taking off in the United States—an ethic calling for awareness and even politeness in our products and technologies. Let's face it, unless we follow the lead of nature in our design strategies, we'll soon become lost in a technological wilderness. If it's genuine convenience we want, we should arrange for it now, before the petroleum-powered train pulls away from the station.

Biomechanics

The word may conjure up a crew of bionic repairmen, but *biomechanics* is also an emerging discipline in the very important field of ecological design. Developing a genuine understanding of the workings of biological species and systems, scientists try to tap nature's unpatented genius for use in human creations. According to biologist and "biomechanic" Steven Vogel, "We've got the answer—the organism—what we have to figure out is the problem."[16] Why are ship portholes round? For the same reason that holes in skeletons are round, says Vogel—to minimize the formation of cracks. Whale blubber is far more than insulation—it's part of the animal's motor. Interlaced with tendons, the blubber stores and releases energy as the whale swims, like rubber bands. (One of the earliest weapon technologies was based on the same idea. The ballista was a Roman catapult that could hurl ninety-pound rocks a quarter of a mile using twisted bundles of animal tendons as the source of power.)

Why are pine cones shaped the way they are? Cornell botanist Karl Niklas used a wind tunnel and sophisticated photography to find out. Though the conventional understanding of female pine cones was that they are passive "catcher's mitts" that intercept whatever pollen happens by, Niklas observed a far craftier design strategy at work. The aerodynamics of the cone actually *pull* pollen grains toward them by setting up a spiral, corkscrew-like current.

Enlightened agriculture can benefit from biomechanics. Pesticides are typically not applied directly at pests but at the ecosystems that happen to contain those pests. By knowing exactly *how* the pest fits into its ecosystem, we should be able to outwit it. As EPA entomologist Dallas Miller explains, "All of the pesticides we commonly use today attack systems in the insect that are identical to systems that you and I rely on—our nervous systems—rather than picking on a system that mammals don't have. The exoskeleton of an insect is an ideal target for that reason. If you can scratch or damage the exoskeleton of an insect, he desiccates and dies, because he doesn't have any veins." In other words, the strategy is tailor-made for the purpose, posing far fewer health threats for nontarget species like humans.

Ideally, a designer's research meshes the intended use with a survey of existing designs—some of which have been around longer than we have. Buckminster Fuller, for example, devised the geodesic dome by following the pathways of natural geometry to discover the shape that would permit "the closest packing of spheres." Similarly, designer Victor Papanek is a proponent of the "tetrakaidecahedron," a fourteen-sided crystal-like shape with eight hexagonal and six square faces. This shape is the only one that makes "a stable, fully three-dimensionally integrated space grid possible." Papanek envisions several different applications for these shapes, from modular grain storage containers and car radiators with lots of surface area to space stations that become instant space colonies when they land.[17]

Papanek predicts some rather visionary housing concepts on earth, too, using crystalline shapes: "With breakthroughs in Russian crystallography since 1970 and our increased abilities to grow large hollow crystals, it may become possible to seed an entire city and move in when it is fully grown."[18] (This notion is reminiscent of certain biotechnologists whose goal is to "grow" computers with *organic* integrated circuits.)

In the game of futuristic poker, physicist Freeman Dyson sees Papanek's bet and raises him one. In *An Agenda for the 21st Century*, Dyson speculates, "If you have advanced biotechnology, I don't see any difficulty in getting all the energy you want from the sun. It's only a question of redesigning trees so that they produce something other than wood. Gasoline, for example. Alcohol. Convenient fuels."[19] When author Rushworth Kidder asks if the trees could be tapped like sugar maples, Dyson replies, "I wouldn't do it so crudely. I would have a sort of living, underground pipeline system, so that the gasoline would be delivered where you want it."

Dyson's speculations, though fun to think about, go beyond biomechanics and biologic into biofiction. Still, we need to have scouts like Dyson reporting back from the future, or we risk having no future at all.

**SPECIAL FOCUS
The Blooming Wastewater**

Wastewater treatment, like many other technologies mentioned in this book, is gradually becoming a *design* science in which knowledge replaces heavy energy and equipment use. Newly emerging biological techniques for treating wastewater combine several of the design strategies mentioned above, primarily the strategies of rice paddy and compost. By using aquatic plants in conjunction with microorganisms, fish, snails, and other species, treatment efficiencies matching those of high-tech facilities are routinely being achieved at a fraction of the cost of conventional wastewater treatment.

Since the passage of the Clean Water Act in 1972, nearly $120 billion has been spent to build and upgrade the nation's sewage plants. These facilities have been successful in removing nitrogen, phosphorus, and human pathogens from our wastewater, but they haven't solved the problem of what to do with all the sludge that's removed. It's sort of like a kid's arithmetic problem: if you have ten billion tons of sludge, and you take away nine billion (by settling them out in a treatment plant), what do you have? You have nine billion tons that nobody is willing to make use of.

The EPA estimates that the sludge in the United States has a total nutrient value equivalent to 10 percent of the chemical fertilizers purchased in the country. But because the sludge is accumulated in urban areas and often contains toxic substances from industry (such as cadmium, copper, and PCBs), it doesn't come back into natural circulation the way it needs to. For this reason, Worldwatch researcher Marcia Lowe describes conventional sewage treatment as "an expensive way of turning fertilizer into pollution."

The first step in more logical wastewater treatment is to maintain "clean sewage." Many people think that putting our wastes into huge volumes of water is dumb, but it's even dumber to contaminate our resources with toxic chemicals. A recent EPA study indicated that the typical wastewater treatment plant actually controls only about half of the toxic chemicals that go into it. Fifteen percent remain in the sludge, 20 percent become air pollutants, and another 15 percent are discharged into receiving waters.[20]

What's wrong with this picture? What does conventional treatment overlook? Research being done by NASA and Ocean Arks International, among others, indicates that plants, fish, snails, and other macroorganisms may be key omissions. The typical treatment plant uses an activated sludge process, a trickling filter, or sometimes both. These systems encourage the growth of microbes that then do the cleanup work by ingesting contaminants. But these microbes are a kind of monoculture, and when toxic surges come through a given plant, entire microbial populations can be wiped out. The same is true when aerators break down or when certain engineering ratios, such as food/microorganism rate, are not met. Most conventional plants also use large amounts of chlorine, which combines with organic compounds to form cancer-causing agents. And some plants use aluminum to make phosphorus settle out. Aluminum may be a structurally good design material, but in chemical form, it can be very toxic. For example, it has been associated with the increased incidence of Alzheimer's disease.

Pioneering work by NASA's B.C. Wolverton in the 1960s indicated that natural systems, such as marshes and wetlands, could efficiently remove contaminants *without* chemicals, mechanical equipment, sanitary engineers, and heavy-duty fuel bills. Working for the Defense Department on biochemical warfare, Dr. Wolverton "saw toxic chemicals disappearing into wetlands without a trace and with no apparent harm to the ecosystem."[21]

Wolverton later went to work for NASA, where ongoing research into closed ecological life-support systems for space travel and colonization overlapped with his previous work. When the sewage treatment plant at the large space lab began to perform poorly, Wolverton suggested, "Rather than spend millions on a new mechanical plant, why don't we just grow some wetland plants? The engineering group laughed at the idea." But the scientist is quick to point out that in the last ten years, millions of dollars in construction and operation costs have been saved using the man-made wetland systems.

Natural systems, like the one at the NASA lab, use such plants as the water hyacinth, duckweed, bulrush, and the ornamental canna lily to convert sewage into high-quality water that's comparable to that produced by advanced treatment methods used in standard plants. Harvested plant material can be used for animal feed, compost, or biomass for the generation of methane. At the San Diego wastewater facility, electrical power is generated from the methane gas produced by water hyacinths.

Wolverton summarizes the advantages of marsh treatment over conventional plants: "They are less costly to install in most locations. Operational and maintenance costs are lower. Nontechnical personnel can operate and maintain the system. There is more flexibility and less susceptibility to shock-loading, and the systems are more reliable." The one disadvantage of a marsh system is that it generally takes more surface area than a standard plant to achieve the same results. If flowering plants are used, however, the system might be a good addition to a municipal park. Typically, the systems work so effectively that there is no noticeable odor.[22]

In the wintertime, the systems continue to function even in cold climates, despite the die-back of vegetation. This is because the plant *roots* don't die, and the microbial colonies that live on those roots continue to function.

Another approach, being perfected by Ocean Ark's John Todd, is more sophisticated, ecologically. It emphasizes the strategy of the rice paddy for additional diversity, flexibility, and productivity. Todd's prototype design for an "aquatic ecosystem" treated the pumped septage of Harwich, Massachusetts. Typically, septage wastes are as much as one hundred times less diluted than regular wastewater, also containing concentrated toxic substances, restaurant fats and greases, and industrial and hospital wastes.

Explains Todd, "We used complex photosynthetically based systems to absorb toxic shocks and organic loading. Fecal coliform levels in the effluent were as low as one one-hundredth those allowable for swimming water. Nitrate levels were below well-water standards. We found that fourteen out of the EPA's hit list of fifteen volatile organics were entering the system, three in very high concentrations. After ecological treatment, thirteen were 100 percent removed and the last, toluene, was 99.9 percent eliminated. The fish at the downstream end of our facility were free of aromatic hydrocarbons, PCBs, and dioxins."

Lifting a corner of a small floating raft full of watercress, Todd points out a colony of snails and eggs, remarking, "Here are the hard workers of this place. They clean up sludge. No one could believe that sludge wasn't accumulating at the bottom of the pool, but we drained it to see. There was almost no sludge. It sticks in the roots of the plants, and the snails and shrimp graze it away."[23] In keeping with the name New Alchemy, the institute Todd founded in the late 1960s, "wastes are transformed into pure water, plants, fishes and diverse life forms."[24]

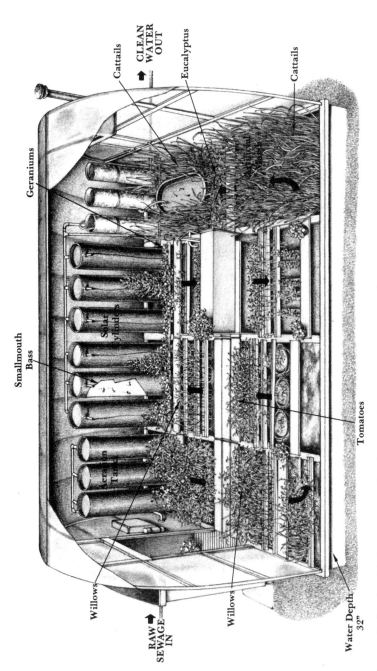

Instead of using high-energy technology and hazardous chemicals to treat our wastewater, many scientists are experimenting with plants, snails, fish, and microbes. *Illustration courtesy of Ray Maher.*

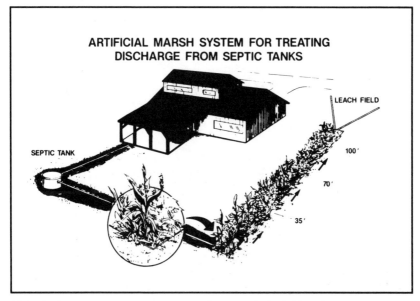

ARTIFICIAL MARSH SYSTEM FOR TREATING
DISCHARGE FROM SEPTIC TANKS

LEACH FIELD

SEPTIC TANK

100'

70'

35'

Biological wastewater treatment can be used in individual homes as well as community systems. This type of system is already being used in many homes in Mississippi and Alabama.

What about heavy metals, which can't be destroyed, but only moved around? Todd has a three-tiered strategy for them:

- Use rapidly growing plants to take up the metals, so the level per plant is low, and they can be safely composted.

- Locate and use plants that are "hyper-accumulators" and mine metals from the wastewater past the hazardous stage to the ore stage.

- Use slow-growing trees to store metals, putting tags on the trees: "Don't cut me down, I'm full of metals."

A second Ocean Ark experiment is taking place in Sugarbush, Vermont, inside a greenhouse filled with eucalyptus, willows, cattails, tomatoes, snails, and tanks of smallmouth bass, among many other species. The ecosystem treats the wastewater from the Sugarbush ski resort. The temperature often hovers near zero during short winter days, but the system is resilient and is performing on a parallel with the chemical treatment plant next door. The state of Vermont is compiling comparative data on the two systems. The steady stream of visitors from all over the world to Todd's system indicates which of the two systems is more popular. Todd explains with a certain amount of pride, "The two buildings sit side by side. One of them is square and squat, made of concrete blocks. Strange chemical smells come out of it, and people are afraid to go to work there. Next to it is an arched greenhouse, transparent, with sun streaming in all sides. It's full of flowers and green plants. People flock to it."[25]

Biologic vs. Technologic: Repairing the Two-legged Stool

One orientation says, "Make it work," while the other says, "*Let it work.*" One says, "We can conquer nature!"; the other says, "Go with the flow." Since ancient times, one of the orientations has been associated with the military and with centralized government, while the other is more closely linked to crops, crafts, and villages.

For lack of better terminology, I call one discipline *technologic* and the other *biologic*. In the last century, technologic has been personified by the engineer with a "can do" attitude. Of course he can do, with a million years of stored-up petroleum at his disposal. There are good, creative engineers out there—I don't mean to come down on just one profession. But the field in general is less sensitive to living things than it should be, and the engineering mentality (that has also invaded other professions) deserves some scrutiny. The word *engineer* actually has the same origins as *ingenious*, but those origins sprang from a time when nature was not as well understood as it is now. Back then, engineers were life-savers, armed with new scientific principles that attempted to meet disease, drought, tornadoes, and floods head-on. The question is, has the engineering mentality steadily developed into more of a threat than nature itself?

In *The Control of Nature*, John McPhee quotes the narrator's words in a vintage U.S. Army Corps of Engineers film about strategies for the Mississippi River: "This nation has a large and powerful adversary. Our opponent could cause the United States to lose nearly all her seaborne commerce, to lose her standing as first among trading nations. We are fighting Mother Nature . . . It's a battle we have to fight day by day, year by year; the health of our economy depends on it."[26]

Barry Commoner identifies a "fatal flaw" of technologic thinking, especially in the years since World War II. Modern technology
is like a two-legged stool: "[Our science was] well founded in
physics and chemistry, but flawed by a missing third leg—the biology of the environment."[27]

Engineers tend to be problem-solvers, not problem-avoiders. If
you want to get from point A to point B, they can muscle you up
a superhighway, but they're not expected to give a damn about
how scenic the trip will be. Their focus is on the destination, not
the journey; the product, not the process. "You want to make the
dog happy? No problem, we'll rig you up a mechanical tail-wag-
ger." Ecological designers see the absurdity of such a contraption,
and relate to the other end of the dog, where those brown eyes
are saying, "Just let me *fit in.*"

In a nutshell, conventional engineering is *logical* enough, but
it's not *bio*logical. Its precision is blind to whole systems. It's looking at the proposed dam, not the native birds or the vegetation
that is interconnected with those birds and the soil that relies on
that vegetation.

This mind-set isn't limited to engineers. Technologic, or jack-in-
the-box logic, is also a familiar characteristic among many
economists, planners, architects, and politicians who prefer to
function by following badly designed rules and assumptions rather
than forging new ones. Sometimes the old rules of one profession
bind up the behavior of another, as in the case of a builder who
wanted to use CFC-free insulation but the city building codes
would not permit it.

An inflexible attachment to a two-year payback is another example of rule-bound behavior: corporate economists consistently
make technologic choices based on the short-term return on
investment rather than long-term durability and sustainability.
Overall economics, also known as life-cycle economics, is sorely
neglected in the race for quick gratification. "If you can't afford to
do something right the first time," asks one enlightened architect,
"how can you afford to do it twice?"

What are some of the characteristics of each type of mentality,
and which type should we put our money on?

Technologic	**Biologic**
No need to know nature, just conquer it	Natural knowledge enriches the device's function

Products and profits	People as output
as output	
Positive feedback:	Make products smart
get more	enough to last
Don't rock the boat,	Actively preventive; devise
just shut up and adapt	better systems
What can our technologies	What do we *need?*
profitably provide?	
Destination oriented	Journey oriented
Overly productive, resulting	Highly protective,
in excess, waste, and pollution	conservative, nurturing
Brute force (geometry,	Finesse (martial arts,
telemetry)	guerrilla approach)
Monolithic, monocultural	Flexible, diverse

Denver's recent experience with the proposed Two Forks Dam is a good example of the ongoing duel between technologic and biologic. The city's consortium of water providers wanted to plan ahead, to make sure there was ample water for the coming years. It seemed like an admirable goal, but in the opinion of ecologists and designers, the proponent's definition of "ample" meant "water enough to waste."

The EPA essentially vetoed the construction of the huge "bathtub in the foothills" because the strategy of the cactus had not been properly examined. Native landscapes should be more widely used, the agency said, in conjunction with water-conservation devices, such as low-flow showerheads and toilets. In addition, there should be a more comprehensive metering system which forces people to *pay* for the exact amount of water they consume. A blend of cheaper, less damaging alternatives was available, said the ecologists, including cooperative exchanges between water users, sustainable use of groundwater, and smaller structural projects.

In other words, pro-development engineers assured Denver that there need be no shifts in thinking, no alternatives to worry about. "Just add water" was their simplistic attitude. Ecology-minded opponents, on the other hand, wanted to know why a priceless gold-medal fishery and scenic canyon had to be sacrificed forever so the engineers could have their technological fun.

Ecologists recognize that nature is "over-booked." Instead of acid-rain-resistant trees and pesticide-resistant bees that accommodate business as usual, they favor an immediate reduction of acid rain and pesticides. Pollution can't just be contained and carted away, they argue, it must be prevented with better design.

Chemical engineers experiment with the addition of limestone into lakes to counteract acid rain's effects. But ecological designers, coming from a different perspective altogether, present a hierarchy of solutions with prevention as the bull's-eye. The method of choice for counteracting acid rain begins long before it hits the lake. Higher efficiency devices will draw less power, they say, which will result in far less acid rain to begin with. Slight upgrades in lifestyle also make energy use less of a dragon. Solar and other clean technologies can provide the same services without pollution hitchhiking along, and habits such as walking and recycling can make life more meaningful.

If you've got to combust, the designers continue, why not design technologies and institutions that permit the use of the cleanest fuels available, such as natural gas and low-sulfur coal? Why not use fluidized bed combustion, a much more efficient means of burning? And if oxides of sulfur and nitrogen are *still* escaping, then we'd better design more efficient scrubbers, precipitators, and bag-houses to catch the pollutants (but at this stage, biologic begins to merge with technologic).

The technologic/biologic dichotomy is all around us. Scientists on the agribusiness payroll are working on genetically altered crops that will have greater resistance to pesticides and herbicides, allowing chemicals to be used with oblivious abandon since they no longer threaten crops. If genetic engineering has to come into the picture at all, doesn't it make a lot more sense to build *pest* resistance into crops rather than *pesticide* resistance?

This point brings up still another bias against the technologic mind-set: engineers, economists, and scientists are often "hired guns." Their mission is to sell pesticides, get more water, arrive at point B as quickly as possible, and so on. The mission of ecological designers (which we *all* must become) is interwoven and omnidirectional. Their goal isn't necessarily a better return on investment, or even higher productivity. They want higher quality of life, more elegantly provided. They realize that the protection of what we already have substitutes admirably for the production of *more*. If this deprives billionaires of additional billions, ecological designers aren't worried.

Barry Commoner made a convincing argument for better design in a speech he gave to a surprisingly receptive EPA audience in

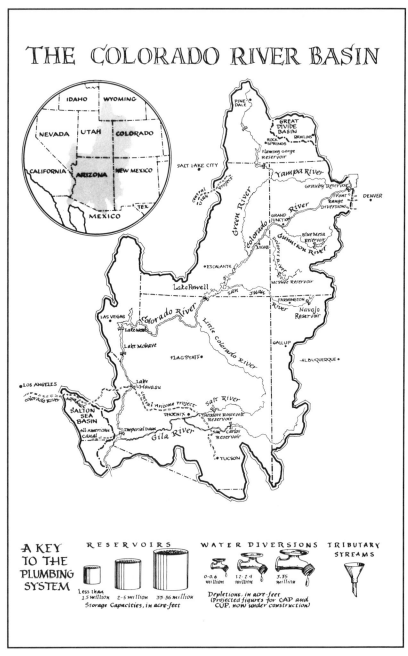

If western water users had been more efficient in their use of water, the engineering of the Colorado River (and its resulting impacts) would not be so extensive. *Illustration from* Western Water Made Simple, *courtesy of Island Press.*

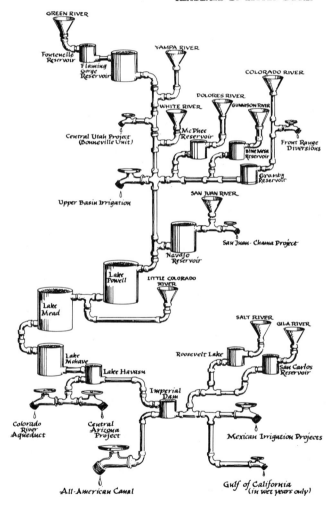

...AND ITS PLUMBING

MAP AND PLUMBING COMPILED
AND EDITED BY MARY MORAN
RENDERED BY LESTER DORÉ

1988. He argued that environmental quality has merely been running in place, not actually improving. "In a few scattered instances, pollution levels have been significantly reduced, by 70 percent or more: lead in the air, DDT in wildlife and people; mercury pollution in the Great Lakes; strontium 90 in the food chain; and in some local rivers, phosphate pollution." He emphasized that these reductions have taken place not because of stricter regulations or more precise high-tech controls, but because the pollutant's production or use was *discontinued.* Airborne lead has decreased by 86 percent because its use as a gasoline additive has been reduced. The production and use of DDT and PCBs has been banned. Mercury is no longer used to make chlorine. Strontium 90 no longer falls out from atmospheric nuclear testing.

Commoner believes that the disease of pollution is defined by national law as a "collection of symptoms." The laws don't discuss the *origin* of the pollutants, only their effects and who is responsible for cleaning up. Like a tourniquet or painkiller, these laws are only meant to stop the bleeding and discomfort, not to prevent the knife wound to begin with.

A Very Disturbing Weather Report

One of the best examples of technologic is the high-tech "fix-it-up" attitude some people have with regard to global warming and ozone depletion. Basically, there are two basic directions we can go with these megaproblems: prevention or adaptation. Most biologic designers are strongly in favor of the first, recognizing a blind alley when they see one, while many technologists seem to see the problems as comic book or video game challenges in which they can play the role of super hero.

If the sea level rises because the greenhouse effect melts the polar ice caps, these engineers are confident they can quickly construct Dutch-style dikes to protect our coastal cities. Space engineers propose huge shields (some call them parasols) that would orbit the planet, blocking the sun's rays like the shading that's sprayed on greenhouses in mid-summer. A few scientists have come up with startlingly stupid ideas, such as transporting dust into the atmosphere with a fleet of jumbo jets. Observing the slight cooling effect that followed the 1982 eruption of the volcano El Chichón in Mexico, a Columbia University professor suggested that thirty-five million tons of sulfur dioxide particles could be deposited annually as a reflecting curtain, even though it would cost billions, result in an increase in acid rain, and fade our blue skies to whitish.

Some of the engineering proposals to counteract ozone depletion are just as lame-brained, including searchlight-like lasers to thin out CFC concentrations ("atmospheric processing") and high-tech missile-launchers to fire frozen "ozone bullets" into the atmosphere. A few urban-dwelling scientists aren't especially worried about depletion of the ozone layer, which will cause increased skin cancer and immunological deficiencies. As long as our cities remain polluted, they feel protected from the sun's ultraviolet rays because the excess ozone at the ground level will compensate for its shortfall in the atmosphere. A similar attitude was expressed by former President Reagan's Secretary of the Interior Donald Hodel, who advised individually engineered protection—dark glasses and wide-brimmed hats.

Because of global warming and ozone depletion, the saying, "the sky's the limit," has taken on a new meaning. The statement is still true, but for a completely different reason than before. The sky has literally become an ecological, geophysical limit, and because of such realities as global warming and ozone depletion, our culture must *change directions*, not just tinker with the same old valves.

A little historical perspective might help illustrate this conviction. In the 1930s, two apparently unrelated scientific activities were taking place. The basic chemistry of ozone formation and its concentration in the earth's stratosphere was first observed. In the same decade, a chemical compound known as chlorofluorocarbon (CFC) was developed as a safe, efficient refrigerant for use in homes. The CFCs were nontoxic, inert, and virtually indestructible. No one ever imagined that their structure was on a time-release collision course with the ozone layer. It wasn't anybody's responsibility to track the journey of CFCs up into the stratosphere, where we now know they persist for up to a hundred years before the sun's rays finally tear them apart, at which point the chlorine atom in them tears *ozone* apart.

I remember a very graphic experiment on a TV documentary many years ago. Hundreds of mousetraps had been set, with Ping-Pong balls loaded on top. When one trap was manually sprung, the whole room became filled with flying Ping-Pong balls from "tripped traps." When I learned the basic mechanism of ozone destruction, it reminded me of those mousetraps because each chlorine atom set free by the sun's rays can destroy up to 100,000 molecules of ozone.

But I need to go a bit farther back in history to make my point—about two billion years ago, when the earth's worst life-caused pollution event occurred. The planet's most highly evolved species, the purple and green photosynthesizing microbes, were running out of a readily available supply of hydrogen, which they required as a basic cellular building block. Their population had by this time increased to the point where the most reliable source of hydrogen, the hydrogen sulfide emitted from volcanoes, was no longer enough to support their habit.

It took a mutant strain of cyanobacteria to devise a brilliant yet "ecocidal" innovation that solved the resource shortage and paved the way for air-breathing mammals and other animals. Their invention was a "technology" within themselves that could break apart the hydrogen-oxygen bond in water. The microbes gobbled the hydrogen they needed and simply dumped the "waste" oxygen. (Does it remind you of carbon dioxide?) The pollution crisis that followed wiped out many of the planet's existing species as the oxygen that was highly toxic to them increased from .0001 percent to 21 percent in the atmosphere.

It *can* happen again. Combustion, CFC Tinkertoys, deforestation, and other favorite hobbies of ours are defining the course of all future life on the planet. If we want our species to be part of the planet's future, we'd better start rethinking and redesigning. Instead of trying to answer social and ecological questions with technical equations and engineering blueprints, we've got to put our heads together and decide what it is we want and the *simplest* way to get it.

Property Shopping: The People vs. the Products

Ozone-busting is only one of chlorine's many talents. It also plays a major role in plastics, pesticides, bleach, and water purification. Chlorine was routinely built into the structure of pesticides like DDT to prevent decomposition and lengthen residual time. Microbes and chlorine don't get along. Nature never certified a carbon-chlorine combination until humans came on the scene.

The "stubbornness" of this bond meant that DDT would hang around for years, building up in plant and animal tissue. The same is true of PCBs, which are poly-chlorinated. The catch to using chlorine to purify water is that it can form toxic compounds when it combines with organic particles in water or wastewater. And the drawback of having chlorine in plastic is essentially the same as with pesticides: it makes plastic a hard guest to get rid of. Can we live with the bad properties of chlorine in order to benefit from its *good* properties? Ultimately, I don't think so. The most intelligent thing we may be able to do with chlorine is to avoid it entirely (like we avoid AIDS viruses, nerve gas, and electrocution), unless it's bound up in partnership with sodium to form salt.

We're getting smarter in our chemical designs, but we still have a long way to go before we reach nature-compatibility. Two recent innovations insert hydrogen into chlorine-containing molecules to make them less objectionable: "biodegradable" plastics that make the chemical bonds slightly more destructible, and certain substitutes for CFCs (HCFCs) that use hydrogen atoms to make molecules break down in the stratosphere in less than ten years (rather than a hundred). We've really just begun tinkering with chemicals and their "pathways," and we haven't yet developed much of an understanding about the interaction of biology and chemistry. (After all, the biggest bottle in our chemistry sets has been petroleum, and we used it in just about all our experiments.) Industry wants compounds that can survive high process temperatures, resist decay, and are lightweight, non-flammable, impermeable to gas, moldable, quick-drying, and so on—properties that "defeat nature." Consumers want products that perform well, but in terms of chemical properties, nontoxicity is higher on the list than indestructibility. Nonpersistence in the environment is up there, too, after our experiences with CFCs, DDT, and PCBs.

Plastics have their advantages, but they'll have to be more sensitive molecules, providing a better fit with natural systems. Likewise, we may need liquid fuels, but simpler-structured ones that combust more completely in better-designed engines.

We're moving toward a compromise in chemical properties. West German environmentalists have referred to an evolving "soft chemistry" industry that will fit better in the environment. But they realize that the world expects high performance in products because of the amazing properties of certain chemicals. Oil-based paints, for example, go on smoothly and dry quickly because they contain stabilizers and VOCs, or volatile organic compounds (the same is true of correction fluid). But these VOCs present indoor air-quality problems and contribute to the formation of ground-level ozone, which pollutes many American cities. Several states have passed regulations to limit the amount of VOCs in paints and varnishes.

The health and environmental effects of asbestos are infamous, yet this mineral has incredible properties that will be missed as regulations continue to phase out its use. Cars have been able to quickly decelerate from sixty miles per hour to a dead stop partly because of asbestos brake linings.

Substitutes are out there, but finding them takes time. When certain heavy-hitting pesticides were banned, we were fortunate to find replacements that were less persistent in the environment, were more precise in attacking a given pest, and required lower rates of application. (For example, using a timed-release of pesticides contained in starch pellets may be a good idea because this can decrease application rates by up to 90 percent.)

As usual, the best solutions may be *composite* ones, weaving strategies together like an ecosystem weaves species. Asbestos may bring us from sixty miles per hour to zero the quickest, but why are we up at sixty to begin with? More deaths have occurred on the highways than in all of America's wars, yet we still pilot our "guided missiles" as if we were being chased. (Which, of course, we *are*, in a social sense.) The point is, maybe the best brake lining is one that does not allow safe speeds over fifty-five miles per hour, and is at the same time not toxic.

Architect William McDonough observes that although the common TV set contains 4,300 different chemicals (including 9–18 grams of toxic mercury) and has a potentially explosive glass tube, we place it directly in front of our children at eye level and walk away unconcerned. Clearly, we aren't seeing the whole picture.

The problem of household hazardous waste is being perceived as a solid-waste problem and an indoor health/child poisoning problem, fundamentally, though, it's a design/demand problem. The properties that manufacturers design into our air fresheners, oven cleaners, bug sprays, polishes, strippers, and other home products are intended to dazzle us. They dissolve grease instantaneously, they dry quickly, their colors are brighter than bright, they kill pests on contact, they smell better than wildflowers, and so on. They give results you can *see* instantly, in trade for health effects that you *can't see*. But the question is, do we need results as quickly as these chemicals provide? Do we really need to *see* insects falling dead from the air? And strictly for the sake of fashion, do we have to use one toxic ingredient (oil-based paint or nail polish) to put the veneer on and another (paint stripper and nail polish remover) to take it off? Can't we find naturally occurring "super molecules" in citrus, cedar, and eucalyptus that get the job done less dramatically but also less hazardously?

We're trained by advertising to jump back in alarm if grease overflows the pan and drips onto our ovens. Passively, we let the grease bake onto the oven's surface, and then reach for the extra strength oven cleaner days later. Why can't we just wipe it up when it spills? With just a little more common sense, couldn't we bake that turkey in a slightly larger pan, so it wouldn't slop over to begin with?

Corporate Designers on the Loose

"It's not my department where they come down," rocket inventor Werner von Braun once said. His job in the pioneer days of space flight was simply to get the rockets up. In much the same way, many corporate managers inherited an agenda that stresses getting *profits* up, regardless of where discharges and pollutants "come down."

The good news is that this approach is becoming obsolete and the corporate world knows it. Governmental officials and environmental groups are calling one aspect of the new thinking "source reduction," the deliberate redesign of products and processes to reduce the amount and toxicity of this country's wastes. The Polaroid Corporation's significant reduction of the mercury in its batteries is an example of source reduction. Before regulations required it, the company voluntarily decided that since mercury causes problems when solid waste is incinerated, an alternative would be found.

The ink industry took the same approach with the lead that has been a routine ingredient in its products. The incentives for the actions on lead were both ethical and practical. The companies wanted to reduce the risks of lead poisoning to their workers and in final products, such as the printing on diaper boxes; they wanted to reduce company liabilities at dump sites where ink wastes are disposed (the Superfund law provides that even a small company can be held liable for the cleanup of an entire landfill); and the industry wanted to avoid a negative public image. The alternative product costs a few cents more per pound of ink, but large companies, such as Procter and Gamble and Campbell's, were quick to see the benefits of lead-free labeling.

Meanwhile, the Newspaper Publishers Association has successfully penetrated the newspaper industry with inks made from 70
percent soybean oil. With far fewer environmental problems from
wastes, a good reputation for "brighter, cleaner colors" than
petroleum-based inks and good performance on the presses, the
new products are already being used by the *Los Angeles Times* and
Boston Globe, among many other publishers.

The overall message is that things are changing faster than any
of us fully realizes. As Sim Van der Ryn states in *Sustainable Communities*, "We appear to be moving away from a society based on
iron ore and fossil fuels to one based on sand, plant matter, and
sunlight. Sand, the basis for our electronics industry, solar collectors, and solar cells, is the only commodity produced in every state
in the nation. Plant matter can provide the feedstock for the same
materials now made from petroleum. Sunlight, in its direct and
indirect forms, will be the basis for our energy system."[28]

A recent phone conversation with researcher Henry Fogle at
Allied-Signal Company left me feeling better about corporate acceptance of this "megatrend" toward biologic. Starting out with research
on substitutes for CFCs (which his company currently produces in
abundance), our discussion soon came around to the solar-collect-
ing properties of polar bear fur, the medicinal potentials of snake
venom, and the tensile properties of spider webs.

Fogle told me his company was actively looking for substitutes
for PCBs, asbestos, and degreasers that contain chlorine and other
halogens. The company is also looking for ways to minimize its
use of such compounds as benzene and formaldehyde (products
containing this life-embalming compound currently account for
around 8 percent of the national economy).[29] As with Polaroid and
the ink companies, Allied-Signal's motives are a blend of the practical and the ethical. "My office is right at the plant where chemicals are produced," Fogle told me, "and when I come to work in
the morning, the night shift is just getting off. Even though these
people don't know that my job involves chemical substitutions,
I get a good feeling knowing that *their* jobs will be safer."

Corporate designer Stewart Mosberg voices similar sentiments.
President of the Package Design Council, Mosberg believes that
nature-compatible design is "going to be a market position in the
1990s, and the words *New!* and *Recyclable!* on packages will be
tickets to product success." At the same time, he sees the designer
as a critical element in solving the landfill space problem, for the

right reasons. "We can do something," Mosberg says. "We have a responsibility as human beings. We're systems oriented. Solving problems is what we do for a living."[30]

Reinventing the Bikini:
Designer Packaging Hits the Mainstream

The rules are changing for designers, just as they are for the rest of us. Designers need guidelines for products that will more closely resemble orange peels and nut shells in function. They need to know things like:

- Is the package even necessary? Can it use fewer materials?

- Is the package "monomaterial," or is it multimaterial and thus difficult to recycle?

- Is it compactible to reduce landfill space needed or will it "float" in landfills like plastic milk jugs do?

- Can the package be incinerated without harmful emissions?

- Does it use recycled materials in its manufacture?

- Does existing or proposed legislation affect the design of the package?

- Can the package be reused in its present form, or will energy be required to bring a second life into being?

In general, package designers are being called upon to pay attention to a slogan they learned in design classes: "Form follows function." Writes designer Karrie Jacobs, "Our products come in packages that are more beautiful than the contents, more durable than the objects we buy for permanent use. And we throw them away."[31]

We need new packaging schemes that fit neatly into our backpack like a nestled-together mess kit. A small company named I-Corp has developed a container that seems to be right on track. I-Corp's recyclable plastic bottles have tongues and grooves so that they interlock in any quantity desired, eliminating the need for plastic yokes and auxiliary packaging, such as shrink wraps, cardboard dividers, and basket carriers. The blow-molded bottle also has a potential reincarnation. When compatible wall-mounted brackets are fastened to a wall, the bottles can serve as spice containers, nail organizers, or refillable shampoo bottles. (Why not buy in bulk if you have the perfect home container in place?)

A friend of the inventor even made a successful raft out of them. After a three-year wait to receive a patent, the interlocking bottle is now on the market. I-Corp is looking for products to bottle in the container, although the inventor held it back for two years until he was satisfied that there were uses for the recycled plastic and that the recycling industry was prepared to handle the volume.[32]

There is a growing trend to reduce the amount of packaging used in the *distribution* of products as well. When a company receives a truckload of production materials or a retailer receives a load of finished products, there are usually great mounds of corrugated boxes, metal strapping, wooden pallets, and polyethylene sheeting to be thrown away. Since the costs of disposal have gone up so dramatically, companies are starting to rethink distribution packaging, especially when the sender and receiver are owned by the same company. General Motors, for example, has adopted returnable plastic baskets to distribute parts, which suppliers can sell back to GM. After complaints from retailing customers about

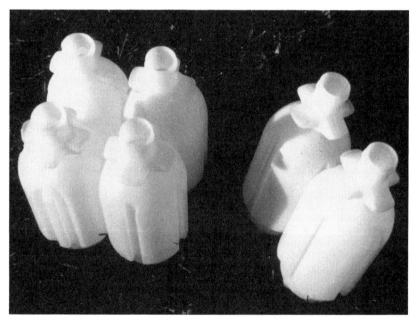

This interlocking bottle design eliminates packaging and creates possibilities for a "second life" for the products. *Photo courtesy of I-Corp.*

disposal costs, Kimball International began shipping its custom-built office furniture "uncartoned," using a combination of blankets, straps, and decks to replace packaging.[33]

One of the most challengeable assumptions about packaging is that we will continue to demand products from two thousand miles away. How much packaging would not even be necessary if much of our food was grown locally and many of our manufactured products could be purchased right at the factory? We *are* making progress. Coming from several different directions at once, we're homing in on sensible design that costs less, fits better, and feels right.

SPECIAL FOCUS
A Plastic Fork in the Trail

Durability or degradability? That's the big consumer-products question of the 1990s, and the design of plastic is right at the center of the debate. Because much of our landfill space is disappearing and our regulations have made it expensive to put trash into landfilled "storage," the country is in the midst of a massive rethink about the *strategy* of plastic design.

Even more important than the landfill question but not as commonly discussed are the environmental impacts from constantly having to "get more stuff" because we've thrown everything away. The extraction and refining of raw materials is using almost half of our total energy (in mining, processing, and distribution) and destroying irreplaceable natural systems such as Amazonia, but we seem more concerned with where to dump the converted resources than with saving the systems from which they're extracted.

A "superplastic" of some kind might be recyclable numerous times (helping eliminate the need to tear apart Alaska for oil), but what kind of process would be used to *create* such a product? And what kind of natural process could effectively break it apart?

Biodegradable plastics make good sense for certain applications, but their design competes with the plastic recycling industry, and assumes two things: that degradation *won't* take place during ordinary use, and that it *will* take place in landfills. What if the wrapper on a pound of ground meat started decomposing before the meat was consumed, or if a garbage bag degraded just enough to rip apart en route to the garbage dumpster?

The genetic instructions we issue to plastics should specify exactly when degradation can take place. But those instructions have to take the product's entire life cycle into account. If degradable plastics are destined for a landfill site, designers have to consider what the conditions will be in that environment. Because of the potential for chemical leaching and methane formation when trash decomposes, landfills are routinely kept as dry and microbe-free as possible. In fact, thirty-year-old newspapers that are still readable have been found in landfills because the lack of moisture, air, and microbes did not permit breakdown.

The first generation of biodegradable and photodegradable plastics has not yet hit the mark, although it *has* made us start thinking about design. The basic idea has been to place easily degradable starch between plastic molecules to speed up decomposition. Studies have shown, however, that "biodegradable plastic" is a misnomer; many small pieces of plastic remain—they're just tinier and far more dispersible. (Because of plastic's ability to fit into odd shapes and remain intact, tiny pieces are already clogging natural nooks and crannies all over the planet.)

One intelligently designed polyester called PHBV is literally *manufactured* by microbes and thus is "biofamiliar." So far, however, its price tag limits use to premium applications such as surgical sutures and slow-release medicines. At the Argonne National Laboratory, another smart plastic is emerging from piles of cheese and potato wastes. According to Argonne spokesman Bob Schwabach, huge mountains of cheese whey go to waste every year, while an estimated ten billion pounds of potato waste are created annually to keep the United States in french fries.[34]

Part of plastic's problem is that it takes so many different shapes. Since plastic is so lightweight and there are at least fifty basic types of plastic, it's a difficult material to recycle. Every year, new techniques are introduced that extrude plastic in layers and blend it in alloys with other materials, such as glass. These techniques pack a lot of structural properties into the plastic, but they are not necessarily *relevant* properties from a natural design standpoint. Like a ten-foot-tall man, these combination products don't fit in their environment. They essentially lock out the possibility of recycling.

In the automobile industry, the use of plastics has approximately doubled in the past few years. Auto salvagers make their income from metal scrap, and have to pay disposal costs for shredder residues, or "fluff." Because of the added plastics, those costs have gone sky-high in recent years, right along with the level of some of our landfills. What can be done to prevent the demise of the eleven thousand auto salvagers in the country? We need them. Part of the answer is to make recycling feasible by keeping plastics in cars relatively pure, easily detachable, and identifiable. Car handles, for example, are made of recyclable zinc and are easily detachable to yield a very high recycling rate.[35]

We need to put name tags on our products just like the ones we sew onto our kids' camp clothes. In fact, the coding system implemented by plastics manufacturers is making plastics recycling a reality. The two most readily recyclable plastics, soda bottles and milk jugs, get "1" and "2" in the code, but certain other resins are also stamped with the triangular arrow. Another identifying system under consideration uses fluorescent dyes or other chemicals that can identify different resins under ultraviolet light.

The central question about plastic still seems to be, what do we *really* need it for? Its moldability and hardness make it a great material for computer chips, and its inertness is a good match with artificial hearts and limbs. Plastic gears and machine parts don't require lubrication, and the advantage of plastic shampoo bottles over glass ones becomes apparent the first time a bottle slips out of soapy hands. Before the appearance of nylon-bristled toothbrushes in the late 1930s, hog bristles were standard fare. Another fitting use of plastic seems to be the tiny little hoses that make water-conservative drip irrigation feasible. A friend who did volunteer work in the African nation of Malawi told me how valuable plastic sheeting is there: U.N. officials offered it as an incentive to each family that built a latrine. The families used it for food storage, moisture insulation in their huts, and many other functions that we take for granted.

But do we really need six layers of plastic packaging on toys, tools, and cosmetics? Do we need plastic diapers of any description? The manufacturer of a "biodegradable" diaper doubled its sales after it began using the slogan, "Change the world one diaper at a time." Cute slogan, but what's wrong with cloth diapers? Diaper services routinely cost only half as much as disposables and are softer on baby's bottom, too.

What we need is mediation between profits and pollution. For example, why can't we subsidize research on plastics made from materials like keratin (found in shells), lignin (the hard substance in trees), and other "heavy hitters" of the natural molecular world? Are we trading "shelf life" for real life?

No Place Like Home

Have you ever noticed how a baby tends to be more impressed with the box that a present came in than the present itself? (It would save time and money just to wrap up an empty box.) Maybe infants recognize intuitively that life is a whole *series* of tubes and containers. After all, they've just recently emerged from one themselves.

A few years later, we find them setting up shop inside a refrigerator box in the front yard, and before we know it, the container has expanded into a huge two-story monster, devouring energy and expelling trash. Connected by a series of umbilical cords, the house is dependent on remote, computerized sources of power. The U.S. Department of Energy estimates that the average home uses the equivalent of twenty-two 55-gallon drums of oil per year. (We can imagine the drums stacked out in the yard where the woodpile used to be, next to the driveway where the *stable* used to be.)

We'll need to stack another twenty-five drums of oil next to the car, which also dumps its own weight in greenhouse-forming carbon dioxide into the air every year. And the refrigerator humming its monotone tune inside the house burns the equivalent amount of coal per year as could be packed inside it.[36] In fact, if all of America's fridges were state-of-the-art efficiency, about twenty large power plants could be shut down altogether.[37]

Living Rooms, Living Houses

Houses, cars, refrigerators, and the other "containers" in our lives eat energy, store design mistakes for many years at a time, and can cause pollution hundreds of miles away. They are *designed* to be gluttonous units of consumption and waste. We spend the majority of our lives either *in* these containers or working to pay for them. Yet we have taken very little control over what they're made of, what they look like, or how efficient they are.

William Stumpf, a Minneapolis designer, believes that the house should be less of a container and more of a functional organism. "Our bodies do a good job of taking in oxygen, food and water, getting nutrition, and dispelling waste," he explains. "Our houses

Bottle deposit laws in more than eleven states give an incentive for consumers to recycle polyethylene terephthalate (PET) bottles, resulting in a reliable supply of the durable plastic for recyclers. Pictured are a few of the products made from recycled PET. *Photo courtesy of Wellman, Inc.*

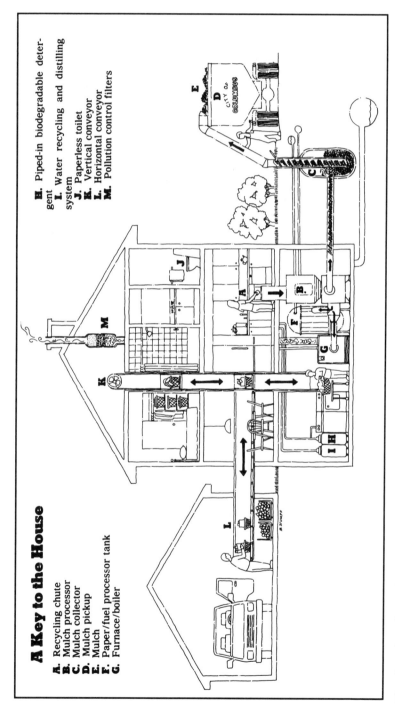

A Key to the House

A. Recycling chute
B. Mulch processor
C. Mulch collector
D. Mulch pickup
E. Mulch
F. Paper/fuel processor tank
G. Furnace/boiler
H. Piped-in biodegradable detergent
I. Water recycling and distilling system
J. Paperless toilet
K. Vertical conveyor
L. Horizontal conveyor
M. Pollution control filters

The American household can be far more than a passive, wasteful unit of consumption. Industrial designer William Stumpf envisions some design possibilities to make our homes more productive.

don't do that very well. They should have digestive systems just like we do." In Stumpf's Metabolic House, various "organs" facilitate this digestion. Vertical and horizontal conveyors, dumbwaiters, and compost chutes help transport supplies from the car through the "techno-mulcher," from which usable compost is pumped at regular intervals.

Instead of regarding the house as an insatiable container designed for rapid conversion of consumer goods into short-lived convenience, Stumpf advocates modeling it after vintage houses that had built-in flour bins, hampers, clothes chutes, and pantries. He also includes a carbonated water tap and cola syrup dispensers to reduce the need for packaged beverages. In the basement is a tank filled with biodegradable detergent, delivered and pumped in by a supplier. Spokane architect Nicolee Bradbury is on the same wavelength. She has a recycling gadget "wish list" that includes an automatic label scraper, built-in can flatteners and a designated recycling pantry.[38]

But why assume that everything that comes *in* needs to go back *out* into the world? Which will come first—a human settlement on the moon or garbage disposals connected to a family or community compost pile? Why can't newspapers be conveniently made into fuel pellets? And instead of plastic garbage bags that are not "digestible," how about a gadget that instantly converts double-layered newspapers into origami trash sacks that last just long enough to get unrecyclables to the trash can or dumpster?

Even crazier in a very sane way are biologic humidifiers, which Victor Papanek has tinkered with: "By combining a mix of deliquescent and antibacteriological crystals, we were able to develop a theoretical surface that would store twelve to twenty-four atoms of water to each crystal atom and release it again when humidity was unusually low. This material could be sprayed onto a wall or woven into a wallhanging."[39] Since the relationship of humidity and temperature is critical in human comfort, these crystal humidifiers could help make a home pleasantly warm and humid without using any energy.

Current research at the Solar Energy Research Institute uses human-made plastic structures and silica gels to accomplish essentially the same function: storage of humidity when there's too much in the indoor environment, and release when there is too little. According to SERI's Tom Potter, "desiccant wheels" also have the capability of filtering out molecules of air pollution. Tiny holes in the structure of the wheels could be precisely matched to resemble a huge hunk of Swiss cheese large enough to admit a mouse but too small to admit the pursuing cat. Formaldehyde, for example, could be selectively filtered out while oxygen remained in the environment.

Another possibility in housing is the decentralization of power. Solar cells, neighborhood power plants, "district heating" (community-scaled use of heat such as power plant effluent), and fuel cells (high-tech "fuel-burning batteries") all promise to decrease our reliance on centralized, invisible energy suppliers. Recognizing this trend, the Edison Electric Institute will fit fifty demonstration homes with mini-cogenerators in 1991. These natural gas-fired units will be only 5 by 2 1/2 by 2 1/2 feet, and will be incorporated in the Institute's "smart house" design, which trades electricity with the electrical grid in the off-peak hours when utility power is cheapest. (In other words, the houses will sometimes generate more than they need, transferring surpluses to the utility; they will sometimes *buy* cheap electricity from the power plant.) The mini-cogenerators' internal combustion engines will each generate five to seven kilowatts of electricity while also capturing waste heat for hot water and house heating.[40]

With the advent of sophisticated systems that will monitor air pollutants, compare indoor and outdoor temperatures to select the cheapest source of heat and ventilation, and automatically dial emergency numbers, we're really not that far from having houses with high IQs that eat, breathe, and sunbathe just like humans.

Icebox Follies

Refrigerators play several roles. They are storehouses of food supplies and food-like substances, cooling in spite of the flame underneath them (the compressors). They're miniature art galleries and shopping-list display units, and they are steady customers of the nation's power plants. America's humming fleet of six-foot-tall refrigerators consumes about 7 percent of the country's electricity, an amount that experts claim could easily be cut in half.

Maybe what we need in our refrigerator doors is a highly efficient window, to be able to peer inside without letting cold air escape. It has even been suggested that mounting a Polaroid-like camera in the door to take instant pictures of the interior would be cheaper than opening the door.

Certainly, our refrigerators need better insulation and top-mounted compressors (since heat rises). Both of these qualities used to be standards back before convenience became the country's primary design criterion—they were scrapped for the sake of spacious compartments and handy freezers. Refrigerators will also benefit from an upgrade in a variety of features, such as better door seals, more efficient motors, and shell designs that don't have heat-conducting metal bridges between inner and outer walls.

A little common sense goes a long way, too, such as not placing the refrigerator right next to the oven or in front of the house's sunniest window. If we shop for the most efficient model in the store when Whitey finally dies, we can prevent a lot of pollution and energy use. Assuming the refrigerator lived to a ripe old age of ten to fifteen years, it most likely has a PCB-containing capacitor in its innards that inhibits the recycling of the scrap metal it contains. (Fortunately, specialists in capacitor-removal have sprung up.) It also contains CFCs, both in the "circulatory" system (the refrigerant) and in the "jacket."

In fact, the need for alternative insulation systems to eliminate CFC use in refrigerators was one of the primary goals of the "Golden Carrot" competition co-sponsored in 1993 by U.S. utilities, the Environmental Protection Agency and the Department of Energy. Whirlpool collected $30 million for coming up with the best prototype for a CFC-free, super-efficient unit that could ultimately cut electric bills by 10 to 35 percent.

Other designs being researched include vacuum panels whose narrow (one-quarter-inch) vacuum cavities are filled with silica powders or glass fibers. These panels, which also have great potential for building insulation, offer an R-factor ten times greater than that of conventional polyurethane foam. Another innovation, Aerogel, is a loosely connected human-made solid that is more than 98 percent air. Because this insulation can also be used as a transparent glazing material, one engineer imagines imbedding an autumnal maple leaf or butterfly within the structure of an Aerogel window. (Why not use Aerogel for the window in our refrigerator doors?)

Prototypes of these new refrigerators—using vacuum panels and Aerogel—are being built and tested in conjunction with the Solar Energy Research Institute, EPA, and the Electric Power Research Institute. At the Rocky Mountain Institute, a SunFrost refrigerator that uses only one-fifth the energy of the average new model was installed, along with a "heat pipe" accessory that uses cold winter air to reduce power needs.

Refrigerators will remain a familiar feature in our kitchens, but don't rule out the possibility that they may be powered by something other than electricity in the future. Heat pumps and exchangers may combine with natural gas or hydrogen to keep the beer and potato salad cold. It is not likely we'll revert to Roman refrigeration—carrying ice and snow from mountaintops—but some variation of an Egyptian ice-making scheme might just play a role in the passively heated and cooled home. Egyptian women of past millennia placed water in shallow clay trays at sundown. The temperature drop as darkness fell combined with cooling from rapid evaporation to form ice, even though ambient temperatures never fell near the freezing point.[41]

The Beast in the Garage

How can we get what we need more efficiently, with less pollution and stress? A related question is how can we tame the beast in the garage, at least until we can replace it?

We need fewer beasts and *cleaner* beasts. The controls we have applied so far have had dramatic results—today's vehicles are at least 90 percent cleaner than their counterparts in the 1950s—but we've got three or four times as many cars now, and we're forty years further down a path that can only lead to even *more* cars since we've designed our built environment to accommodate them.

It is well documented that prototypes exist that are far more efficient, with some getting more than eighty miles per gallon. Our first strategy should be to *insist* that they be put on the market. Burning far less fuel will automatically reduce pollution. The problem is that the idea of fuel efficiency has in recent years had neither consumer nor government support. Consumers have drifted back to midsize cars, and Congress has failed to be aggressive about efficiency standards.

Car companies tell us the consumer doesn't want to pay the extra four or five hundred dollars that the more efficient cars will cost, but a combination of incentives and subsidies would go a long way toward making that extra cost disappear. An increase in gasoline taxes would be a first step in repaying some of the many hidden costs of the automobile, and if those revenues were returned as rebates to buyers of highly efficient cars, the attractiveness of buying an intelligent model would be twofold. Why not legislate rebated fuel savings to the savers—the "Robin Hood Strategy"—by taxing gas guzzlers and transferring those taxes to the gas misers? Instead of spending billions to defend oil in the Middle East, why shouldn't we spend it in America, by subsidizing the development of "ultramobiles" that are less abusive to their environment, and less threatening to world peace?

186,000 Miles per Second—
It's Not Only a Good Idea, It's the Law

What can applied biologic and "physiologic" do to improve the country's 150 million vehicles? Where are the opportunities from the standpoint of thermodynamics and aerodynamics? According to a 1993 report by the Rocky Mountain Institute, when you design a car like an airplane, not a tank, magical things happen. One of the most simple, effective innovations, says the report, is to make car bottoms as smooth as car tops, lowering the "drag coefficient."

The automobile is a composite of friction losses, inefficient combustion, and unused heat potential. The strategy of the athlete comes in handy here. (Where there's friction, heat, and pollution, there's opportunity.) The automobile is also a very heavy beast—far heavier than it needs to be. Worldwatch researcher Michael Renner estimates that, on the average, a 10 percent weight reduction will yield a 6 percent fuel economy gain.[42] Materials that offer weight-reduction potentials without strength or safety reductions include magnesium, plastics, aluminum, and high-strength alloys.

Transmission efficiency can also be improved. The continuously variable transmission, which fits the right gear to the requirements of speed and terrain, has been around for forty years but has been neglected, despite demonstrated fuel savings of 10 to 20 percent. Aerodynamics, tire rolling resistance, energy dissipation in the brakes, and energy consumption in accessories are other targets for upgrading. Such features as "skirted" front and rear wheel openings, dorsal fins, hidden wipers, a sculpted underbody, low-profile radiator and headlights, and a lens-mounted interior mirror system (instead of friction-fighting side mounts) are also being explored. General Motors has looked into a hydraulic height-adjustment system that "low-riders" will love: car height is automatically adjustable according to vehicle speed. A better match between natural laws and car design can also be achieved by making use of idling and braking energy. Advanced designs store energy that would otherwise be wasted in a "flywheel" in much the same way a child stores toy vehicle energy in a rubber band or wind-up gear system.

The possibilities for space age "electrochromic" windows (like changeable lens eyeglasses), ceramic engines, lubricants that are more slippery, electronic sensing, and so on all use biologic to make cars smarter. In effect, we're all driving cars that are a hundred years old since nothing has fundamentally changed in car design since the days of Ransom Olds. The *appearance* of cars changes often enough to shame us into new purchases every four or five years, but the internal combustion engine still punches pistons through cylinders, dumping unused gases out the back.

According to Barry Commoner, the world has overlooked an opportunity to significantly upgrade engine performance by bypassing the "stratified charge engine." Commoner argues that the best place to control car pollution is at the point of origin—that is, in the engine, *not* the tailpipe. The stratified charge could go a long way toward satisfying that strategy, but "the engine would have to be considerably redesigned, and this would mean extensive retooling in the manufacturing plants."[43] Instead of using biologic to *prevent* pollution, the auto industry has thus far appeased us with catalytic converters as an "end-of-pipe" control measure.

From a technologic versus biologic perspective, the problem is that many of us don't understand physics or even basic mechanics well enough to demand better cars. As representatives of the demand/design side, citizens and politicians have to give the engineers general instructions on what we *want* in a car, rather than let them tell us what we can have. I can guess that a petition containing ten million signatures would have some effect on the auto industry: "Create this car by the year 2000 and you will have ten million customers." If I could recommend a few of the qualities to be listed on such a petition, I'd include several of the criteria strategies already mentioned in this chapter—the strategies of steel (durability, recyclability), cactus (conservative), the rice paddy (integrated, efficient), and lover (appearance secondary to essence). My list of requirements for a nature-compatible "ultramobile" would include the following features:

- It would be fueled by a hybrid of hydrogen, electrochemical (batteries, fuel cells) and stored power (flywheels, hydraulics).

The car lets nothing be wasted. Heat pumps convert waste heat to cooling or stored heat to be used in houses (portable columns filled with heat-storing, high-tech salts and alcohols could provide radiant heat on "heat racks"). Cars could be outfitted with tiny built-in wind turbines to take advantage of highway speeds, and air compressors that automatically adjust tire pressure to eliminate "rolling resistance."

- If not fueled by hydrogen, other alternative fuels should be used, such as methanol, ethanol, or natural gas, whose chemical structures are simpler than gasoline and consequently emit fewer pollutants. In this way, conventional pollutants (CO, NOx, hydrocarbons) as well as CO_2 (the major greenhouse gas) are minimized.

- The "ultramobile" should be highly durable and weather resistant. Henry Ford once built a prototype car out of recyclable soybean-based plastic, demonstrating its resistance to impact and nicks by beating on it with a sledge hammer. Since the car's paint was incorporated within the plastic, it wasn't vulnerable to damage from impacts. The plastic was also lighter than steel, thus improving energy efficiency.

- The "ultramobile" should contain no toxic materials. The hazardous chemicals that make up that "new car smell" should be off-gassed before the new owner has to be exposed. Cadmium bolt-coatings, asbestos brake linings, sodium azide in air bags, CFCs in air conditioners, and potential fumes inside the car from the engine should be reduced or eliminated completely.

- The car parts and assembly should be designed specifically for recycling. Components would be modular and highly recyclable. If plastic is used, it must be in readily detachable units that are easily separated. The purchase price of the car would include a deposit on the body and all recyclable parts, such as the battery, catalytic converter, and engine block. Tire casings should be made from a material that is either more durable or less—the existence of tire mountains all over the country indicates a design opportunity. (In Ford's "biological vehicle," the tires were made from goldenrod.) Since it's really just the tread we need, why can't we design replaceable treads for permanent, lightweight tires?

I know, this all sounds hopelessly optimistic. What we may be looking at here is a high-cost vehicle that's designed to reliably last a decade or two, just like major appliances, and that is financed for a longer term like a house mortgage.

But we're dealing with an industry that controls at least a sixth of the economy. How can we dictate our design demands to a monolith so obsessed with—and successful at—the shaping of those demands? A more relevant question is "How can we afford *not* to?" We've become too sophisticated to fall for the idea that "design" is shape, color, acceleration, and TV sex symbols *only*. Automobile design should focus on durability, efficiency, and nature-compatibility.

We don't *want* only one type of car. We need electric cars for some uses and organically fueled cars for other uses. And we need to think about leasing, sharing, and co-owning vehicles, too. Several apartment complexes across the country have successful car-sharing programs. Participants sign up for "cartime" and make their travel arrangements accordingly, thus avoiding the need for families to own second cars. This works especially well when a car is only used occasionally for long-distance travel. In such a case, a "city car" (maybe electric) could meet most of a family's requirements with high efficiency.

Inventing Institutions That Nurture Smart Design

What humans do best is design and create. But just as a silkworm needs the right materials in order to weave silk, we need the right information and assumptions to weave a high-quality society. We also need a flexible institutional structure that bends when needed but never breaks, like a California home designed to survive earthquakes. Thomas Jefferson had some good words on this subject: "Laws and institutions must go hand in hand with the progress of the human mind. As that becomes more developed, more enlightened, as new discoveries are made, new truths discovered and manners and opinions change, institutions must advance also to keep up with the times."

Jefferson seems to have acknowledged that society is in constant evolution and that the rules must change to fit the game. To get better houses, we've got to demand smarter architects. If it's regulatory compliance we want, those regulations have to accommodate human behavior, a very critical element of nature. For example, referring to the many leaking gas station storage tanks, EPA underground storage tank expert June Taylor writes, "Whatever system the EPA chooses for leak detection, record keeping, reporting, and the like, it has to be understandable and doable by a high school student in the freezing cold and dark of a Minnesota winter morning. Otherwise, it may look good on paper, but it won't work in the real world, and that's where the leaks are."[44]

To work, our institutions have to resemble ecological networks, passing useful information around like nutrients. Telephone, mail, and weather systems do this on a planetary scale already. We have plenty of operating experience in implementing sensible strategies—we really just need to agree on what's "sensible."

The following chapter explores technologies, attitudes, and procedures that are flowing into the mainstream from nature-compatible rivulets and tributaries throughout our society. In hazardous waste treatment, water and power efficiency, and renewable energy supply, biologic is inch-by-inch becoming an American characteristic. And not a moment too soon.

CHAPTER 5

IMPLEMENTING

It's the end of the beginning for America and its western colleagues. From here we move into a more advanced ecological
stage, just as a child ultimately makes the fearful yet exciting shift
to junior high. This transition might happen relatively smoothly or
it might not, but in any case it won't happen mindlessly. We'll have
to decide exactly what we want—based on what nature can spare
on a continuing, sustainable basis—and devise methods that don't
make a mess out of our lives and our environment.

In the powerful realms of high finance and collective decision-
making, the fundamental design strategy has to become symbiosis—the interlocking cooperation of social and economic species,
rather than the competitive, energy-depleting strategy that has
characterized our pioneer ecosystem. In any ecosystem, there are
certain rules that all members honor because it would be suicidal
not to. One example is soil maintenance—each plant species
"invents" methods to help the team either build soil or keep it in
place, because if it erodes away, the whole system goes broke.
Animal species, too, tend to be soil-conservative in one way or
another, or else they disappear right along with the soil. Human
values are the *cultural* resource that needs protection above all
else. If our values and goals become self-defeating (such as "bigger

is better"), our techniques will follow right along.

Another ecological model for our society is the nitrogen-fixing bacteria that live on the roots of a particular species of plants, the legumes. The earth's atmosphere is 79 percent nitrogen (a primary plant nutrient), but not many plants live in the air. So, a certain strain of bacteria made legumes an offer they couldn't refuse: in return for starch from their root systems, the plants receive nitrogen, which the bacteria somehow pull right out of the air like magic. Why shouldn't more of our social arrangements be win/win, dovetailed arrangements like this one? If our values and goals demand environmental coherence, then we can find a way to make that coherence happen by satisfying everyone's needs (the critical word, of course, is *needs*, not *cravings*).

A Declaration of Interdependence

In this final chapter, we look at different kinds of mainstream partnerships—both social and technical—from an ecological perspective. Ecologists remind us that evolution encourages even parasites to become progressively more cooperative or symbiotic, because if a parasite is greedy and saps too much vitality from its host, it eliminates its own niche. Many industries and cities are on the verge of doing just that. For example, by drawing down groundwater levels, some coastal cities are causing salt water infiltration because of negative pressure. Other cities are experiencing surface collapses as water is overused.

Sometimes the coalitions between social species (institutions, companies, and so on) are very curious ones. One unlikely symbiosis involves a waste disposal company that will bury low-level radioactive wastes in California's Mojave Desert and a nature group that wants to save an endangered species of tortoise. To get its disposal permit, the company has agreed to build a two-foot-high, 7.5-mile-long fence across one edge of the tortoises' habitat, which will enable the tortoises to come out ahead, since the fence will keep them from getting squashed on the nearby interstate highway. Trades like these are becoming routine in America, as environmental assessments, city council meetings, and legal settlements increasingly incorporate give-and-take into the process.

Adaptability is another critical element on the road to a stable ecosystem. The Chinese character for "crisis," which includes signs for both "danger" and "opportunity," recognizes the importance of adaptability. Resource shortages, stock market crashes, and environmental pollution resemble natural crises such as hurricanes or forest fires—they spell danger but also present opportunities for new species to come onto the scene. Where there's energy waste, we need adaptive new species to scavenge efficiently. For example, wherever methane escapes from landfills or natural gas pipelines, we need to devise ways to capture it, not only because it can be a source of fuel but because if it gets into the atmosphere in that form it can substantially contribute to global warming. Where there are existing mountains of dead tires, we need to develop ways to recycle them. (We also need to design tires that have less waste built into them.) The strong card of our species is the ability to intentionally *design* symbiosis into our social ecosystem. As in nature, it's a trial-and-error proposition, and as everyone knows, experiments don't always work. Species (both natural and cultural) often become extinct because they are unable to fit in. Even huge dinosaur technologies such as nuclear energy are not exempt. We have a clear incentive to strive for a better-designed world: either we learn to go with the flow, or we don't go.

In the areas of energy, water supply, and hazardous wastes, that panicky feeling of crisis has already surfaced in the 1970s and 1980s. The dangers have been at least partially acknowledged in each case, and many of the opportunities have been identified. This chapter looks at some of the social and technical innovations already in the mainstream that can help move us away from danger and toward opportunity.

Pioneer America's biggest collective screw-up has been its separation from nature. From a design perspective this is the fundamental flaw, because the less contact we have with our environment, the less natural our designs will be. We continue to design artifacts and systems for sale to humans, but humans whose values are slightly off-the-mark. The fact is, we've gotten downright creepy in the flickering half-light of the TV and the mechanical, resigned cadence of the commute. What else can our *designs* be but creepy?

Hitting the Mark:
Pollution Prevention by Design

The sport of archery and the pursuit of environmental protection are alike in at least one respect: once we know exactly what we're shooting at, we rely on expertise to help us hit the mark. We can no longer expect to maintain a high-quality environment by accident, just as we can't expect to consistently shoot arrows into the bull's-eye without practicing our archery.

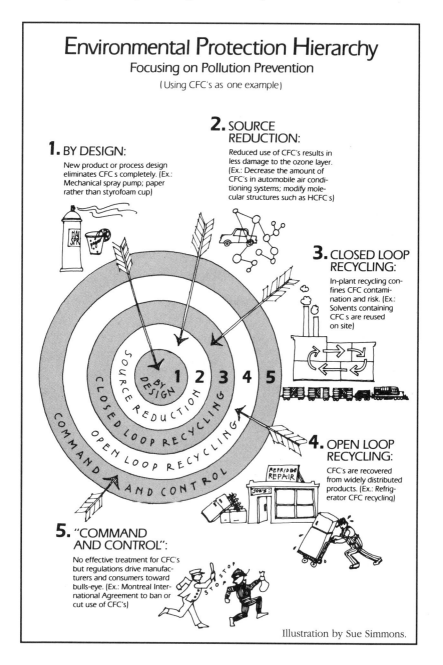

Environmental Protection Hierarchy
Focusing on Pollution Prevention
(Using CFC's as one example)

2. SOURCE REDUCTION:
Reduced use of CFC's results in less damage to the ozone layer. (Ex.: Decrease the amount of CFC's in automobile air conditioning systems; modify molecular structures such as HCFC s)

1. BY DESIGN:
New product or process design eliminates CFC s completely. (Ex.: Mechanical spray pump; paper rather than styrofoam cup)

3. CLOSED LOOP RECYCLING:
In-plant recycling confines CFC contamination and risk. (Ex.: Solvents containing CFC s are reused on site)

4. OPEN LOOP RECYCLING:
CFC's are recovered from widely distributed products. (Ex.: Refrigerator CFC recycling)

5. "COMMAND AND CONTROL":
No effective treatment for CFC's but regulations drive manufacturers and consumers toward bulls-eye. (Ex.: Montreal International Agreement to ban or cut use of CFC's)

Illustration by Sue Simmons.

This final chapter elevates the concept of evolved design and expertise up to the corporate and national level, where it may be useful to the American mainstream of business and government. To organize our roster of design strategies and our menu choices from Chapter 3, let's use an Environmental Master Plan as a rough, suggested guideline for mainstream America.

The Master Plan takes the form of an archery target with sensible, nature-compatible design as the bull's-eye. ("Design" includes both inspired ideas and well-executed actions.) Expert aim reduces pollution and environmental abuse, *by design*. The closer our designs and strategies come to the center of the target, the less environmental damage there will be. In the past, a given company may have generated pollution which then proliferated out into the world from the source—in effect, "escaping" from the conceptual bull's-eye. But expert design, firmly based on ecological reality, eliminates that pollution in the planning stages while proportionally reducing health and environmental risks. (Bob Simmons, director of the Continued Success Foundation, encourages corporate designers, politicians, county planners, and architects to mount a dartboard Master Plan right on the conference room wall.)

For example, a hydrogen-powered car emits very little pollution, and qualifies for the inner circle. Similarly, organic or "low-input" farming does not pollute its surrounding environment because knowledge of natural systems is deployed instead of polluting chemicals: appropriate tillage methods and crop rotation minimize erosion and soil depletion. Solar-powered water heaters are bull's-eyes because they eliminate pollution from coal-burning power plants or other fuel-related sources. Consumer products manufactured from appropriate molecules that fit rather than fight the environment are also bull's-eyes, because design has killed the problem before it could multiply. (Consumer goods containing toxins multiply their effects by causing problems at the factory, at the point of use and beyond, and at the point of disposal.) Groundwater protection and water efficiency are right on the mark, too. In Brookings, South Dakota, a comprehensive wellhead protection plan prohibits industrial activity near the source of the city's water, while in Santa Monica, California, a $100 rebate is given to every resident who installs a highly efficient toilet. Each of these examples incorporates biologic: knowing the full implications of a product or process enables a closer match between natural and cultural systems.

The advantages of precise aim encompass everything from survival of the species all the way down to a higher rate of return on stocks and bonds. (For example, the inspired layout of Village Homes, mentioned in Chapter 3, not only enhances the quality of life and reduces environmental impacts, but also increases property values.) If pollution is prevented right from the start, we can dodge the iceberg-like crises that loom ahead while at the same time creating a more pleasant world with less stress and cleaner, greener profits.

Obviously, being slightly off the mark is preferable to missing the target altogether. Toxic discharges into waterways and mountain-side clear-cuts are so far from the bull's-eye that stringent regulations are required to mandate better aim. When arrows whiz *past* the target, environmental impacts are extensive, sometimes approaching irreversible effects. CFC-containing designs and devices, for example, threaten the entire planet, and only better aim can reduce that threat.

The outer ring of the target is characterized by engineered "fixes" that try to *contain* environmental impacts rather than eliminate them. They attack effects rather than causes. As a last resort we battle environmental impacts using conventional, engineering-oriented means: hard-to-enforce regulations, expensive pollution-control devices, drawn-out litigation, desperate cleanups in Alaskan fiords, and so forth. We haven't *prevented* pollution, we're just trying to keep it from getting even further off-target.

The strong point of well-designed regulations is that they discourage pollution by making sloppy design cost too much, or just flat-out making it illegal. (Figuratively, they give incentives to polluters to practice their archery or else risk stiff penalties.) If our environmental laws are good ones, the regulatory ring gets progressively smaller as America's aim improves on a given issue. For example, a Connecticut law requires that newspapers published or circulated in that state will use increasing amounts of recycled paper, starting with 20 percent in 1993 and rising to 90 percent in the next ten years.[1]

The entire area between the bull's-eye and the outer ring of the target represents relatively good aim that could still be improved with practice. For example, by rethinking an existing process or product, we may be able to reduce the pollution that "tags along." For example, decreasing the amount of phosphates that are used in detergents also decreases the premature death of lakes by algae build-up. Another example is a reduction in the amount of materials used in a given package, which also reduces the impacts from resource extraction and product disposal. Several detergent manufacturers have now designed refillable containers, which will cumulatively reduce the amount of waste going to our landfills. Government agencies and corporate designers refer to this concept as "source reduction." It's not a bull's-eye, but it's a definite improvement.

We might refer to the territory outside source reduction as "closed-loop recycling." Products and pollutants continue to be generated as always, but their proliferation is reduced by recycling that occurs right at the point of origin, such as when an automobile manufacturer reuses process scraps to make engine blocks. This kind of recycling is far more effective than the next concentric space (open-loop recycling) for three reasons: the materials don't have to be re-collected; they haven't yet been contaminated by other materials in the world and are therefore are easier to recycle; and they don't pose risks and create hard-to-control impacts in the environment. Companies are discovering (with high disposal costs as an incentive) that many hazardous wastes can be reduced with closed-loop recycling.

Open-loop recycling is further out from the center because more energy is required to achieve it, and because pollution still occurs. In addition, we never completely get the materials back—some remain as environmental contaminants. For example, millions of cars roll off our production lines each year, but only a small percentage of the original materials are ultimately recycled. Better design would take cars closer to the target's center—design that makes recycling easy, attractive, and mandatory.

Design excellence tends to expand outward, effectively making the bull's-eye larger, just as a hardy new species proliferates from its point of origin. If a community or company has a good idea, other social species will adopt it. One example is the wellhead protection plan mentioned above. This good-sense idea is expanding outward from its origins in Brookings, South Dakota, into North Dakota, Montana, and Wyoming just like ripples from a stone thrown into a pond.

Nature aims for the bull's-eye, too. Starting at opportunistic slovenliness (like a bulldozed construction site quickly covered over with nutrient-wasting weeds), a given ecosystem gradually develops more efficient ways of using resources so that nothing is wasted. For an ecosystem, the bull's-eye is waste-free stability. For a company or community, the bull's-eye is exactly the same: waste-free stability.

Let's take a specific product, chlorofluorocarbons (CFCs), and develop a Master Plan to reduce their impact on the planet's ozone layer (CFCs are also a "greenhouse gas"). The major uses of CFCs are as aerosol propellants, in refrigerants, as blowing agents in foams, and as solvents to clean things like circuit boards during manufacturing processes.

Master Plan for CFC Reduction

1. Bull's-Eye (pollution prevention by design): the best thing to do with CFCs is eliminate them altogether, by design. U.S. industry has shifted to other propellants such as hydrocarbons, but these also have environmental impacts. A better design is the use of mechanical spray bottles, such as described in Chapter 1. Substitutes for CFC solvents, such as citrus-based cleaners, are right on target because they don't use CFCs and have few environmental effects. Refrigerators are also being designed to be CFC-free, as well as highly efficient. Egg cartons and paper cups that don't contain CFCs are also direct hits on the bull's-eye.

2. Source Reduction: Several large companies have developed a less-harmful substitute for CFCs—HCFCs—which still are harmful to the ozone layer, but only about a tenth as much. Thus, better design improves a bad situation. Consumer awareness can reduce the volume of CFCs in the environment, too: if we buy cardboard rather than styrofoam egg cartons, we help drive industry toward the center of the target, where no CFCs are manufactured to begin with.

3. Closed-loop Recycling: Some industries recycle the CFCs used as solvents in processes, keeping the compound from getting into the air.. This is far better than discharging CFCs into the environment.

4. Open-loop Recycling: If CFCs are already out in the world, the best approach is to figure out ways to collect products that contain them and recycle the compound. For example, some companies have developed equipment that will recycle CFCs contained in used car radiators and refrigerators—

a far better (if cumbersome) response environmentally than letting the chemicals escape.

5. Regulation and Engineered "Fixes": If CFCs are not being eliminated or recycled by Steps 1 through 4, "command and control" methods become necessary. If CFC manufacturers continue to make money selling the compound, even though our environment is threatened, regulations come into play as a last resort. For example, the international agreement reached in Montreal to reduce CFCs became necessary because CFC use was completely missing the target, and CFCs were drifting up into the stratosphere, where they remain for one hundred years, ripping apart protective ozone molecules. As mentioned in Chapter 4, outlandish, desperate methods such as the use of laser beams have been suggested as a means of "mopping up" the chemicals, but efforts to drive our aim inward toward the bull's-eye make much more sense.

Former EPA Administrator William Ruckelshaus summarized how the Master Plan approach must be implemented when he wrote:

> To get anything done in a free society three things are needed. First there has to be agreement on a set of values, some public consensus that there is a goal worth pursuing. Next must come a set of incentives, by which society can reward those who pursue the values and sanction those who do not. Finally, institutions must be able to adopt the values and administer the incentives.[2]

Overcoming the White House Effect

Our lives are cluttered with laws and customs that contradict the overall neatness of nature. Our partly concealed national agenda calls for high rates of consumption to build the GNP (Gross National Pile) even higher. As a result, whole-systems efficiency and resource sustainability are simply not part of the mainstream strategy.

In fact, the laws we put in place were *intended* to make extraction and exploitation easy. The idea was to get that ore out of the ground, get that timber out of the forest. But now that resource scarcity and pollution have entered our national consciousness, the rules are changing.

New coalitions are emerging to take advantage of nutrients and energy now squandered in pointless pollution and conflict. Cooperative arrangements are springing up between utilities and environmental groups, which until now have tended to be enemies. Other new developments include partnerships between counties to facilitate regional recycling; "negotiated rulemaking" (regulations by consensus); the use of efficiency experts to tune up our electrical and chemical processes; "soft chemists" who provide nature-compatible molecules for use in processes and products; "debt-for-nature" swaps that absolve debts in trade for ecological preservation; land use plans that balance quality of life with industrial needs; and so on.

The handwriting is on the wall, in the form of graffiti, newspaper articles, and technical monographs. It reads, *"Paradigm Shift."* By changing paradigms (collections of assumptions and operating procedures), we're changing from a social ecosystem that maximizes both production and waste into one which optimizes resource protection and efficiency. Unfortunately, the "White House effect" (political inertia in the executive branch) sometimes gets in the way, as when President Reagan declared that "No nation has ever conserved itself to greatness." Reagan's weakness was not being able to perceive the new efficiency paradigm: we can have lifestyles that are *higher* in quality if we use our heads, not just our oil rigs.

Winston Churchill observed, "First we shape our buildings, then our buildings shape us." The same is true of laws and procedures—they'll distort everything in our lives if they are poorly conceived. Furthermore, if we become preoccupied with following outdated rules, we may never get around to *changing* them. Fortunately, there are a few enlightened politicians and environmentalists on the scene experimenting with new rules. The Tim Wirth and John Heinz "Project 88" strategy is one example. The two senators (from Colorado and Pennsylvania, respectively) argue that creative solutions can emerge from our existing economic framework. They propose economic and social mechanisms calculated to hit the bull's-eye without even rocking America's boat. The fundamental notion is that "consumers and producers must face the true costs of their decisions—not just their direct costs but the full social costs." Among the methods they propose are tradable permits for industrial pollutants (which set a ceiling on a chemical's production and allow companies to trade production "coupons"), the removal of subsidies and market barriers that promote inefficiency and waste, and the use of "offsets" to maintain environmental quality. (For example, when a utility emits a given level of carbon dioxide, it must plant a given number of CO_2-reducing trees in compensation.) Some of these strategies were incorporated into the Clean Air Act amendments of 1990.

Other political representatives have proposed tightening efficiency standards for cars, appliances, and buildings; requiring more effective government procurement of recycled paper, oil, and other materials; and promoting better channels of technology transfer from government to industry. Perceiving the need to do an "end run" around the defensive line of old-paradigm politicians, these enlightened political representatives seem to be demanding, "What's the connection between the Greenhouse Effect and the White House effect?"

Barbed Wire and Branding Irons: Regulations That Fence Pollution In

Environmental regulations are essential tools in the conversion of sloppy design into well-crafted design. In a sense, the world of business and industry needs to be regulated just like a thermostat regulates a furnace. Without feedback from the thermostat, the furnace would run continuously, because that's what it's been programmed to do. Its mission is the conversion of natural gas into heat—it doesn't know anything about human comfort or impending energy shortages.

The implicit mission of environmental regulations is to herd pollution out of our common environment and into the corral. Barbed wire and branding irons were used to enclose the Great Plains in the 1890s; we rely on environmental regulations to define ecologically constructive boundaries in the 1990s. The ultimate goal would be to have an ethical, self-regulating society in which everyone behaved responsibly and there was no pollution or resource abuse. But we may as well expect cows to round *themselves* up, knowing exactly which corral to report to at what time.

Things change so quickly in our world, and new problems emerge so abruptly that we'd be lost without regulations. Our challenge is to forge creative regulations that help us evolve better ways of doing things, from transportation through manufacturing. We need not just rules, but *tools* that help identify opportunities for good aim, and that nurture constructive partnerships.

Now more than ever, we need these creative regulations to be *behavior-changers* that feed back clear signals to polluters about society's demands. The EPA's posse raid on the federal nuclear weapons plant at Rocky Flats, Colorado, in the summer of 1989 is an announcement of things to come. About fifty criminal investigators descended unannounced on the plant and conducted an in-depth audit of its methods and practices. The "raid" resulted in an abrupt change of management. A new initiative, criminal prosecution for environmental crimes, is finally getting the attention of the country's chief executive officers. Environmental negligence is one precedent already in place—a company president can be held personally responsible for the actions of his or her employees and can be thrown in jail if an employee knowingly pollutes the environment. Several years ago in Illinois, two executives were indicted on murder charges when an employee died from work-related cyanide poisoning.

Many environmentalists view litigation as the single most important tool they have. John Adams, of the Natural Resources Defense Council, believes that the value of the judicial system lies in its centralization. The country is huge, and diverse, but our legal system is a unifying, precedent-dependent mechanism. Frederic Sutherland and Vauter Parker of the Sierra Club Legal Defense Fund list some of the key things that environmental lawsuits have done:

- Saved millions of acres of land from inappropriate development, sometimes with last-second injunctions that halted bulldozers and chainsaws.
- Put teeth into environmental laws and credibility into the environmental movement.
- Provided leverage for citizen activists to wage David vs. Goliath battles against both industry and government.
- Brought issues into the news media and attracted support for various causes.
- Established precedents and legal principles that have steadily changed the rules by which environmental decisions are made.[3]

The Coevolution of Ecology and Political Will

Coevolution is the choreography of ecosystems. One example is the evolutionary dance performed by insects and plants, which seems almost deliberate. Over the course of time, a plant species evolves and retains a deterrent chemical in its make-up, and the insect pest gradually develops some way to deal with the chemical, sometimes drawing a third dancer onto the stage. Over time, evolution provides still *another* intricacy, further embellishing the dance. Coevolution, then, is the fine-tuning that continually takes place among species in response to each other's changes.

The coevolution of the mimosa tree and the oncideres beetle is a model for the way our culture needs to advance: by mutualistic self-interest (with altruism sprinkled in, in our case). The female oncideres will lay her eggs only in that one species of tree, and she neatly cuts a slit around the limb that contains the eggs, which kills the limb, because the offspring can't survive in live wood. The self-interest of the beetle also happens to be in the best interest of the tree, because without the maintenance the limb-pruning provides, the tree will die in about twenty-five years, but with it, the tree may live a hundred years or more.[4] The technologies, policies, and designs we choose need to mimic the inherent logic of the mimosa and its beetle caretaker.

Our designs and strategies are not acceptable unless they enhance *other* designs and strategies. Sometimes this will require a "pruning" or replacement of some of our institutions. Hazel Henderson says it well: "Just as the decay of last year's leaves provides humus for new growth the following spring, some institutions must decline and decay so that their components of capital, land, and human talents can be used to create new organizations."

Coevolution is a central theme in environmental protection as well as in nature. Mirroring increasing complexities in industry and society, America's regulatory structure is more complex than ever. (The Superfund law, for example, has tremendously increased the demand for attorneys to interpret and administer the complex regulation.) We grumble to ourselves as we sit obediently at a stoplight (especially if there's no other traffic), but it doesn't usually occur to us that the traffic lights are *coevolving with population density*. A graph showing an increase in the number of traffic lights would undoubtedly show an increase in several other variables: number of cars, road expenditures, and automobile accidents. Similarly, the graph of environmental regulations tracks pollution control expenditures.

Hazardous waste regulations as well as treatment technologies are in constant coevolution with the chemicals contained in the wastes. Incinerators are becoming increasingly efficient in direct proportion to the complexity of human-made molecular structures. Advanced biological treatment of hazardous wastes is now turning

Current Regulations: An Economic Incentive for Waste Reduction

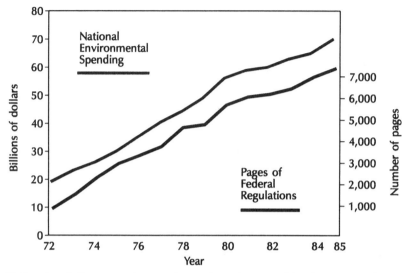

National pollution control expenditures have increased in direct proportion to the number of pages of environmental regulations. No doubt other variables are following similar upward trends, such as stress-related illness and habitat loss. *Illustration from Congressional Office of Technology Assessment report,* Serious Reduction of Hazardous Waste, *courtesy of COPIRG.*

to the field of biotechnology to respond to these structures; in order to take apart what humans have created, even microbes are being redesigned. For example, biotechnologist Ananda Chakrabarty proposes that for every chemical permitted to come into the marketplace, there should be an "antidote" in the form of an engineered bacteria or fungus, with the skills to "untie" that chemical compound.[5]

Clearly, such advanced design schemes need to be carefully regulated. We need regulatory custodians to make sure our antidote designs are less hazardous than the original designs they replace. More important, we need less complex designs in the world that *require* antidotes.

Bull's-eye Biologic

As environmental protection continues to evolve, it becomes increasingly a process of quality control—making sure the ingredients and techniques are correct. One experiment in quality control is "negotiated rulemaking." Rather than waiting for lawsuits to appear on the desk of an EPA administrator (there are currently close to five hundred), the EPA is sitting down with industry and environmental groups to forge workable laws. Currently, something like eight out of ten environmental laws are challenged in court, which squanders resources, causes delays, and erodes the effectiveness of the laws.

The conference table is becoming a central symbol of environmental problem-solving. Instead of hurling grenades in the shape of lawsuits and civil penalties, opposing factions are becoming used to the idea of sitting around a table and asking, "What can we *agree* upon? What will it take for all of us to be satisfied?" Government, public interest groups, and industry aim for the bull's-eye in the center of the table: consensus. The EPA's first attempts at negotiated rulemaking have been moderately successful, as have the efforts of several state rulemaking sessions. In Massachusetts, for example, industry helped create a new toxic chemical reduction law. For their trouble, they got an innovative mechanism for information-sharing (although they themselves will pick up the tab for its expenses through chemical user fees).

This networking, bartering approach resembles an interconnected ecosystem, because in a sense it is one. Coevolution can provide multidimensional tongues and grooves in our social affairs, as cultural coevolution mirrors the give-and-take characteristic of evolution in the natural world.

Frederic Krupp, executive officer of the Environmental Defense Fund, acknowledges the need for cooperative efforts to protect the environment. He suggests that we are in a new stage of environmentalism that is not satisfied with the precast role of opponent to environmental abuses. Its practitioners recognize that behind the waste dumps and dams and power plants and pesticides that threaten major environmental harm, there are nearly always legitimate social needs—and that long term solutions lie in finding alternative ways to meet those underlying needs.[6]

This orientation is not a familiar one to Americans, who seem more comfortable with white hats and black ones (representing the people vs. industry). The more conciliatory trend that Krupp refers to makes us feel a little nervous because it requires that agencies and environmental groups help direct profits like police officers direct traffic. As Barry Commoner has pointed out, this begins to sound like the "S" word—socialism—a word that makes many politicians and businessmen choke on their cocktails. For example, if we specify exactly what type of automobile the manufacturers must produce, is this tampering with private enterprise, or ensuring the common well-being?

Economist Hazel Henderson cautions that there is inevitably a lot of inertia and friction to overcome before opposing factions can reach consensus: "The old order cannot see what is being born. They say, in effect, 'We have created such a dangerously unstable system that you must keep us in power, since only we understand and can manage the dangers we have created.' Thus, one can never expect new alternatives to emerge from dominant cultures and their elites."[7]

We're in the habit of paying for the economic growth to which we are addicted with some form of aggression. But if we're clever, we can barter for contentment instead, with good design. Realistically, though, the change won't take place overnight. If we demand better cars and different kinds of cities, there are going to be people losing their jobs and their investments. On the other hand, if we don't demand better cars and cities, we'll lose far more than jobs. The attractive part about shifting our environmental focus is that there is money to be made in pollution *prevention—* both in avoided costs and in substitute products.

If American industry willingly makes the paradigm shift to better design and higher efficiency, overall corporate profits will be up, and the country can retire its debt within a few years with money saved on its cumulative energy, water, and waste collection bills.

America's regulations, economic incentives, and social customs *are* steadily becoming more compatible with natural laws. In hazardous waste treatment, regulations acknowledge the ecological limitations of land disposal and create such stringent requirements that disposal costs have escalated from about $20 a ton to $200 a ton, making waste minimization very attractive economically. In energy supply, the long-held assumption that more energy is the answer to any and all power-related questions is being successfully challenged by efficient devices and innovative financing schemes. And in the area of water supply, the strategy of the cactus is now a respected approach for maintaining both the quantity and quality of water. In all three areas, we can solve problems by working smarter, not harder. And the costs we *avoid* by substituting information for resources will pay the bill.

We'll look first at the opportunities that efficiency and renewable sources offer for streamlining the country's carbon-snorting, dragon-like energy system.

SPECIAL FOCUS
Playing Hardball with the Soft Path

Perhaps our best biologic success story in recent years is the rediscovery of what the sun can do for us, if we let it. Solar and other renewable energies fit into our Master Plan because they prevent the severe pollution produced by fossil fuel extraction and combustion. With the spectre of global warming clouding humanity's future, fuel combustion is a burning issue in more ways than one.

Incorporating biologic concepts such as orientation, thermal storage, and the use of high-tech glasses and plastics, American builders have sold well over a million solar-heated houses in the past ten years. One of the best examples of an effective sun-powered building is Amory and Hunter Lovins' home, which is also the office of the Rocky Mountain Institute they founded. A 4,000-square-foot facility in Snowmass, Colorado, where temperatures can fall to forty-five degrees below zero, the building is a showpiece of good design, both in structure and fixtures.

The Lovinses refer to the building as "the equivalent of a small oil field that pumps two-thirds of a barrel a day." Its heating bill is typically zero, while the monthly electricity bill for the large building is only about $40. The Lovinses are true pioneers of a new paradigm, the "soft energy path," which is decentralized and focused on efficiency and renewable energy. Rather than try to perpetually increase supply of nonrenewables, the soft path focuses on a steady-state, recyclable society. Correctly predicting in the 1970s that efficiency would reduce the nation's energy demands, Amory Lovins presented a well-documented alternative to centralized power in the book, *Soft Energy Paths*.[8] Renewable energy sources, such as solar heating and electricity, geothermal, wind, hydroelectric, and biomass, can reliably supply the nation's energy needs—*if* those needs have already been tuned up with the most efficient devices and techniques now available.

Reprinted courtesy of the *Rocky Mountain News.*

The most basic step is using the sun's heat directly. There's no reason our houses can't be as temperature-conservative as picnic coolers. In Sweden and other places such as Minnesota in the United States, new superinsulated houses require only one-tenth the energy for heating and cooling as the average American house. Bigelow Construction company in frosty Minnesota guarantees that yearly energy bills in its thermos-like houses will not exceed $200 a year.

Electricity by the Express Route

A more technically sophisticated use of solar energy is a process using photovoltaics, which is in effect a technological analog of photosynthesis. Photovoltaic (PV) cells are coming into full flower in the nation's research labs, where higher efficiency cells are consistently being developed.

The biologic of PV cells is extremely attractive. "No heat, water, or moving parts are required, just a photon to jar an electron from its orbit, causing an electric current to flow," writes Worldwatch researcher Cynthia Pollack Shea.[9]

PV cells are already economically competitive with the most expensive components of the nation's electrical system, such as gas turbines and remote power needs that make distribution from centralized plants very expensive. Worldwatch Institute researcher Christopher Flavin describes the current PV cell climate:

> Photovoltaics is a world of high-tech laboratories, secret plans, patents, and weekly rumors of the latest breakthrough. Solid-state physicists are quickly being joined by back-to-nature homesteaders, environmentalists, venture capitalists, and bankers. Increasingly, photovoltaics is becoming a world of big business, with oil companies and large electronics corporations investing heavily.[10]

Flavin cautions that no single technology can solve the world's energy problems, but that photovoltaics appears ready to start playing a major role. A pioneering use of PV cells has been solar watches and calculators. In 1987 alone, 200 million solar calculators were sold. More than 15,000 homes worldwide receive their electrical supply from PV cells, and the U.S. Coast Guard has pressed more than ten thousand PV systems into use to power navigational aids.[11]

Scott Sklar of the Solar Energy Industries Association believes that in the next century, 25 percent of the nation's electricity could be supplied by solar cells and solar-thermal technologies. He cites two major advantages to solar power plants, once their costs have become competitive with fossil fuel plants: solar plants can be built as large or as small as needed, and a solar plant "can get all the needed permits and be built within eighteen months, because it has no emissions."[12]

Already, several full-scale PV power plants are coming on line, in addition to a cluster of solar-thermal power plants that focus sunlight to create generator-turning steam.

The Renewable State

California has been responsible for a large percentage of the renewable energy brought on line in the last ten years. In fact, from a total of less than 50 megawatts of electrical generation in 1979, the state's renewable energy capacity has jumped to over 5,000 megawatts in 1988. These energy sources include the

Advanced technologies combine with traditional good-sense design at the Rocky Mountain Institute in Aspen, Colorado, providing a building space that gains rather than consumes energy. *Illustrations courtesy of Rocky Mountain Institute and Aspen Design Group.*

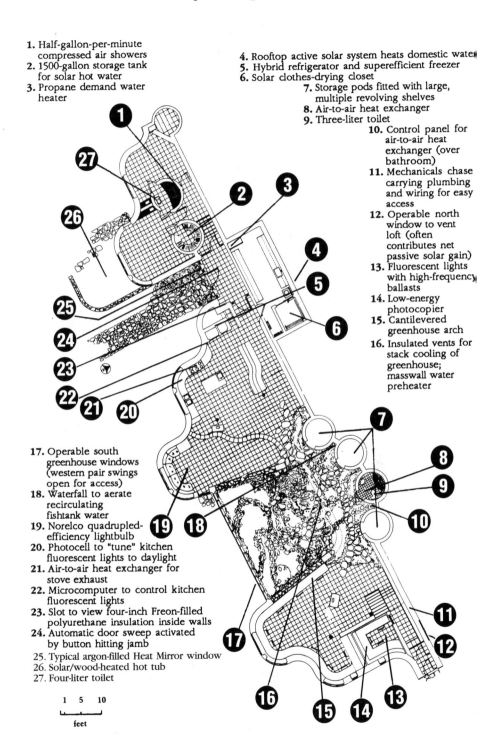

1. Half-gallon-per-minute compressed air showers
2. 1500-gallon storage tank for solar hot water
3. Propane demand water heater
4. Rooftop active solar system heats domestic water
5. Hybrid refrigerator and superefficient freezer
6. Solar clothes-drying closet
7. Storage pods fitted with large, multiple revolving shelves
8. Air-to-air heat exchanger
9. Three-liter toilet
10. Control panel for air-to-air heat exchanger (over bathroom)
11. Mechanicals chase carrying plumbing and wiring for easy access
12. Operable north window to vent loft (often contributes net passive solar gain)
13. Fluorescent lights with high-frequency ballasts
14. Low-energy photocopier
15. Cantilevered greenhouse arch
16. Insulated vents for stack cooling of greenhouse; masswall water preheater
17. Operable south greenhouse windows (western pair swings open for access)
18. Waterfall to aerate recirculating fishtank water
19. Norelco quadrupled-efficiency lightbulb
20. Photocell to "tune" kitchen fluorescent lights to daylight
21. Air-to-air heat exchanger for stove exhaust
22. Microcomputer to control kitchen fluorescent lights
23. Slot to view four-inch Freon-filled polyurethane insulation inside walls
24. Automatic door sweep activated by button hitting jamb
25. Typical argon-filled Heat Mirror window
26. Solar/wood-heated hot tub
27. Four-liter toilet

1   5   10

feet

Recent advances in wind generators reduce metal fatigue and capture renewable energy far more efficiently.

simultaneous production of heat and electricity ("cogeneration"), the combustion of biomass materials (such as wood chips), wind turbines, hydroelectric, geothermal, and solar electricity.

Wind farms now provide about 1 percent of California's electricity—enough to power 280,000 homes. In the last nine years, wind power costs have dropped by two-thirds, partly because mass production has brought their price down.[13] The search for a "nickel wind machine"—a wind generator that costs five cents a kilowatt-hour has produced extremely efficient technologies in recent years, that can compete favorably with fossil fuel power.

The California Energy Commission has predicted that these renewable sources will account for 25 percent of the state's energy supply by 2000.[14] The renewable energy program has been so successful that the state legislature is gearing up to begin marketing renewable energy expertise and technology throughout the world.

Power Plants or Powerful Plants?

The Department of Energy estimates that "biofuels" (including woody and herbaceous crops, agricultural and forestry wastes, and oil-producing plants for conversion to burnable fuels) could supply 20 percent of current U.S. energy consumption. Approximately 3 to 5 percent is already supplied by wood and wood wastes, compared to 4 to 5 percent for nuclear power and 4 percent for hydroelectric power. In addition to helping heat a fifth of all American homes, wood provides 8 percent of all energy used by industry.[15] Another contribution from biofuels is the 850 million gallons of corn and sugar crops that are converted to ethanol every year for use in gasoline blends. The ethanol raises octane while reducing carbon monoxide emissions from vehicles. Organic wastes are another energy resource. At more than eighty facilities nationwide, municipal solid waste and refuse-derived fuels are being burned to provide electricity and heat for industrial processes.

Biomass is an attractive energy strategy in terms of global warming, the nastiest troll among environmental problems. Because carbon dioxide (the major greenhouse gas) is both produced and consumed in the growth and use of biomass, biofuels offer a

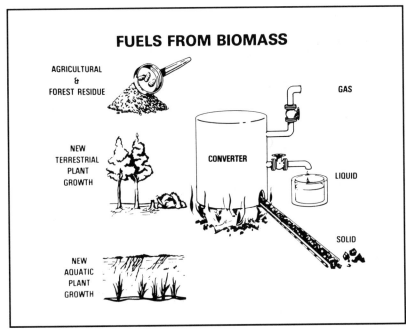

FUELS FROM BIOMASS

AGRICULTURAL & FOREST RESIDUE

GAS

NEW TERRESTRIAL PLANT GROWTH

CONVERTER

LIQUID

SOLID

NEW AQUATIC PLANT GROWTH

Energy supplied from plant materials will never run out. Many fuels from biomass burn more cleanly than petroleum fuels, and the plants that supply the fuels can also reduce carbon dioxide levels, which in turn reduces the threat of global warming. *Illustration courtesy of Solar Energy Reasearch Institute.*

renewable energy source that doesn't increase carbon dioxide levels in the atmosphere. A World Resources Institute study titled *Growing Power*, points out that:

> Thanks partly to a 1978 law that requires utilities to buy electricity from small private producers, biomass-fueled power projects planned in the United States steadily increased from 235 megawatts in 1981 to more than 1000 megawatts in 1985, and further development of fuel from wastes seems almost certain.[16]

In the same report, however, the authors respond to valid concerns about the environmental impacts of biomass as an energy source:

> Such large-scale production of energy crops does call environmental consequences, conflicts with food production, and the distribution of costs and benefits into question. But these problems are not unique to bioenergy projects; the same issues writ large surround export agriculture. The trick is to undertake these programs carefully, and to avoid environmentally sensitive areas.

The Brazilian experiment in biofuels has been a success in many respects, although critics claim that biofuels are still not as viable economically as petroleum, and that Brazil's program has required massive governmental subsidies. Still, the production of automobile fuel from vast sugar cane plantations has resulted in a 30 percent reduction of oil imports and has created employment opportunities, an export market for ethanol-powered vehicles and distilleries, and an improvement in Brazilian air quality—which needs improving in many areas due to the burning of forests to clear land.

A Niche in Time

By honoring age-old advice not to put all eggs in a single basket, decentralized, soft-path technologies will put power precisely where it's needed. They will also subdivide several hundred prime military targets into several million. The inherent security of renewable energy is especially evident when mainstream power systems fail, but alternative systems keep going. For example, a Great Plains farmer whose house was powered by a wind generator was watching TV and saw a report that his whole area was blacked out due to a power failure. He went outside and verified the report: the familiar dots of light from neighboring farms were dark.

Another incident that occurred eight or ten years ago illustrates the potential vulnerability of our electrical system. A power failure occurred in Ohio, and the plant's computer went looking for surplus power to take up the slack. But all the nearby plants were running at peak demand, and the first utility to respond was in Arkansas, where a hydroelectric plant was "idling." The Arkansas plant was automatically controlled, and when the request for power came in, the plant started up. The opening of its massive gates released a large volume of water below the plant, capsizing a meandering boat and instantaneously killing the fisherman in it. So interconnected has our system become that a power outage in Ohio can kill a man in Arkansas.[17]

Because of the pivotal, underlying role which energy plays in our world, renewable energies and efficiency may be as critical to world peace as the world's entire stockpile of warheads. (Indeed, the caulk gun may be a far more valuable defense item than all the world's M-16s.) As actor/producer Robert Redford phrased it at a senate hearing, "It's important to raise the environment to the same level as national security, because if we poison our planet, what is there left to defend?"

Aside from offering the country (and the world) a greater measure of genuine security, renewable energy supplies are in general less polluting, potentially less expensive, and more "humanly scaled." Woven into the fabric of life, renewable technologies are powered by the planet's most basic, most thoroughly dependable mechanisms—sun, wind, water, and plants. What they cannot power may not *need* to be powered. (If fusion power does emerge from our labs, will it cause more *con*fusion than it's worth? The more we feed the monster, the bigger it will get. And don't the gigantic uncertainties and social question marks of nuclear power make it *unclear* power?)

Despite the "solar eclipse" that the Reagan administration attempted to stage during the lost decade of the 1980s (cutting back drastically on solar research and development) renewable energy implementation has demonstrated that the soft path is not "flaky"—systems *can* be designed that will power our world without hydrocarbons.

The fact is, it's the "hydro" part of hydrocarbons we need—the "carbon" part is what's making the mess. Inevitably, we will move out of our "hydrocarbon economy" and into a less constricted, renewable "carbohydrate economy." One of our highest priorities should be the clean production and use of hydrogen, the simplest, most abundant element in the universe. The problem is there are fewer than forty people in the country doing full-time research on hydrogen as an energy source. Out of a $2 billion federal energy budget, only about $3 million goes to hydrogen research.

Scientist H. Ti Tien from Michigan State University may be on the right track toward the inexpensive production of hydrogen: an electrochemical/photovoltaic cell modeled after the process of photosynthesis is now producing hydrogen directly from seawater, with no power inputs other than the solar spectrum. The membrane device is currently undergoing efficiency improvements and may be ready for use sooner than fusion, the heavily subsidized "perpetual experiment" that has received so much hopeful press.[18]

Most proponents of renewable energy sources believe that ninety-three million miles (our distance from the sun) is about the closest we need to be to a fusion reaction. Controlled fusion might be less dangerous than fission (now used in conventional nuclear plants), but wouldn't abundant, unlimited energy supplies permit us to make an unlimited mess? Is it really vast energy supplies we want, or more intelligent, relevant ways of using *sufficient* energy supplies?

Substituting Wits for Watts

All ecosystems aspire toward efficiency. The emergence of energy efficiency as a central focus in our culture is analogous to the sudden appearance of a new species or survival skill in an ecosystem. An interesting example is coconut-cracking among monkeys. One bright individual learned how to throw coconuts onto rocks to break them open, and within several years, monkeys all over the Pacific had somehow picked up the skill. A species of bird, the titmouse, accomplished a similar feat in England in the 1950s: one advanced bird somehow acquired the ability to pilfer milk by puncturing the foil lids on front porch milk bottles, and the trick became widespread not only within its own species but among distant cousins as well.

It's the same with lighting, heating, motor efficiency, cooling, and all the rest of our electrical needs. Individuals such as Amory Lovins and Art Rosenfeld are proponents of "new ways to crack coconuts," and the rest of us will soon follow suit. It's not kilowatts we're after, they remind us, but lights, motor-power, and the other things that *run* on kilowatts. So if we can make our products and processes smarter and less energy-hungry, we'll need fewer kilowatts, not more. Fewer kilowatts means less pollution, and it also means that fewer expensive power plants will have to be built in the future.

Lovins writes, "The efficiency revolution has taken place in so many millions of small, unglamorous places—an insulated attic here, a plugged steam leak there—that its full dimensions are seldom realized. Yet by 1986, the thirteen-year-old 'energy efficiency industry' was producing the equivalent of two-fifths more oil per year than the century-old oil industry was extracting."[19] In the past few years, energy efficiency has stalled (largely because the price of oil has come down), but the potentials are still awesome—equivalent to the discovery of a workable fusion technology but far less imposing.

Lovins also states that "negawatts" (as he terms electrical efficiency), have yielded seven times as much energy as new supply

By substituting state-of-the-art lighting technologies, America could be just as brightly lit but close down over a hundred power plants. *Photo produced from USAF Defense Meteorological Satellite Program film transparencies, archived for NOAA/NESDIS at the University of Colorado. Reprinted with permission.*

sources in recent years, and that of the new supply which has been brought on line, more has come from renewable sources like solar, hydroelectric, and geothermal than from conventional, highly polluting sources such as oil, nuclear, and coal.

Lighting the Way to a New Paradigm

Energy-efficient light bulbs are a perfect symbol for the evolutionary jump our society is about to make. Because energy has been so cheap, we used Edison's primitive design throughout the light bulb's first century. Yet the new designs now on the market (compact fluorescents and others) offer a direct pathway to pollution reduction, cost savings, and resource protection. In effect, they hit the center of the bull's-eye by substituting wits for watts, and craftiness for coal. They provide the same level of light with 18 watts that the common light bulb does with 75, and they last ten times as long.

The conventional light bulb puts out heat right along with the light because it isn't efficient at converting electricity to light. That

The EverX exit sign uses only half a watt, compared to standard 12 to 50 watts in the millions of exit signs throughout the country. When power fails, the electro-luminescent plate will continue to glow if previously exposed to light. *Photo courtesy of QNX, Inc.*

"heat pollution" can make a building's air conditioning system work overtime, which in turn requires more coal to be burned, resulting in air pollution, acid rain, and more power demand for air conditioning, because the coal-burning heats the entire environment. State-of-the-art light bulbs are much cooler, emitting five times less heat than incandescents. The person sitting at his/her desk sees just as well (the compact fluorescents don't have the flicker of conventional fluorescents) and at the same time, effortlessly contributes to cleaner air.

If these smart bulbs were screwed into our country's millions of light fixtures instead of incandescents, close to a hundred coal or nuclear power plants could be shut down! Worldwatch researcher Christopher Flavin writes, "If utilities or energy efficiency companies were to invest in efficient lighting in homes and offices, and split the savings with occupants, compact fluorescents could sweep the market."[20] In fact, the Southern California Edison power utility has now *given away* more than half a million such bulbs after discovering that it was cheaper than generating new electricity to power inefficient bulbs. "Operation Lightswitch" in the state of

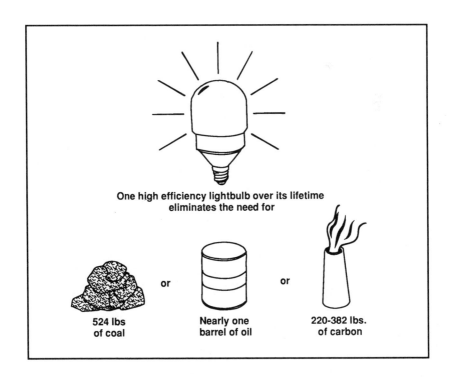

One high efficiency lightbulb over its lifetime eliminates the need for

524 lbs of coal or **Nearly one barrel of oil** or **220-382 lbs. of carbon**

Maine is a partnership between Central Maine Power and the Maine Lions Club. The utility wanted to avoid building another expensive power plant, so it purchased (and made available to the Lions) 90,000 light bulbs that each use 75 percent less energy than the bulbs the Lions usually sell in their annual door-to-door campaigns.

One of the most successful social experiments concerning lighting technologies has been EPA's "Green Lights" program. Launched in 1991, the program enlists the voluntary participation of corporations, utilities and government agencies to upgrade existing lighting. More than a thousand partners have already installed new lighting systems, and EPA estimates that by 2000, at least 50 billion square feet of U.S. facility space will be committed to high-efficiency lights, chasing the ghost of Thomas Edison out of our office buildings and factories.

Buildings with High IQs

In cities such as Phoenix and Los Angeles, pavement and buildings serve as heat batteries or thermal mass to hold in solar energy. The average nighttime temperature in Phoenix has increased by some seven or eight degrees since the 1950s—an increase that upsets neither the air conditioning industry nor the utilities. The "heat island" effect of urban areas is an energy glutton, eating coal and uranium to produce coolness.

Arthur Rosenfeld of the Lawrence Berkeley Laboratory estimates that cooling cities with natural techniques, such as planting more trees and using light-colored paints and shingles to augment reflection, could save about 1/160th of our annual energy needs, decreasing the emission of CO_2 by about twenty million tons of carbon per year. The addition of light-colored sand to asphalt would also increase a city's reflectivity, further lowering its cooling bill.

At the Solar Energy Research Institute in Colorado, photochromic window glazings are under intensive development and could offer another design strategy for reductions in energy used to cool buildings. Using the same technology as eyeglasses that darken when the wearer goes outside, these windows could prevent a given office or living room from becoming an oven.

Already in wide use are "low emissivity" windows with a thin, invisible, reflective film (about 70 atoms thick) which acts as a "mirror" to heat but not light. In the winter, this kind of glass will prevent heat from escaping from a building, while in hot southern

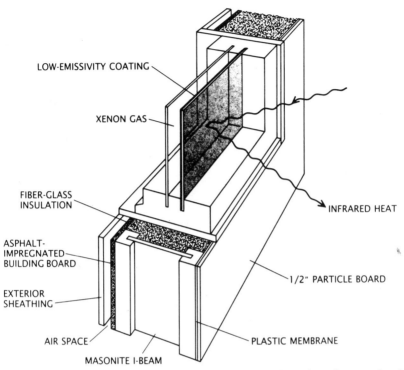

LOW-EMISSIVITY COATING

XENON GAS

FIBER-GLASS
INSULATION

INFRARED HEAT

ASPHALT-
IMPREGNATED
BUILDING BOARD

1/2" PARTICLE BOARD

EXTERIOR
SHEATHING

AIR SPACE

PLASTIC MEMBRANE

MASONITE I-BEAM

State-of-the-art windows offer roughly double the insulating value of conventional double-paned windows. A reflective, invisible film allows light in but doesn't let house heat get out. Inert gases between the panes further reduce heat loss.

climates, the windows can prevent heat from entering a building. With low-E glazings, windows help buildings take advantage of the natural daylight, which can reduce the use of light bulbs. According to Rocky Mountain Institute:

> The low-E coatings, coupled with the injection of special gases between the panes of glass, have yielded R-values (a measure of insulating power) roughly double that of traditional double-glazed windows. The readily available superwindows typically cost 10 percent to 20 percent more than the traditional double-glazed window. This extra cost, however, is soon recovered through decreased heating and cooling costs.[21]

Energy audit experts remind us not to overlook the less glamorous potentials in our homes and other buildings. There are still great energy savings to be "mined" in the billions of tiny air leaks in American homes: all the little caulkable leaks in the typical "unconserved" house add up to a 4' x 4' open window.

The renovated headquarters of the Natural Resources Defense Council is a model of what can be done with high-efficiency lights, windows, and heating/air conditioning. The 30,000-square-foot office space, completed in early summer 1989, demonstrates technologies that are "easily available, financially sound, and aesthetically pleasing," according to NRDC scientist David Goldstein. "We're not pushing the outer limits of technology here." Yet if all American offices came up to this standard, the energy saved would allow us to shelve the entire U.S. nuclear energy industry.[22]

Among the features at the NRDC office are motion sensors that automatically turn lights on when someone enters the office and shut them off ten minutes after the last occupant leaves. "Another side benefit of these sensors," says Goldstein half-whimsically, "is that if there's ever a break-in, the police can follow the burglar's progress through the building by watching the lights go on."

The NRDC's office also includes individualized heating controls. This bypasses energy-wasting differences that always seem to occur in the standard office: one corner is freezing because the air conditioning is going full-tilt, while in another corner employees are roasting because of the heat produced by afternoon sun, 100-watt human bodies, copy machines, and computers.

Sensors track outside temperatures and make use of cool ambient air instead of air conditioning whenever possible. Eight to fifteen changes of air per hour are provided in the building, instead of the standard four to five. Lighting is designed so that most of the light hits the work space. Instead of a standard 3 watts per square foot, NRDC eliminates glare and energy waste with good design and .5 watt per square foot. Varying thicknesses of low-E coatings in the windows reflect unwanted heat from sunny exposures and permit light and heat to enter through north-facing windows. (They also prevent the escape of building heat in the winter.) In short, the office space fits in with its environment rather than trying to overpower it. NRDC's Robert Watson comments that the office disproves the belief that energy efficiency means workers "have to show up in miners' helmets." At the same time, says Watson, it reduces the skepticism of developers who say, "It's a nice idea but it can't be done economically." NRDC's payback is slightly longer than conventional renovations (because initial cost is higher), but once the efficiency measures have paid for themselves, the environmental group's utility bills are going to make the rest of Manhattan look foolish. (The $100,000 grant that

An ingenious system of louvers at the Albany County Airport enables building owners to balance light gain and heat loss. A microcomputer continually gauges the indoor and outdoor environment, and selects the most energy-efficient position for the louvers. The skylit solar court provides 40 percent of the lighting and 20 percent of the heating in the new passenger terminal in Colonie, New York. *Photo courtesy of The Fleming Group and Einhorn, Yaffee, Prescott, PC, Albany, New York.*

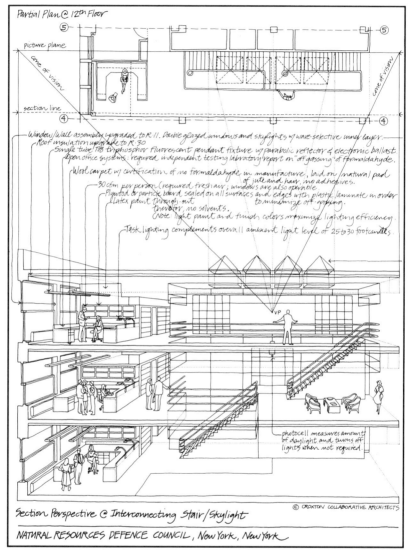

Partial Plan @ 12th Floor

Section Perspective @ Interconnecting Stair/Skylight

NATURAL RESOURCES DEFENCE COUNCIL, New York, New York

© CROXTON COLLABORATIVE ARCHITECTS

Using natural daylighting to its fullest advantage, as well as high-tech lighting and individualized office heating, the new headquarters of the Natural Resources Defense Council in New York City is a model of efficiency.

NRDC got from Consolidated Edison, the city's utility, also sweetened the deal.)

Many utilities are realizing that the cheapest place to generate electricity is right in the fixtures of their users. And, as discussed in the following section, the same principles can be used in water supply.

Substituting Wits for Wasted Water

By building an oversized, disruptive dam smack in the middle of an ecosystem, we require demand to rise in order to meet—and finance—the new water supply. Rocky Mountain Institute's John Woodwell explains the pitfalls of increasing the price of water to cover a dam's cost: "As the Washington Public Power Supply System (WPPSS) so spectacularly demonstrated with electricity, a rise in a utility's tariff encourages efficiency and reduces demand. Reduced use in turn forces an additional price hike which further reduces demand, and so on. This financial 'death spiral' has buried WPPSS and several utilities."[23]

But with easily achievable, inexpensive efficiency measures, you "pay as you go." A more highly evolved notion than monkish conservation, efficiency doesn't require deprivation. For example, one dramatic water-saving technique is "xeriscape," a biologic strategy that uses natural landscaping, soil building, and tuned-up awareness to minimize water needs. Homeowners who have converted from "monoculture" lawns to xeriscape comment that summer weekends are no longer devoted to grass mowing and lawn pampering. "I can go out and play golf instead," said one xeriscaper, "and let someone else take care of the grass."

Xeriscaping is a good example of how good ideas can radiate in several directions at once. By reducing the square footage planted in grass, it can also reduce an arid city's trash ("solid waste") problem. Nationwide, close to 20 percent of our municipal garbage is grass clippings, leaves, and other yard wastes.

Just as cooler light bulbs reduce air conditioning needs, water efficiency in general can reduce the energy needed to heat more water. High-efficiency showerheads and faucet fixtures fall into this category. If a one-gallon jug can be filled by your showerhead in less than fifteen seconds, you need a more efficient fixture. By shelling out between $15 and $20 at the hardware or home center store, you can take home an easy-to-install, high-tech showerhead that delivers the same quality of shower using a third of the water. Sacrifice and deprivation don't come into the picture: high-velocity pulsing jets substitute good design for superfluous water, saving the average four-person family at least twenty-five gallons of water a day that doesn't have to be heated (more like fifty gallons total). Citywide, the potentials are very attractive indeed. By saving millions of gallons of water, a city can reduce its need to build dams, pump ground water, and treat both drinking water and wastewater.

In fact, many water utilities are now creating supply on the demand side by subsidizing water efficiency. If their ultimate product is customer and shareholder satisfaction, water supply is not the bottom line. Services provided by the water are the bottom line, and if they can be supplied more efficiently so less water is used, everybody wins. (Including the utility, which doesn't have to acquire more water and treat unnecessary water.)

The city of Aurora, Colorado, passed a law specifying a certain organic content in real estate lots, to conserve water. (The dry, sandy soils typical of the area do not hold water well.) Complying with this law means that developers and builders have to add compost to their properties. Unfortunately, many of the builders have been adding peat moss mined from mountainous wetlands, which upgrades one land use (suburban housing) at the expense of another (subalpine habitat).

A very innovative scheme in Morro Bay, California, requires would-be builders to save more water in existing structures than will be used in a proposed new structure. Builders become efficiency scavengers, replacing sections of leaky water mains and installing high-efficiency fixtures like showerheads, toilets, and aerators in houses all over the city, by arrangement with their owners.

Another California scheme, facilitated by the Environmental Defense Fund, made partners of water users and water providers. The Metropolitan Water District of Southern California and the Imperial Irrigation District teamed up to line leaky irrigation canals and carry out other conservation measures. The water district paid the bill in exchange for rights to the recovered water that had previously been wasted.

What do we do with the majority of our water? We eat it. More than 70 percent of the world's water, and up to 90 percent of the water in western states, is used for irrigation. A little biologic can go a long way in saving large percentages of this irrigation water. By using gravity and soil moisture wisely to prevent excessive evaporation, farmers can not only save water but also prevent pollution resulting from runoff and infiltration of fertilizers and pesticides. For example, by using lasers to precisely level their fields, farmers can make sure irrigation water goes directly onto their crop and not into the drainage ditch, heavily laden with wasted, hazardous pesticides.

Rather than spraying irrigation water high into the air where it evaporates quickly, smart farmers are now using precision application techniques: drop tubes that hang from rotating sprinkler systems and drip water that efficiently "spoon-feeds" root zones.[24]

Another method of substituting wits for water is a small device that looks like nothing more than a marshmallow. Made of water-absorbing gypsum, the small blocks can save up to 58 percent of applied water by electronically communicating when a given crop *needs* water. Sort of like periscopes in reverse, the gypsum block is ingenious in its simplicity: a farmer connects a calculator-sized instrument to the probe attached to the buried block, and immediately knows how moist the soil is.

At Colorado State University, several researchers have succeeded in getting the plants themselves to report when they're thirsty. Using a miniature microphone, the scientists listen for an increase in clicking sounds emitted by thirsty plants when vapor bubbles form in the plants' stems. It may not be too fanciful to imagine that one day whole fields of crops will be able to warn, "We're thirsty!"[25]

Sort of like periscopes in reverse, marshmallow-sized gypsum blocks hooked up to electrodes are a reliable indicator of how much moisture soil contains, removing the guesswork. Water use can be reduced substantially, sometimes resulting in healthier crops. *Photo courtesy of Gail Richardson.*

Harvesting the Opportunities

A television commercial for snack chips summarizes current-day America in seven words. Comedian Jay Leno devours a crisp chip and invites us to "Crunch all you want, we'll make more." America is obsessed with the supply side: raw materials extraction, mass production, and mass marketing. In our pioneer ecosystem days, the supply side has admittedly been dazzling, sort of like the colored lights and cotton candy at a carnival. There's no doubt that our most awesome hour from an output standpoint was the mobilized, mandated production during and immediately after World War II. We demonstrated a real aptitude for supplying, and we had the resources to supply. Plastic packaging, for example, was an outgrowth of our need to feed and clothe distant soldiers. After the war, our mobilization efforts had far too much momentum to sit down and relax. We continued to mobilize highway systems, bomb shelters, suburbs, pesticides, and so on, never questioning whether the new designs fit the environment.

We were set loose and encouraged to have all the pop and candy we wanted, because it would knock the GNP sky-high, like in one of those carnival booths where you ring the bell at the top of the pole by using a sledge hammer and Paul Bunyan-like muscles. The carnival GNP bell continues to ring in the 1990s but many Americans are not sure we're having any fun. Since the "bads" are lumped together with the goods and services, it's difficult to tell if those bell rings indicate frenzy or fulfillment. The cost of car crashes figures into that GNP, along with pollution control, liability insurance, and prescription drugs. Now it's the carnival's price of admission that has gone sky-high—so high that we now spend most of our working hours buying carnival tickets.

America's giddy Ferris wheel days are over. Instead of always relying on the environmentally depleting supply side, we're making the inevitable jump to a new paradigm. From a pioneer, Paul Bunyan society we are progressing to a more highly evolved, mature society.

Where the Money Comes From: Avoided Costs and Waste-free Lifestyles

The question that nags well-intentioned consumers, agencies, and businesses in recent years has been, "How can we afford to do all these creative, efficient things that hit the bull's-eye when there are children to raise, insurance bills to battle, rivers to be cleaned up and stockholders to satisfy? *Where does the money come from to do the right thing?"*

One emerging response, rising over the American horizon like a high-efficiency light bulb over our cartoon heads is, "Let the market pay for them!" If an idea is genuinely good, chances are it's also marketable. The trick is to trace the flow of expenditures. What money is now being misspent on out-of-tune services such as waste collection, wasteful energy, and wasted water? The avoided costs of building and operating power plants, water distribution systems, and waste disposal sites can foot the bill, if intelligent political and economic arrangements can be made.

Rather than make society pay for waste, the new paradigm says, "Let's create ways we can instead spend our money on a *lack* of waste." Collectively, we can refuse to pay for waste by not generating it, or at least by reusing what we have. And we can change our standard ways of doing business to avoid waste, too (not strictly because we're angelic, but also because our laws and markets demand it).

For the same reason that Reynolds Aluminum opted to encourage recycling in the United States rather than continue alumina and bauxite production overseas, utilities are paying customers to become more efficient—because efficiency is often cheaper than production. Northeast Utilities paid Calder department stores $300,000 to install 9,500 energy-efficient light bulbs at ten of its stores. Throughout the country, consumers of electricity are being paid for volunteering to have their air conditioners and other appliances automatically turned off by the utility during peak hours— brief interruptions which they won't notice except in lower bills. In fact, the sale of "negawatts" (efficient devices and strategies) is so lucrative right now that about a dozen investor-owned utilities are selling efficiency expertise in the territory of other utilities.

Amory Lovins suggested during the energy crises of the 1970s that it might be cheaper to supply high-efficiency cars free of charge to everyone who drove an old gas-hog than it would be to seek out, deliver, and clean up more oil. In fact, cities such as Denver are now subsidizing the phase-out of gas-hogs. The "eat all you want, we'll make more" mentality is beginning to be questioned. Lovins is still making provocative, paradigm-shifting comments as we head into the 1990s. "Putting a proper price on depletion and pollution cannot replace a proper regard for our moral obligations to beings in other places, forms and times," he acknowledges. "But prices imaginatively combined with flexible, accessible markets can at least apply to corrective mechanisms the same vigor and ingenuity—the same diversity and adaptability—that have got us into this mess." Expanding this logic into other realms, he asks wryly, "How much is it worth paying people to stay *off* the roads so we needn't build and mend them so much?"[26]

Who has the money and what are they doing with it? An increasing percentage of Americans agree that pumping our resources into military devices that can only kill is not very bright. If one-tenth of our military budget was instead devoted to alternatives in energy, vehicles, farming, and manufacturing, we could reduce environmental impacts rather than create them. (The U.S. military is perhaps the nation's largest single source of pollution.) The insurance industry is another resource-eating monster. Why shouldn't the insurance industry shift its focus from claim-payer to claim-*preventer* and still turn huge profits? Most large corporations have already diversified to "cover their assets." Why shouldn't the insurance industry, which controls such a large percentage of the country's money, be "born again" in the preventive mode? By using capital of that magnitude *constructively*, we could be buying health rather than illness.

For example, how much money could that industry have *saved* if they had invested in alternatives to asbestos and Agent Orange? The American Lung Association estimates that the country has already saved $4.4 billion in health care costs because of the Clean Air Act, but that another $17 billion could be saved if sulfates and particulates in our air could be cut by another one-fifth. Why doesn't the insurance industry coevolve with health care, and save itself *lots* of money by using preventive maintenance—not just for heart disease and lung cancer, but the overall well-being of the whole culture? This may sound naive, but what I am suggesting is a fresh approach—a new paradigm for the insurance industry. Rather than betting on diseases like cancer, the insurance industry's capital could far more profitably be utilized betting on a clean environment. (Estimates of how much cancer is environmentally caused range from 10 percent all the way up to 75 percent.)

As the National Clean Air Coalition has pointed out, "The cost in economic terms alone of living in a polluted environment is higher than the price tag for cleaning up."[27] How much would we save if we paid neither health costs *nor* cleanup costs? The point is, we don't need to be dicing up resources or performing surgery to be living high-quality lives. We'll need less money to begin with if we can resolve to wipe out pollution and environmental damage at their sources by using a higher level of thinking.

The marketplace is where cans of worms are traded as live bait—where things like avoided pollution and resource depletion become business opportunities. In the process of fishing for good-sense designs, many "movers and shakers" are now realizing the scope of money to be made in America's evolution to a higher quality of life.

In his pioneering book, *The Closing Circle: Nature, Man, and Technology,* Barry Commoner pointed out correctly that from an ecological standpoint, there's no such thing as a free lunch. Everything costs either money or energy.[28] Responding to this ecological postulate, Amory Lovins playfully characterizes a shift in focus from the supply side to the demand side as not just a free lunch, but "a lunch we're *paid to eat!*" Rather than pouring money down the drain in the form of pollution, waste, and overkill, focusing on efficiency can provide a net gain. He writes, "Far from being costly, abating global warming should, on the whole, be immensely profitable. Improving energy productivity can save the world upwards of a trillion dollars a year—as much as the global military budget."[29] How can this be accomplished? One motor and one motor vehicle at a time, enabled by enlightened federal, state, and local regulation, and enlightened individuals.

How do we locate other opportunities for avoiding costs? We simply look for smoke, and stress, and weird-colored industrial discharges. Wherever there's pollution and other bad stuff bloating the GNP and wasting our money, there are opportunities for better design as well as lucrative investment. Tom Eichhorn of California's South Coast Air Quality board reports that his office has gotten hundreds of calls from foreign entrepreneurs who see business opportunities in the lifestyle-changing measures of the Los Angeles Plan. (The plan, to be phased in over the next fifteen or twenty years, mandates alternatives in everything from vehicles and lawn mowers through paint and deodorant.)

Instead of supplying just chemicals, pesticide companies need to see the opportunities for supplying agricultural biologic instead; some companies have already diversified into this area. Soil maintenance, crop rotation, and pest monitoring accomplish the same

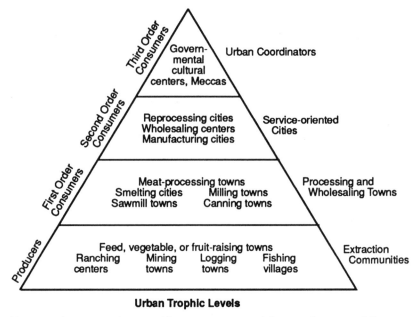

Urban Trophic Levels

Human culture not only resembles an ecosystem, it is one. *Courtesy of Spenser Havlick,* The Urban Organism, *MacMillan and Company, 1974. Reprinted with permission.*

thing that pesticides do but more intelligently. If this industry correctly perceives the coming changes discussed in Chapter 3 in the section called Organic by Choice, they will go with the flow of both nature and culture rather than resist.

Along the same lines, the petroleum industry is slowly evolving into an efficiency-information industry that preserves its own petro-profits by extending the supply. In the past few decades, this industry has acquired patents for many alternative energy devices such as solar cells and electric vehicles, to the dismay of many "true believers" in a more sustainable world. The concern is that these devices will languish on company shelves and be kept out of production so as not to compete with the companies' primary products. But when our persistent demand for such devices is heard, the companies will have no choice but to respond. By putting such alternative technology into production, the companies can begin to prevent oil spills by transporting less oil to begin with.

Municipal tax dollars might be better spent on water conservation and wellhead protection than on water and wastewater treatment and pollution clean-up. Recycling is not yet an incredible money maker, but it can certainly avoid many of the escalating costs for disposal. Another community-level initiative that can protect the environment by design is zoning. Once a given town has mustered the political will, it can prevent water and air pollution associated with transportation, agriculture, water supply, energy use, and industry—all by implementing more sensible land use.

In the private sector, the sky-rocketing costs of hazardous wastes can be slashed by as much as 90 percent, according to Denny Beroiz of General Dynamics Corporation, where a directive from top management forced the pollution-preventing, cost-avoiding redesign of several key processes. Because the hardware did not exist to clean electronic circuit boards with as little waste as they had targeted, General Dynamics invented their own process. They saw an opportunity and went for it, saving themselves millions of dollars, and at the same time, reducing environmental pollution substantially.

Sweet-talking the Wicked Witch

The phrase "hazardous wastes" sounds agreeable to only one faction of our population—those who make a living disposing of it. For the rest of us the notion is about as pleasing as, say, a flat tire on the way to an appointment, or the Wicked Witch of the West. Wouldn't it be nice if we could stumble on a way to be rid of hazardous wastes like Dorothy was finally rid of the witch? Sprinkle water on them and they vaporize into steam, leaving clean, empty black drums behind?

I don't think we should count on this happening. Hazardous wastes are hazardous precisely because they *won't* go away. They don't fit anywhere in our world. Their origins are misdesigned, and so are their destinations. Half of the country's drinking water now comes from beneath the ground, yet most of the 300 million tons of hazardous waste generated each year goes *into* the ground— into injection wells and leak-prone lagoons and landfills. Obviously, hazardous wastes and the nation's water supplies are on a collision course, with American society right in the middle.

Federal regulations of the 1970s and 1980s defined the problem of hazardous wastes and set a framework for dealing with it, but the issue is still out on the fringes of our conceptual target in most cases—in the "control" mode rather than the "prevent" mode. Regulations such as RCRA and amendments to Superfund call for permanent treatment of the wastes by incineration, chemical and biological treatment whenever possible. But the fact is, many of these chemicals need to be eliminated right from the start—we can't let them get out into the world because they're nearly impossible to herd back in. The only realistic way to take apart certain chemicals is never to put them together in the first place.

This is a new concept in human evolution. Until this century, we've never had technologies that "advanced" beyond usefulness in the way that nerve gas, nuclear weapons, and some of the more stubborn pesticides have done. Like a kid who's seen his parents strike matches, we know enough to set fires, but we haven't yet proved that we know how to contain them.

In hazardous waste treatment and other areas, we are at a turning point in the realm of design. We need to make sure that our technologies are not just off-course kamikaze pilots, hitting the wrong target. We have to know the *context* of their mission and use them as infiltrators and guerrillas, going with the flow of nature. We've never really considered that chemicals had to be precisely fitted—until now, strong was enough.

Just as the plant-eating insect and the plant have coevolved over the millennia, microbes and molecules have undergone an incred-

Instead of paying expensive disposal costs, many companies are now recycling chemicals such as solvents, preventing pollution at its source. *Illustration of solvent recycling system courtesy of Finish Company, Inc.*

ible coevolution in the last hundred years. An interesting example of this coevolution occurred at the Homestake Gold Mining Company in South Dakota, the largest gold mine in North America. The mine's discharge into Whitewood Creek was so full of pollutants that the creek had been virtually lifeless for several generations. Cyanide used in the mining process was one of the culprits, accomplishing not only ore refinement but creek sterilization as well. State and federal regulations—and sizable penalties—made Homestake take a closer look at the problem. A discovery that several of their scientists made down in the mine was almost as valuable as the gold itself: a bacteria that had evolved a tolerance, even a *preference*, for cyanide. Engineers rigged up a series of bioreactors that serve as "all you can eat" cafeterias for the patented microbes, leaving the mine's wastewater clean enough to meet discharge standards. Fish and other organisms have returned to the creek, and the Homestake management has plans to market its new technology.

A similar approach is being tried in Alaska, at the site of the Exxon Valdez oil spill. EPA scientists applied two kinds of fertilizer to beaches in Snug Harbor to encourage the growth of oil-eating microbes that occur naturally in the environment. Although it's hard to document how much of the oil has decomposed (as opposed to finding its way into the bodies of organisms other than the oil-eaters), the project seems to be a success. In Minot, North Dakota, soil microbes successfully removed 95 percent of the pesticide residues resulting from a warehouse fire, eliminating the need to cart away thousands of tons of contaminated soil for burial in a hazardous waste landfill.

But microbes have more important things to be doing than just mopping up after bad design. They should be more widely incorporated into design schemes that *prevent* wastes to begin with. The critical role of microbes in processes such as wine fermentation is well known; why not expand on that expertise, using microbes for metal plating, plastic production, and the manufacture of things like adhesives? Microbial pesticides such as *Bacillus thuringiensis* are already competing with chemical ones for a share of the market. Their advantage is specificity: they hit the bull's-eye by attacking a narrow, focused characteristic of the pest, and leaving the rest of us alone. If microbes are not used as information-loaded *substitutes* for chemicals, they can at least become a more common feature of manufacturing processes (far better aim conceptually and physically than land disposal).

James Patterson, of the Illinois Institute of Technology, says, "It is likely to be simpler, more economical, and advantageous to genetically engineer a biological system to handle a waste stream at its point of generation, where it is in its most consistent and concentrated form, prior to blending that stream with others for end-of-pipe treatment. We might consider this approach as more of a manufacturing process than pollution control."[30] The Johns-Manville Company markets Biological Detoxification Systems to other companies as process components. Diatoms are used as microbe carriers in processes that destroy wastes predictably and in many cases, very economically—*before they get out into the world.*

Microbes have beneficial uses in other areas as well. At ski resorts throughout the country, armies of ice-forming microorganisms under the flag of "Snomax" manufacture snow when weather patterns are not cooperating. Genetically-altered cousins of these microbes have been proven to *inhibit* the formation of frost, because the ice-forming gene has been removed. If "Frostban" can outcompete naturally occurring bacteria that cause frost, an extra 6 or 7 degrees of frost protection might be achievable, which would translate into a multibillion dollar industry. However, federal agencies have wisely taken a cautious approach here to make sure there are no hidden side effects as a result of the genetic tinkering.

Don't Let Them Crash the Party to Begin With

Just as electrical efficiency and informed agriculture can save money, so can "waste minimization," EPA's term for smart manufacturing. In response to cost-saving opportunities, governmental regulations, and legal liabilities that make disposal very unattractive, companies are gradually bringing biologic into their design flowcharts. If they want to continue to sell their product, as well as bypass a lot of litigation, most companies now know to make some quick substitutions, such as replacing lead solder with tin or silver solder; arsenic oxide (a refining agent for glass) with antimony trioxide, and so forth.

In some cases it's possible to convert a "can of worms" into bait, as Meridian National in Ohio does. The steel-processing company reprocesses the sulfuric acid with which it removes scale from steel sheets and slabs, reuses the acid, and sells ferrous sulfate compounds to magnetic-tape manufacturers.[31] Strategies such as this allow companies to form ecosystem-like webs of exchange in which one company's wastes become another company's resources.

But the best way to deal with rowdy, unmanageable hazardous wastes is to keep them from crashing the party at all. A newly formulated cleaner/degreaser designed by the Coors Company substitutes citrus-based molecules for hazardous chemicals. The new product goes with the flow of both regulatory and natural law: it has low volatility to prevent air emissions; it has a low flash-point, low corrosivity, and toxicity; and is not cancer-causing.

Under the Resource Conservation and Recovery Act, wastes are tracked from "cradle to grave" by means of an extensive paper trail. In many cases, "birth control" might be a far better way to go. The responsibility for such family planning falls under the nation's Toxic Substances Control Act (TSCA), which grants companies approval to manufacture chemicals. The problem is that the volume of applications TSCA staffers receive makes their jobs resemble those of short-order cooks. Rather than scrutinize the possible effects of each chemical, TSCA scientists must often rely on company-supplied data for reassurance that the chemical will be safe. When that data is sketchy, the scientists resort to "Structure Activity Relationships"—a sort of guilt-by-association approach. If the structure of a given compound resembles that of a known troublemaker, TSCA says, "Back to the drawing board." But of roughly twelve thousand applications since 1979, only about two hundred chemicals have thus far been deflected.

Although we can't turn our backs on the Superfund sites that are already out there in the midst of America's towns and cities, we can and should beef up the *other* end of the chemical stream (TSCA) to help make sure that America's molecules are compatible with its life forms.

Let the Seller Beware

For centuries, the slogan "Let the buyer beware!" has echoed through our marketplaces right along with the tolling of the clock in the town square. But that echo is now being silenced by health, safety, and environmental regulations, the court system, and consumer awareness. In direct proportion to the complexities of our industrial world, regulations have expanded to protect citizens from manufactured chemicals, wastes, and other products. These regulations were typically "end of pipe" rules at first. Boilers on steamships must be inspected, discharges from factories must not contain more than a certain level of organic chemicals, American cars must have catalytic converters, and so on. But increasingly, our federal laws are demanding biologic.

At Superfund sites, cleanup remedies must consider permanent destruction of wastes rather than just storage. Dischargers into municipal sewage systems must "pretreat" wastes to protect both the treatment plant and the waters into which its effluents flow. Cities must devise transportation control plans that will ensure compliance with the Clean Air Act. And comprehensive Environmental Impact Statements must be prepared before any federally-linked project can proceed. (Many states have their own EIS laws as well.) These laws all acknowledge the importance of pollution *prevention.* In effect, they require the *seller* to beware, or else face fines and court orders.

Another element forcing sloppy design to take better aim is liability, graphically explained by attorneys Stuart Eisenstat and Jesse Hill in the book, *Environmental Auditing*:

> Your legal department informs you that, some 25 years ago, one of the companies your firm acquired last year made a product that was used, some 15 years ago, by a Mr. Brown. Mr. Brown is now retired, you are told, having had a long career in the construction industry. Mr. Brown's doctor has informed him that he has lung cancer that is inoperable.
>
> As you listen to the sad news about Mr. Brown, you are thinking, "That's too bad, but what does it have to do with me or our firm?" The answer becomes vividly clear when the general counsel informs you that you have been sued for $5 million by Mr. Brown's attorney . . . and that preliminary conversations with your insurance carrier indicate that your firm has no insurance coverage whatsoever for the claims asserted by Mr. Brown.[32]

David Zoll, an attorney with the Chemical Manufacturer's Association, says, "The fact is, insurance companies don't have to take risks with companies or products which present potential liabilities. They can make their money somewhere else."

Another good indicator of the shift in responsibility from buyer to seller is a growing trend in the construction industry: "Let the *builder* beware." Because of potential lawsuits from buyers, developers are much more wary about the history of a building site or building. Two common liability problems are underground storage tanks and asbestos—both lurk unseen beneath the surface. Patrick

Zuroske, whose firm has conducted more than a hundred environmental investigations in the last two years, says, "Out-of-sight can later drive a developer or property owner out-of-mind." Zuroske's environmental audits are performed for buyers, sellers, and lenders, mostly in the Chicago area. Illinois passed the Responsible Property Transfer Act of 1988, which requires sellers to disclose environmentally hazardous uses of property in the past, but Zuroske doesn't put his full faith in the shift from buyer to seller wariness. He conducts a thorough on-site inspection of a property, followed by a search through government records for possible violations in the past connected with the property. If anything seems suspicious, he starts taking samples of soil, groundwater, and air. "An environmental auditor is really an environmental historian," Zuroske explains. "You're trying to understand what has gone on at the site over the years."

Even in states without property disclosure laws, there is an "implied warranty of habitability," under which legal responsibility is shared by the seller, builder, architect, and manufacturer of building materials, each of whom has a professional responsibility to produce a building free of hazards.[33]

A Corporate Cluster on the Paradigm Cusp

Paradigm paralysis can be a fatal flaw, according to Joel Barker, author of *Discovering the Future: The Business of Paradigms.* By becoming locked into an obsolete paradigm ("hardening of the categories," he calls it), a company or individual will not change gears when the overworked engine is lugging. Instead of risking complete breakdown, we need break*throughs.*[34]

Who invented the electronic quartz watch? It couldn't have been the Swiss, Barker reasons, because their watchmakers have set standards for precision mechanical watches for hundreds of years, and their hold on the watch market, which was 90 percent before World War II, was still 60 percent in the 1970s. Not the Swiss, who smugly predicted in the early 1980s that a changeover to quartz watches would be very slow, and that they would have only a 15 percent share of the watch market. Who invented the quartz watch? Barker asks again. The Swiss, he crows. But because it had no gears and no springs, it wasn't really a watch to old-paradigm watchmakers, whose inflexibility concerning the new design buried a three-hundred-year-old industry.

Barker reports a similar story line with a crackpot inventor named Chester Carlson as the central character. Carlson made the rounds of the major photography companies in the late forties carrying a box with a shiny steel plate in it, a secret charging device, and a light bulb. In a separate container he brought a fine black powder. After each demonstration, the management at Kodak and IBM and all the rest of the companies nodded politely and showed him the door. Only one company—now known as Xerox Corporation—had the foresight to see in the photocopied image a new paradigm: xerography.

Barker quotes DNA co-discoverer James Watson, explaining how he was successful instead of somebody else: "Well, you see, I was doing something my peers thought unwise; if they had thought it wise, they would have done it."

Paradigm-shifters are like sailboats. Rather than fight the wind, they go with it. To make America's environmental shift a successful one, we'll need a whole flock of capable "sailors" to lead the way. Fortunately, there's good evidence that we've got them.

Just as the Wright brothers built a prototype airplane using the tools of a bicycle factory, many of America's companies are quickly evolving to fill new niches: electric car manufacturers, efficiency consultants, enlightened architects and scientists, and so on. For example, Mike Corbett had a concept for a new kind of subdivision—one with solar houses, lots of open space, and narrow roads. A development built for people, not cars, where desirable features of village life could be incorporated into a suburban setting. Part of Corbett's passion was prompted by what happened to his boyhood home along a country road in the Sacramento River Valley: all the special places were gobbled up by concrete and suburban homes.

After years of scrapping with bank loan officers (twenty banks turned him down) and the town planning department, he saw his concept finally become a reality. Although every innovative feature created its own set of hurdles ("We kept writing arguments to the staff reports, and just outwrote and out-logicked them"), he finally obtained the variances he needed.[35]

A little company in Ohio, C.S. Bell, exemplifies a flexible, evolving company that has survived for over a century by fitting into the social ecosystem. The company started by manufacturing farm bells to call farmers in to supper, then evolved into cast iron woodstoves for train cabooses when the market for farm bells cooled off. In the 1970s the company adapted its expertise to capitalize on the popularity of whole grain foods. They came out with a line of kitchen-sized grain mills to go along with the industrial-sized hammermills they produced. When the need for recycling began to hit America, the company adapted a hammermill to crush glass bottles, coming up with a special alloy that would be wear resistant to glass. What's next? "The recycling field is full of potential," says company manager Ron White.[36]

Jack Cameron's Major Appliance Pickup Service had to adapt to changing times, too, or else Cameron would have gone broke. When the scrap recyclers to whom Cameron sold appliance scrap metal became alarmed about the polychlorinated biphenyls (PCBs) in appliances, he became an expert in removing the capacitors which contained the toxic compound. By guaranteeing PCB-free scrap, Cameron built his business into a small recycling empire.[37]

Corporate giants Dow Chemical Company and Domtar, Inc. of Montreal plan to cash in on recycling, too, by using a patented Dow process to turn soft drink bottles and milk jugs into a high-grade plastic resin. The two companies hope to recycle up to seventy-five million pounds a year (about one-fifteenth the total national volume) of the plastic containers.

Two paradigm-shifting companies deserve special recognition here. One is a corporate sibling of Dow and Domtar—the 3M Company. 3M has changed gears, developing a reputation as a progressive company with environmental savvy in about fifteen years. Its "corporate culture" has evolved into one with a highly tuned awareness of opportunities that simultaneously prevent pollution and save money. In fact, 3M has saved close to half a billion dollars and prevented massive volumes of discharges and emissions (more than 120,000 tons of air pollutants and 16,000 tons of water pollutants) by making "Pollution Prevention Pays" (3P) its primary target.

This innovative program is the perfect example of how regulations drive design toward the ideal at the center of the target. The 3P program was first conceived when the company was working under government contract to develop instantaneous fire extinguishers for the cockpits of jet airplanes. The product that 3M designers came up with worked extremely well but it didn't meet the EPA's permit requirements because it was harmful to fish and other aquatic life. "The product was brought back to the 3M laboratory for examination. Scientists found that three of the five major ingredients were *not* harmful to aquatic life. After a week of experimentation, researchers found substitutes for the two harmful chemicals. The final fire-extinguishing agent had one-fortieth the toxicity of the original product, but was equally effective. Much to their surprise, 3M officials discovered that the new product formulation was *less* expensive to produce."[38]

A light bulb went on over the head of Joseph Ling, head of 3M's environmental department. "My idea was to construct a company-wide program at 3M which would create incentives for *all* of our technical employees to experiment with their products in an attempt to prevent pollution and reduce costs," said Ling. The program targets four components: product reformulation, process modification, equipment redesign, and recovery of waste materials for reuse.

Ling's program simultaneously became the corporate model for how to avoid conflict, because confrontation with environmental agencies, product users and community activists could all be avoided if the company focused on pollution prevention rather than merely pollution control.

The 3M program illustrates several important themes for successful paradigm-shifting. Pollution Prevention Pays became *institutionalized* from the top down. Employees' ideas were nurtured in the same way that parents nurture a grade school science project. It has been said that corporate executives need to behave as if their mothers were looking over their shoulders, and at 3M, Joseph Ling became that mother. Rather than isolate the line employees—who knew the process—from upper management, who committed corporate funds, Ling got the two factions together to brainstorm. The results have been beneficial all the way around.

Profits and Principles

The Body Shop is a relative newcomer to the corporate ecosystem, and wears the new paradigm as if there had never been any other. Anita Roddick's operational slogan is "a partnership of profits with principles." The company, a cosmetics retailer, has a handful of specific target principles: to sell products with a minimum of hype and packaging (the company spends nothing on advertising); to promote health rather than glamour, reality rather than the dubious promise of instant rejuvenation; to use naturally based, close-to-source ingredients; to never use animals in the testing of ingredients or final products; and to respect the environment, making all products biodegradable and recycling all waste.

In quest of natural ingredients for her company's products, Roddick has lived with Bedouin women in the desert to learn how they protect their skin and with reindeer herdsmen in Lapland to test products in extreme cold. "Moving into societies and speaking to women about rituals like birth, marriage, and death, what happens to your body, what ingredients are useful makes more sense than pulling ideas out of the air or saying, 'What do people want next?' " Roddick believes.[39]

"The cosmetic industry is bizarre because it is run by men who create needs that don't exist, making women feel incredibly dissatisfied with their bodies," said Roddick. "They have this extraordinary belief that all that women want is hope and promise. To me, it's innately dishonest to make claims that a cream that is basically oil and water is going to take grief and stress and fifty years of living with the sun off your face."[40]

Instead of glamour, Roddick's company promises to "cleanse, polish, and protect the skin and hair." The emphasis on health rather than appearance overflows with biologic. What nature and culture have cooperatively cooked up over the millennia is very likely to be superior to the glitziness of petro-products encased in multiple layers of splashy packaging. (The typical package of rouge, for example, consists of nine items: cellophane wrap, a cardboard box, a corrugated sheet to protect the mirror, a plastic container, a metal handle for the brush, and a sponge to apply the makeup itself. In addition, manufacturers use more than five thousand ingredients to make cosmetics, including alcohols, alkalies, dyes, oils, and waxes.) Says Roddick, "It's wonderfully refreshing to go to areas like Morocco and to see not shampoo being used to wash hair but mud." She points out there are more than 200,000 known plant species in the world, of which we have learned to use only 2,500. The expansion of our knowledge can not only provide health for humans but for whales (by using jojoba instead of whale oil) and rain forests, too.

Roddick's new line of products is called Rain Forest, and is made of ingredients from the endangered jungles of Brazil, where she recently visited with the Indians. "There's an interesting fruit that looks like a lychee and when you open it up, it's full of little berries that the Indians use as face paint," she explains. "It might be possible to make this into a solid chalk for a lipstick." If jungle berries seem strange as lipstick ingredients, American women should consider some of the other substances that have been used, including crushed and dried insect corpses, ground-up fish scales, sterilized grease from sewage plants, and cinnabar, a poisonous red sulfide of mercury. The New York Board of Health considered banning lipstick in the 1920s, "not because of what it might do to the women who wore it, but because it might poison the men who kissed the women who wore it."[41] The millennia-long tradition of touching up facial complexion to suit the current fashion is no less treacherous, from lead dusting powder to "Arsenic Complexion Wafers," ingested by eighteenth-century Europeans to achieve a white pallor.[42]

The products of the Body Shop are not poisonous, as evidenced by the longevity of their use throughout the world. In fact, many might qualify for inclusion in survival supply kits—if you run out of food you can always drink your shampoo.

Another paradigm-shifting feature of the cosmetics company is its Environmental Projects Department, which encourages—even demands—that employees take part in local and global activities to help solve environmental problems ranging from soil erosion through global warming. The perfect example of a company that's going with the flow of both nature *and* culture, the Body Shop is not shirking its responsibilities to stockholders either: 1988 sales were $300 million.

What's the Use?

Sometimes a particular industry or land use is simply not suited for an area. For example, Idaho environmentalists have been known to get into some pretty heated discussions with loggers. The National Forest slogan, "Land of Many Uses," has been lampooned in that state as "Land of No Use." After large-scale tree-cutting has taken place, the environmentalists argue, habitats are altered, erosion wipes out fish populations, and access roads scar the wilderness. One outspoken logging opponent said, "You practically have to beat Idaho politicians over the head—with fish—to make them perceive that recreation is a far better use of our public lands than heavily subsidized logging." At the center of the controversy is the idea of proper land use: is logging or recreation more sustainable, with fewer environmental impacts? If government subsidy is required to make timber-cutting economically viable in Idaho, maybe our National Forest policy needs to be rethought.

The siting of dams and hazardous waste treatment plants offer two well-publicized examples of how environmentally sensitive decision-making can be useful concerning the use of land. Former EPA administrator William Ruckelshaus explains how the ECOS company progressed toward the center of the target, trying to match social acceptance with environmental suitability:

> The state of Washington needs a hazardous waste-handling facility—as do many states. ECOS conducted a statewide screening that eliminated almost 80 percent of Washington's area, based on such criteria as sensitive lands and land uses, natural hazards, transportation accessibility, and historical or archaeological importance. Communities in the remainder of the state were then publicly asked if they might be interested in hosting the facility.
>
> The company helped interested communities form citizen advisory committees to represent the community at large and serve as liaisons to the firm. These committees negotiated proposals that included stringent environmental safeguards and substantial economic benefits for the community. This March, two towns put the proposals to a vote. In both places more than 60 percent of the voters favored accepting the proposal and allowing the facility to be opened in their community.43

A similar situation occurred in rural Tooele County, Utah, which was right in the scoping sights of a handful of hazardous waste treatment companies. Rather than permit the companies to build facilities at will (providing they met state and EPA requirements), the commissioners put a Special Use Zone into effect, which spelled out where they would be willing to consider siting a commercial facility. This geographic bull's-eye is remote from population centers and water supplies yet accessible by highway and rail. Several companies are now completing their applications to site facilities, which will bring needed jobs and revenues to the county.

A dam site better than conservation? Not in most cases. In federal regulations concerning impacts caused by river and lake tinkering, four elements are listed for primary consideration when the construction of a reservoir is being considered: Can construction be avoided (by substituting projects or programs that have less impact)? Can damage be effectively minimized? Can the effects be mitigated? Can the "losers" be fairly compensated? Using our Master Plan once again, the bull's-eye is not building the dam to begin with, if it's not really needed. Outward from this conceptual optimum, the hierarchy becomes progressively less desirable environmentally. By the time the project's builders are talking about compensating the victims, they have just about missed the target altogether, because species are potentially being lost and habitat and homes may be eradicated for the sake of increasing the water supply. As has been previously discussed, it might be far wiser to decrease demand with efficiency improvements.

Most species have natural mechanisms to define territory. Ecologist Eugene Odum believes that humans need to implement political territoriality to sustain the integrity of the land we're borrowing. He recommends that we deliberately zone land to optimize high production (for example, intensive cropping) in certain areas and high *protection* (for example, strictly enforced wilderness) in certain other areas. He believes this will necessitate the creation of regional environmental commissions to implement land use plans voted on by the people.

The preservation of wilderness isn't a new phenomenon. Nature preserves were first created for the pleasure of the ruling classes (such as the lands used by the kings of Sri Lanka, the European royal hunting preserves, and Hawaiian and Florida Key reserves controlled by the elite).[44] With the establishment of national parks and wildlife areas, local open space reserves and land trusts, however, the public has literally begun to draw the line in resistance to the homogenization of our nation's land. Why sacrifice prime ecosystems to warehouses, highways, and subdivisions? Why not implement zoning plans, as Boulder, Colorado, has done, that will protect resources and raise the quality of life at the same time? Only by employing a forward-looking Master Plan can a community or region avoid environmental impacts by design.

Pockets of Opportunity

Until just recently, we've been like the child who sees an egg but is totally unaware of the possibility of a chicken inside, or who sees a display counter of oranges and assumes they grew right there in the supermarket. We haven't bothered to trace origins or consequences. We're getting into that habit now, and we're ready to put some of the pieces together in creative ways to form designs for living that are far more efficient.

There are millions of opportunities out there, and I hope this book has made a few of them more understandable, acceptable, and accessible. Everywhere we look there are pockets of experimentation—little seedlings reaching for sunlight. Sometimes, the experiments are reactive, arising out of a backs-to-the-wall situation such as the recycling innovations in space-limited areas like New Jersey and Rhode Island. Sometimes remoteness is a positive factor in trying new ideas. For example, the highly efficient Sun Frost refrigerator (which uses about one-seventh the energy that a conventional refrigerator does) has found a "niche market" with watt-conscious users of photovoltaic panels, which in turn are especially economical way out in the sticks beyond the reach of power lines.

Wilderness areas, national parks, remote islands, and space shuttles, stations, and satellites are all good testing grounds for new ideas, because they are outside the hub of conventional assumptions. A friend of mine does consulting work on the Pacific Island of Utirik, helping install solar panels for natives who have never had reliable electric lights before. These installations are socially symbiotic in the sense that good operational data will be gained while the islanders obtain needed power for lights and refrigeration.

One of the primary elements in our development is the realization that having more *stuff* isn't synonymous with contentment— we don't have to load ourselves down so much to be happy. As Jerry Mander writes, "There's the old story of the native on a Pacific Island, relaxing in a house on the beach, picking fruit and spearing fish in the water. A businessman arrives on the island, buys all the land, cuts down the trees and builds a factory. Then he hires the native to work in it for money so that someday the native can afford canned fruit and fish from the mainland, a nice cinderblock house near the beach with a view of the water, and weekends off to enjoy it."[45]

Sometimes the best pockets for learning are where something *hasn't* worked before, as in highway-scarred Los Angeles. L.A.'s planners apparently did not have a conceptual target in mind. The land and the ecosystem on it must have been spectacular a hundred years ago, but humans aimed poorly in terms of fitting in with that land. The city's quest for breathable air will be a model for many other American cities that are drifting toward "Los Angelization." The hypothesis at the center of the target is that health and well-being are far more important than cars and drive-ins.

Sometimes pockets of opportunity are little centers of proactive excellence—the outgrowth of efforts by enlightened individuals who captured the ears of their neighbors. Davis, California, and Boulder, Colorado, are good examples of communities in which individuals have made the difference. Recently, Boulder's mayor attended a national mayors' conference at which a prototype for a natural-gas-fueled automobile was presented. She returned to Boulder and requested the city's environmental department to check into converting city vehicles to the alternative fuel.

Excellence proliferates—that's the way nature works. The successful experiment or design stands a good chance of being adopted elsewhere. Sometimes a tiny innovation can turn the whole world around, like the computer chip or the first photograph of Earth from space. Buckminster Fuller frequently illustrated this idea with the "trimtab," a small device that activates a ship's rudder and changes the direction of a huge ocean liner with very little effort. Many such devices are mentioned in this book—the solar cell, the water purification indicator on cardboard solar ovens, the water-conserving gypsum block, the recycling code on plastic packaging, the high-efficiency light bulb, and so on. Individually, they're ingenious ideas, but collectively, they can be seen as a Design Revolution.

I've woven different systems and environmental issues together in this book because they're woven together in nature, and because similar design criteria and assumptions can be overlaid on each. One of the most critical criteria of all for nature-compatible design is diversity. There is no *one* solution for anything. As Wes Jackson counsels, "The singular goal breaks the system." We keep expecting a single device or subsystem to do everything, as if we were ordering delivered pizza instead of trying to perfect a culture.

It Depends

Throughout this chapter I've suggested that our intentions and actions should aim for a conceptual bull's-eye in our target or Master Plan. Obviously, the idea is to get our society aiming at the same criteria. To encourage good aim, we need clear regulatory signals and we also need social consensus, including taboos against ecological sloppiness. To develop those taboos we need a sense of connectedness—with each other and with our world. In many cases, the failure to meet basic *needs* keeps us in pursuit of irrelevant *wants*. For example, because junk food does not satisfy us in a basic sense, we continue to crave the many artifacts advertised on TV.

Working intently in a backyard vegetable garden is a bull's-eye because it is self-perpetuating: it not only provides exercise but the food-energy to sustain the exercise and the garden. Driving a block to buy packaged food from 2,000 miles away is completely off-target for obvious reasons, but prices haven't yet caught up with ecological reality. We haven't yet polished up our archery skills. We're still beginners.

We've made the big, easy decisions—put scrubbers on factories, bolted catalytic converters on cars, dammed the rivers with the greatest potential, spent over a hundred billion dollars on wastewater treatment plants, and so on. Our strategy in the future will involve fewer sweeping, generic moves and many more localized, specific ones. For each environmental challenge, there is a particularly good arrow in our quiver. The same idea is expressed in another outdoor sport, fly fishing. The main difference between fly fishing and "random" fishing is that the fly fisherman knows what he's doing. He knows what will attract fish at what time of the year and ties his own flies to meet that need. In contrast, the novice fisherman just casts his line out there, anywhere—one place is as good as the next. Skill doesn't have to improve when supply is continually augmented with hatchery-stocked fingerlings.

I toured a highly efficient farm recently where advanced techniques were being used in soil retention and soil building, water conservation, biological controls, and so on. Someone asked the elderly, enlightened farmer what the best method is for growing corn in Colorado. The farmer paused, thought it over, then replied, "It depends." In dry years, the farmer's methods were completely different than in wet years; if soybeans had been grown in the field the previous year, his fertilization strategy reflected that fact, and so on. The farmer's reply commanded respect among the listeners in the tour group because it revealed that a discriminating, experienced thought process was going on, one that matched specific solutions to specific problems.

One of our greatest challenges is to stamp out generic answers and packaged solutions. It's not just petroleum that's making us dumb, it's a whole prefabricated way of thinking, steadily converting our entire society into a monoculture. We need *more* designs, not fewer. For each different situation, we need a perfectly fitting solution.

Perhaps our most critical design need is towns and cities that are eminently *livable*, so people will want to stay put. Closely knit communities bring social feedbacks into our culture. They bring a sense of responsibility and pride to environmental protection, and give tradition and culture a chance to have a tempering effect on impulse.

When we intend to stay in a place, we start making decisions rather than letting them "make themselves." We tailor-make solutions for each challenge. We begin to design for permanence and interdependence. By persistent trial and error, we learn what we need to know, ultimately sensing that human survival boils down to a single, fundamental notion: plant the right seedling in the right place and the rest will take care of itself.

AFTERWORD
Getting Smart Together

Let's imagine for a moment that everything trivial fell away from each of our lives, and we could see clearly all of a sudden. Let's say one of our children died, or a parent, wife, or husband. Or we're a teenager again, and we just wrecked the brand-new family car.

All of a sudden everything else seems pretty insignificant, doesn't it? We go back to basic feelings, in terms of what's important and what's not. The notion of "having" is far less important than "being." We realize that at a fundamental level, there is nothing more important than *doing things right*. Being rich isn't more important. Having illusory power over others is not. And certainly, driving carelessly in an "automobile" is not.

Have you ever noticed that our most vivid memories are of times when we were forced to be basic, such as when a heavy snowstorm forced our busy world to a sudden halt? Why can't we decide to be basic, and let all the extraneous garbage go?

In one of his philosophical musings, Jean-Paul Sartre imagines a young man who refuses to go to war out of an obligation to take care of his sick mother. Sartre points out that the bonds of loyalty to one's mother are ageless, while unquestioned loyalty to one's government is a relatively recent invention, and what's more, one that is sometimes morally cloudy.

We have a roughly analogous situation in today's world. Our dilemma is between taking care of an ailing Mother Earth or marching obediently in the ranks of an economy with an outdated and misguided mission. Our quest for fulfillment through material gratification has hit the planet like thousands of nuclear bombs. Intuitively we know the battle cannot and even should not be won. It's another Vietnam or Afghanistan—the brute force of our technologies is too blundering and our engineering too blind to successfully conquer nature's tried and true resilience and grassroots persistence.

When things are clear, we suddenly feel the harness of the "hang glider" that's holding us up. Each of us is connected in an awesome, precarious, yet reassuring way to the basic mechanisms of life. We didn't make up the rules, we just follow them. If we're smart.

During our moment of clarity we begin to see that the Biggest Thing is making sure that we take care of things, and that the second Biggest Thing is learning how we can best do it. Individually, our most pressing responsibility is to find that particular niche where our abilities can be most useful and fulfilling.

If we somehow had a *simultaneous* moment of clarity (as sometimes happens after a natural catastrophe or during a shared moment of prayer), we'd realize that we're not very far off, really. Several big, key thoughts, occurring in all our heads at the same time—that's all it will take, along with the vitality and determination to put those thoughts into action.

There are two precedents within our memory span: a massive mobilization for World War II, when nails and rubber and even bones were hoarded and donated to the cause; and the energy crises of the 1970s, the so-called "moral equivalents of war," which launched an energy efficiency bandwagon that held energy use to 1973 levels while the economy continued to expand by 40 percent through the late 1980s. We already know that we can mobilize, we just have to be convinced that now's the time to do it.

We already know a lot about our environment and our part in it. All we really have to do is apply our understanding collectively, combining intuition and rationality. When we get right down to it, it's clear that what we have here is air, land, water, and each other. (In "each other" we of course include the plants, trees, bacteria, and our furry and feathery cousins.)

We realize that life is a continual series of changes—slight hang glider adjustments in response to wind currents and gravity and the desire to maintain a course in the general direction of survival. To expect life to be unchanging is to be thinking unclearly, as is the inability to recognize when things have already changed.

Our world has changed, radically. Individuals from both sides of the human spectrum—the intuitive as well as the rational—counsel that we may be the most important collection of humans ever to live on the planet, because our decisions will to a large degree determine the condition *of* the planet. Our culture's Golden Rule has become an ecological imperative: either we do unto others as we would have them do, or else we're done for.

Species are passing away, and fundamental life support systems are coming unraveled. We no longer have the buffers of wide open spaces, natural resiliency and diversity, and abundance that we had in the past.

What will motivate us into action? If we need a common foe to rally around, we've got one. Our common foe is the destruction of natural systems, both by the world's undernourished and overnourished.

Our assumption as a culture is that "when the chips are down, we'll respond, just like we always have." Well, the chips *are* down. To fail to respond to shifts in the wind is to crash our hang gliders against the solid rock of immutable natural laws. If that sounds impossibly dramatic, just think of it as a movie—but one that's coming right off the screen and into our world . . .

Our task is to design a culture that goes with the flow of nature. It's that simple. We need to use intelligence rather than just massive amounts of stockpiled, once-only energy. Pollution and environmental deterioration are fundamentally a lack of coherence and information, and a lack of will.

All we have to do is get smart, together. What's so hard about that?

> In the next century
> or the one beyond that
> they say,
> are valleys, pastures.
> We can meet there in peace
> if we make it.
> To climb these coming crests
> one word to you, to
> you and your children:
> *stay together*
> *learn the flowers*
> *go light*

—From "For the Children," by Gary Snyder

ENDNOTES

Introduction

1. Abba Eban, quoted by Amory Lovins in the paper, *Energy, People, and Industrialization,* Stanford University, January 1989.

2. Personal conversation with Ted Flanigan, Rocky Mountain Institute, March 1989.

Chapter 1: Biologic

1. Tom Bender, "Sharing Smaller Pies," in *Resettling America: Energy, Ecology and Community,* Gary Coates, editor (Andover, Massachusetts: Brick House, 1981).

2. Eugene Odum, "Input Management of Production Systems," *Science,* Vol. 243 (January 13, 1989).

3. Gary Coates, editor, *Resettling America: Energy, Ecology and Community* (Andover, Massachusetts: Brick House, 1981).

4. Wendell Berry, *Standing by Words* (Berkeley: North Point Press, 1983).

5. Howard Odum, in *Stepping Stones,* Lane de Moll, editor (New York: Schocken Press, 1978).

6. Herman E. Daly, *Steady State Economics* (San Francisco: W.H. Freeman and Company, 1977).

7. "Waste Stopper: Pumice on Copper," 3M Company fact sheet, Environmental Engineering and Pollution Control Department, St. Paul, Minnesota.

8. David Wann, "Biologic: Designing Products with Nature in Mind," *Environmental Action* (November/December 1988).

9. Personal conversation with Jim Starry, Environmental Design, Inc., Boulder, Colorado, June 1989.

10. Nancy Jack Todd and John Todd, *Bioshelters, Ocean Arks, City Farming: Ecology As the Basis of Design* (San Francisco: Sierra Club Books, 1984), 99.

11. Keith Schneider, "Fear of Chemicals Is Turning Farmers to Biological Pesticides," *New York Times* (June 11, 1989), 26.

12. James Gustave Speth, "The Greening of Technology," *Washington Post* (November 20, 1988), D3.

13. Aldo Leopold, *A Sand County Almanac* (New York: Oxford University Press, 1968).

14. Robert J. Cohn, *Advertising Age Magazine* (May 15, 1988), 24.

15. Cynthia Crossen, *Wall Street Journal* (Dow Jones and Co. Inc., 1989).

16. Wendell Berry, *The Unsettling of America* (San Francisco: Sierra Club Books, 1978).

17. U.S. Bureau of Census, Statistical Abstracts of the United States, 109th edition (Washington, D.C., 1989).

18. Thor Heyerdahl, "How Vulnerable Is the Ocean?" in *Who Speaks for the Earth?*, Maurice Strong, editor (New York: W.W. Norton, 1973).

19. Christopher Flavin and Alan B. Durning, "Building on Success: The Age of Energy Efficiency," Worldwatch Paper No. 82, March 1988.

20. Hazel Henderson, *Politics of the Solar Age* (Garden City, New York: Anchor Press, 1981).

21. Lester Brown, *Building a Sustainable Society* (New York: W.W. Norton, 1980).

22. F.H. Bormann, "An Inseparable Linkage: Conservation of Natural Systems and the Conservation of Fossil Energy," *Bioscience* 26 (1976), 754-760.

23. James Parsons, "The Scourge of Cows," *Whole Earth Review* (Spring 1988), 40.

24. Thomas R. McKinney, "United States Feedlots," Rocky Mountain Institute report, 1987.

25. Paul Ehrlich, *The Machinery of Nature* (New York: Simon and Schuster, 1986).

26. Dyan Zaslowsky, "A Public Beef: Are Grazing Cattle Turning the American West into a New Desert?" *Harrowsmith* (January/February 1989), 39.

27. Laura Maggor, "Food and Agriculture," draft manuscript for Rocky Mountain Institute, 1989.

28. Dyan Zaslowsky, "A Public Beef: Are Grazing Cattle Turning the American West into a New Desert?" *Harrowsmith* (January/February 1989), 39.

29. Norman Myers, *GAIA, An Atlas of Planet Management* (Garden City, New York: Gaia Books, 1984).

30. Stewart L. Udall, *The Quiet Crisis* (New York: Holt, Rinehart and Winston, 1963).

31. Brian Tokar, *The Green Alternative* (San Pedro, California: R. & E. Miles Co., 1987).

32. Ian McHarg, *Design with Nature* (Garden City, N.Y.: Doubleday/ Natural History Press, 1971).

33. Kirkpatrick Sale, *Dwellers in the Land: The Bioregional Vision* (San Francisco: Sierra Club, 1985).

34. David Wann, "Thinking Globally and Acting Locally," *Bloomsbury Review* (December 1985).

35. Edward Abbey, *One Life At a Time, Please* (New York: Henry Holt and Company, 1988).

36. Robert Ornstein and Paul Ehrlich, *New World, New Mind: Moving Toward Conscious Evolution* (New York: Doubleday, 1989).

37. James Lovelock, *Gaia: A New Look at Life on Earth* (New York: Oxford University Press, 1979).

Chapter 2: Knowing

1. James Lovelock, *Gaia: A New Look at Life on Earth* (New York: Oxford University Press, 1979).

2. Paul Hawken, *The Next Economy* (New York: Holt, Rinehart and Winston, 1983).

3. Personal conversation with Barbara Blum, Solar Box Cookers International, May 1989.

4. Testimony of Dr. H.M. Hubbard before U.S. House of Representatives, July 8, 1987.

5. Jose Goldemberg et al., *Energy for a Sustainable World* (Washington, D.C.: World Resources Institute, September 1987).

6. Susan Hassol and Beth Richman, *Recycling: 101 Practical Tips for Home and Work* (Snowmass, Colorado: The Windstar Foundation, 1989).

7. Bruce Piasecki and Gary Davis, *America's Future in Toxic Waste Management: Lessons from Europe* (Westport, Connecticut: Quorum Books, 1987).

8. William Broad, "Space Pollution Forces NASA to Change Plans for Key Projects," *New York Times* (December 27, 1988).

9. Robert Ornstein and Paul Ehrlich, *New World, New Mind: Moving Toward Conscious Evolution* (New York: Doubleday, 1989).

10. Tom Crum, *The Magic of Conflict* (New York: Simon and Schuster, 1987).

11. Jerry Mander, *Four Arguments for the Elimination of Television* (New York: Morrow Books, 1978).

12. Garrett be Bell, ed., "To Your Health," in *The New Environmental Handbook* (San Francisco: Sierra Club, 1980).

13. "Science and the Citizen," *Scientific American* (December 1979).

14. Noel Vietmeyer, *Ceres,* No. 109 (January/February 1986), 50.

15. Anna Campbell, quoted by Henry M. Vyner in *Invisible Trauma: The Psychosocial Effects of Invisible Environmental Contaminants* (Lexington, Massachusetts: Lexington Books, 1988).

16. Henry M. Vyner, *Invisible Trauma: The Psychosocial Effects of Invisible Environmental Contaminants* (Lexington, Massachusetts: Lexington Books, 1988).

17. David Bodanis, *The Secret House* (New York: Touchstone, 1986).

18. "Toxin-free Community for Chemically Sensitive Planned," *Arkansas Democrat* (May 26, 1989).

19. Linda Lee Davidoff, "Multiple Chemical Sensitivities," *The Amicus Journal* (Winter 1989).

20. Karen Winegar, "Home Sweet Home May Contain Toxic Building Materials," *Chicago Tribune* (September 10, 1989), Section 16.

21. James Russell, "Suppressing the Office Energy Appetite," *Architectural Record* (October 1989).

22. Health hazard report # HETA 81-150-994, National Institute for Occupational Safety and Health (Cincinnati, Ohio: U.S. Forest Service, 1981).

23. Daniel Grossman, "Pollution Indoors," *Technology Review* (May/June 1989).

24. George Rand, "Indoor Pollution: The Issue Continues to Build," *Architecture* (March 1989).

25. Debra Lynn Dadd, *The Nontoxic Home: Protecting Yourself and Your Family from Everday Toxics and Health Hazards* (New York: St. Martin's Press, 1986).

26. *Unfinished Business: A Comparative Assessment of Environmental Problems* (Washington, D.C.: U.S. Environmental Protection Agency, Office of Policy Analysis, February 1987).

27. David Wann, "On the Firing Line: The Challenge of Environmental Risk in Region 8," *EPA Journal* (November 1987).

28. David Wann, "On the Firing Line: The Challenge of Environmental Risk in Region 8," *EPA Journal* (November 1987).

29. P. Steinhert, "Trouble in the Tropics," *National Wildlife* (December/January 1984).

30. Paul Ehrlich, "Winged Warning," *Sierra* (September/October 1988), 57.

31. Paul Ehrlich, "Winged Warning," *Sierra* (September/October 1988), 57.

32. "Toxic Chemicals Found in Great Lakes Birds," *New York Times* (March 21, 1989).

33. Jane E. Brody, "Is the Air Pure or Foul? Lichens Can Tell the Tale," *New York Times* (August 18, 1987).

34. Morgan Gopnik, Science Corner, *Environmental Action* (September/October 1988), 9.

35. *Chemical and Engineering News* (July 1, 1988), 19.

36. Stephen Sautner, "A Plastics Packaging Primer," *Environmental Action* (July/August 1988), 24.

37. Barry Commoner, *The Closing Circle: Nature, Man and Technology* (New York: Knopf, 1971).

38. Amory Lovins, Competitek Conference, Snowmass, Colorado (September 1989).

39. U.S. Environmental Protection Agency, *Future Risk: Research Strategies for the 1990s,* 1988.

40. Gina Maranto, "Earth's First Visitors to Mars," *Discover* (May 1987), 29.

41. Rick Boling, "Solar Chimney for Low-Cost Desert Cooling," *Popular Science* (May 1986), 16.

42. "Acid Rain's Complex Chemistry," *Christian Science Monitor* (March 14, 1989).

43. Edward O. Wilson, *Biophilia* (Cambridge, Massachusetts: Harvard University Press, 1984).

44. Daniel Yankelovich, *New Rules* (New York: Random House, 1981).

45. Marilyn Ferguson, *The New Common Sense*, in press.

46. Michael Greenburg et al, "Network Television News Coverage of Environmental Risks," *Environment* (March 1989).

47. Bradley Smith and William Thompson, "The Fishermen of the Tittawabassee," *Environment*, Vol. 26, No. 5.

48. Jerry Mander, *Whole Earth Review Anniversary Issue* comments (Winter 1988).

Chapter 3: Choosing

1. Frances Moore Lappé, *Rediscovering America's Values* (New York: Ballantine Books, 1989).

2. Langdon Winner, *The Whale and the Reactor: A Search for Limits in an Age of High Technology* (Chicago: University of Chicago Press, 1986).

3. Langdon Winner, *The Whale and the Reactor: A Search for Limits in an Age of High Technology* (Chicago: University of Chicago Press, 1986).

4. Charles Panati, *The Extraordinary Origins of Ordinary Things* (New York: Harper and Row, 1987).

5. Charles Panati, *The Extraordinary Origins of Ordinary Things* (New York: Harper and Row, 1987).

6. "The Tin Can: Blessing and Nuisance," *Chicago Tribune* (April 29, 1987).

7. Charles Panati, *The Extraordinary Origins of Ordinary Things* (New York: Harper and Row, 1987).

8. "Cars Cars Cars Cars Cars," *Sierra* (May/June 1989), 22.

9. Robert Ornstein and Paul Ehrlich, *New World, New Mind: Moving Toward Conscious Evolution* (New York: Doubleday, 1989).

10. Amory Lovins, *Energy, People, and Industrialization* (Stanford University: Hoover Institution, January 1989).

11. J.C. Furnas, *The Americans: A Social History of the United States 1587-1914* (New York: Putnam, 1969).

12. Richard C. Paddock, "Gillette Agrees to Remove Toxics from Its Liquid Correction Fluid," *Los Angeles Times* (September 29, 1989).

13. Bruce Leigh, "How Green Is Your Company?" *International Management* (January 1989).

14. Robin Knight, "The Greening of Europe's Industries," *U.S. News and World Report* (June 5, 1989), 45.

15. "Decent Clean and True," *Management Today*, February 1989.

16. Meri McCoy-Thompson, "Environmental Seal of Approval," *Worldwatch Magazine* (May/June, 1989), 6.

17. Nancy Shute, "Going Organic," *Amicus Journal* (Spring 1989).

18. Herbert Giardet, *Blueprint for a Green Planet* (New York: Prentice Hall, 1987).

19. Beth Richman and Susan Hassol, *Everyday Chemicals* (Snowmass, Colorado: Windstar Foundation, 1989).

20. Simon Counsell, *The Good Wood Guide* (London: Friends of the Earth and the National Association of Retail Furnishers, 1988).

21. Karen Swisher, "Chlorofluorocarbons Usage Will Be Hard Habit to Kick," *Washington Post* story in *Denver Post* (July 9, 1989).

22. "Promoting Source Reduction and Recyclability in the Marketplace," EPA 530-SW-89-066 (Washington, D.C., September 1989).

23. "The Environment," *New York Times* (July 4, 1989).

24. Paul Hawken, *The Next Economy* (New York: Holt, Rinehart, and Winston, 1983).

25. Susan Meeker-Lowry, *Economics As if the Earth Really Mattered* (Philadelphia: New Society Publishers, 1988).

26. David Wann, "Right Here, Right Now," *Environmental Action* (January/February 1990).

27. T.L. Ferrand, "Mandatory Recycling: Rhetoric or Reality?" (Biocycle Recycling Conference, 1988).

28. "Garbage Magazine Wants to Be Conscience of Throwaway Generation," *Denver Post* (June 17, 1989).

29. James Hillman, *Resurgence* (July/August 1988).

30. "Cars Cars Cars Cars Cars," *Sierra* (May/June 1989), 22.

31. Lester Brown, "Facing the Future on Two Wheels," *World Watch* (July/August 1989).

32. Peter Calthorpe and Sim Van der Ryn, *Sustainable Communities, A New Design Synthesis for Cities, Suburbs and Towns* (San Francisco: Sierra Club Books, 1986).

33. Peter Calthorpe and Sim Van der Ryn, *Sustainable Communities, A New Design Synthesis for Cities, Suburbs and Towns* (San Francisco: Sierra Club Books, 1986).

34. Peter Calthorpe, "Pedestrian Pockets: New Strategies for Suburban Growth," *Whole Earth Review* (Spring 1988), 118.

35. Mark Satin, editor, "Bigger Roads—Or Trolleys, Bikes and Urban Redesign?" *New Options,* No. 52 (October 31, 1988).

36. Marcia Lowe, "Pedalling into the Future," *The Futurist* (March/April 1989), 18.

37. Fred Reid, "Real Possibilities in the Transportation Myths," in *Sustainable Communities, A New Design Synthesis for Cities, Suburbs and Towns* (San Francisco: Sierra Club Books, 1986), 167.

Chapter 4: Designing

1. Victor Papanek and James Hennessey, *How Things Don't Work* (New York: Pantheon Books, 1977).

2. Victor Papanek, *Design for the Real World: Human Ecology and Social Change* (Chicago: Academy Chicago Publishers, 1985).

3. Charles Panati, *Extraordinary Origins of Everyday Things* (New York: Harper and Row, 1987).

4. Karrie Jacobs, "The Design of Garbage," *Metropolis* (December 1988).

5. Martin Pawley, *Building for Tomorrow: Putting Wastes to Work* (San Francisco: Sierra Club Books, 1982).

6. Cynthia Pollack, "Mining Urban Wastes: The Potential for Recycling," Worldwatch Paper No. 76 (April 1987).

7. Office of Technology Assessment, *Facing America's Trash: What Next for Municipal Solid Waste?* (October 1989).

8. Martin Pawley, *Building for Tomorrow* (San Francisco: Sierra Club Books, 1982).

9. Martin Pawley, *Building for Tomorrow,* (San Francisco: Sierra Club Books, 1982).

10. Susan Hassol and Beth Richman, *Recycling: 101 Tips for Home and Work* (Snowmass, Colorado: The Windstar Foundation, 1989).

11. Susan Hassol and Beth Richman, *Energy: 101 Practical Tips for Home and Work* (Snowmass, Colorado: The Windstar Foundation, 1989).

12. Charles Panati, *Browser's Book of Beginnings* (Boston: Houghton Mifflin, 1984).

13. Victor Papanek, *Design for the Real World: Human Ecology and Social Change* (Chicago: Academy Chicago Publishers, 1985).

14. Lynn Margulis and Dorian Sagan, *Microcosmos: Four Billion Years of Evolution from Our Microbial Ancestors* (New York: Summit Books, 1986).

15. Paul Ehrlich, *The Machinery of Nature* (New York: Simon and Schuster, 1986).

16. Bruce Fellman, "An Engineer's Eye Helps Biologists Understand Nature," *Smithsonian* (July 1989), 98.

17. Victor Papanek, *Design for the Real World: Human Ecology and Social Change* (Chicago: Academy Chicago Publishers, 1985).

18. Victor Papanek, *Design for the Real World: Human Ecology and Social Change* (Chicago: Academy Chicago Publishers, 1985).

19. Rushworth Kidder, *An Agenda for the 21st Century* (Cambridge, Massachusetts: MIT Press, 1987).

20. Terry Davies, *The Environmental Protection Act* (Washington: Conservation Foundation, September 1988), 2.

21. George Stanley, "A Scientist's Dream," *Ducks Unlimited* (November/December 1987), 72.

22. Becky Gilette, "Revolution in Wastewater Treatment," *Biocycle* (March 1988), 48.

23. Donella Meadows, "The New Alchemist," *Harrowsmith* (November/December 1988).

24. John Todd, "Adventures of an Applied Ecologist," *Whole Earth Review* (Spring 1989).

25. Donella Meadows, "The New Alchemist," *Harrowsmith* (November/December 1988).

26. Barry Commoner, *The Closing Circle: Nature, Man and Technology* (New York: Knopf, 1971).

27. Barry Commoner, *The Closing Circle: Nature, Man and Technology* (New York: Knopf, 1971).

28. Sim Van der Ryn and Peter Calthorpe, *Sustainable Communities, A New Design Synthesis for Cities, Suburbs and Towns* (San Francisco: Sierra Club Books, 1986), 167.

29. Brobech and Averyt, *The Products Safety Book* (Washington, D.C.: The Consumer Federation of America, 1983).

30. Karrie Jacobs, "The Design of Garbage," *Metropolis* (December 1988).

31. Karrie Jacobs, "The Design of Garbage," *Metropolis* (December 1988).

32. Deborah Abrahams, "Interlocking Bottles Make Enviro-Sense," *Environmental Information,* Vol. 14, No. 1 (February-March 1988).

33. Diana Twede, "Factors Influencing the Reduction of Distribution Packaging Waste." Doctoral Dissertation, Michigan State University, 1988.

34. Reed Glenn, "Vital Signs," *Boulder Daily Camera* (November 16, 1989).

35. LaVerne Leonard, "Designing for Posterity: Are Plastics a 'Good' Choice?" *Plastics Design Forum* (May/June 1988), 27.

36. Christopher Flavin and Alan B. Durning, *Building on Success: The Age of Energy Efficiency,* Worldwatch Paper No. 82 (March 1988).

37. "The Most Energy-Efficient Appliances–1988," (Washington, D.C.: American Council for an Energy-Efficient Economy, 1988).

38. Patricia Leigh Brown, "Ingenuity Is Creating a Home for Waste," *New York Times* (July 27, 1989).

39. Victor Papanek, *Design for the Real World: Human Ecology and Social Change* (Chicago: Academy Chicago Publishers, 1985).

40. Ted Flanigan, *IRT Newsletter,* Aspen, Colorado (February 2, 1989).

41. Charles Panati, *Extraordinary Origins of Everyday Things* (New York: Harper and Row, 1987).

42. Michael Renner, "Rethinking the Role of the Automobile," Worldwatch Paper No. 84 (June 1988).

43. Barry Commoner, "Failure of the Environmental Effort," (Flushing, New York: Center for the Biology of Natural Systems, January 1988).

44. June Taylor, "Tackling Pollution from Underground Storage Tanks," *EPA Journal* (April 1986).

Chapter 5: Implementing

1. John Holusha, "Old Newspapers Hit a Logjam," *New York Times* (September 10, 1989).

2. William Ruckelshaus, "The Politics of Waste Disposal," *Wall Street Journal* (September 5, 1989).

3. Frederic P. Sutherland and Vauter Parker, "Environmentalists at

Law," in *Crossroads: Environmental Priorities for the Future,* Peter Borelli, editor (New York: Island Press, 1988).

4. Kirkpatrick Sale, *Dwellers in the Land: The Bioregional Vision* (San Francisco: Sierra Club Books, 1985).

5. Gilbert S. Omenn, *Environmental Biotechnology: Reducing Risks from Environmental Chemicals through Biotechnology* (New York: Plenum Press, 1988).

6. Frederic Krupp, "New Environmentalism Factors in Economic Needs," *Wall Street Journal* (November 11, 1986).

7. Nan Stockholm, *Corporations and the Environment: How Should Decisions Be Made?* (Stanford University, 1980).

8. Amory Lovins, *Soft Energy Paths: Toward a Durable Peace* (New York: Harper and Row, 1979).

9. Cynthia Pollack Shea, "Renewable Energy: Today's Contribution, Tomorrow's Promise" Worldwatch Paper No. 81 (January 1988).

10. Christopher Flavin, "Electricity from Sunlight," *The Emergence of Photovoltaics* (Solar Energy Research Institute, December 1984).

11. Christopher Flavin, "Electricity from Sunlight," *The Emergence of Photovoltaics* (Solar Energy Research Institute, December 1984).

12. Larry Tye, "Solar Energy: A Technology Whose Time Is Coming?" *The Boston Globe* (April 11, 1989).

13. Ted Flanigan, *IRT newsletter,* Vol. 4, No. 1 (January 5, 1989).

14. *California's Energy Outlook, 1987 Biennial Report* (Sacramento, California: California Energy Commission, 1988).

15. Solar Energy Research Institute, "Science and Technology in Review" newsletter (Winter 1988-89), 2.

16. Alan S. Miller et al., *Growing Power: Bioenergy for Development and Industry* (Washington, D.C.: World Resources Institute, April 1986).

17. Gary Coates, *Resettling America: Energy, Ecology and Community* (Andover, Massachusetts: Brick House, 1981).

18. Ward Worthy, "Solar Cell Produces Hydrogen from Seawater," *Chemical and Engineering News* (June 26, 1989).

19. Amory and Hunter Lovins, "Oil Risk Insurance: Choosing the Best Buy," *GAO JOURNAL,* No. 2 (Summer 1988).

20. Christopher Flavin and Alan B. Durning, *Building on Success: The Age of Energy Efficiency,* Worldwatch Paper No. 82 (March 1988).

21. Rocky Mountain Institute Newsletter (February 1989), 5.

22. Rick Lyman, "For Office Buildings, the Future Is Now," *The Philadelphia Inquirer* (April 26, 1989).

23. John Woodwell, "Plugging the $1 Billion Drain: The Efficiency Alternative to Two Forks," (Snowmass, Colorado: Rocky Mountain Institute, September, 1989).

24. Sandra Postel, "Conserving Water: The Untapped Alternative," Worldwatch Paper No. 67, (September 1985).

25. Sandra Dillard-Rosen, "Scientists Listen to Roses to Keep Them Happy," *Denver Post* (May 27, 1989).

26. Amory Lovins, "Making Markets in Resource Efficiency" (Snowmass, Colorado: Rocky Mountain Institute, June 1989).

27. "In Our Opinion: Conservation: Good Politics and Good Economics, Too?" *Deseret News* (September 3, 1988).

28. Barry Commoner, *The Closing Circle: Nature, Man and Technology* (New York: Knopf, 1971).

29. Amory Lovins, Rocky Mountain Institute Newsletter, Vol. 5, No. 3 (Fall 1989).

30. Gilbert Omenn, *Environmental Biotechnology* (New York: Plenum Press, 1988).

31. Robert A. Frosch and Nicholas E. Gallopoulos, "Strategies for Manufacturing," *Scientific American* (September 1989).

32. Lee L. Harrison, editor, *The McGraw-Hill Environmental Auditing Handbook: A Guide to Corporate and Environmental Risk Management* (New York: McGraw Hill, 1984).

33. Personal conversation with Patrick Zuroske, June 1989.

34. Joel Barker, *Discovering the Future: The Business of Paradigms* (Lake Elmo, Minnesota: ILI Press, 1985).

35. Berger, John, "Optimal Suburbia," in *Restoring the Earth: How Americans Are Working to Renew our Damaged Environment* (New York: Knopf, 1985).

36. Gene Logsdon, "Adapting Old Know-How to New Products," *BioCycle* (May 1989).

37. Dan Goldberg, "Recycling Used Appliances," *Waste Alternatives* (September 1989).

38. Nan Stockholm, *Corporations and the Environment: How Should Decisions Be Made?* (Stanford University, 1980).

39. "Anita Roddick: More Than Skin Deep," *International Herald Tribune* (September 12, 1988).

40. David Oates, "Keeping Body and Soul Together," *Director* (June 1988).

41. David Bodanis, *The Secret House* (New York: Simon and Schuster, 1986).

42. Charles Panati, *Extraordinary Origins of Everyday Things* (New York: Harper and Row, 1987).

43. William Ruckelshaus, *Wall Street Journal* (September 5, 1989).

44. Edward Wilson, *Biophilia* (Cambridge, Massachusetts: Harvard University Press, 1984).

45. Jerry Mander, *Four Arguments for the Elimination of Television* (New York: Morrow, 1978).

APPENDIX: SOURCES AND RESOURCES

This section is a sampling of innovative products and resources, providing information and access to the designs and designers mentioned in this book.

HIGH EFFICIENCY LIGHTING

Information:
International Association
of Lighting Designers
18 E. 16th Street Suite 208
New York, NY 10003
(212) 206-1281

American Home
Lighting Institute
435 N. Michigan Avenue,
Suite 1717
Chicago, IL 60611
(312) 644-0828

Sales:
Many lighting stores and hardware stores now carry compact fluorescents and other high-tech bulbs. Other sources are:

G.E. Company
Jim Jensen
Lighting Business Group
Nela Park
Cleveland, OH 44112
(216) 266-2121
(800) 626-2000

North American Phillips
Dan Calleo
Phillips Square, CN6800
Somerset, NJ 08873
(201) 563-3492
(800) 543-8167

Osram Corp.
Jack Hoffman
P.O. Box 7062
Newburgh, NY 12550
(800) 431-9980

Rising Sun Enterprises
Robert Sardinsky
P.O. Box 586
Old Snowmass, CO 81654

Energy Conservation Products
Barry Zellen
511 Canal Street
New York, NY 10013
(212) 925-5991

EverX one-half watt exit signs
QNX Inc.
67 Sanford Street
East Orange, NJ 07018

BIOLOGIC IN THE HOME
Super-efficient refrigerators
Many mass-produced refrigerators now achieve high degrees of efficiency—one Whirlpool model uses only half the kilowatt hours (750) as the average model now in homes. A source for one of the most efficient of all (200-plus kw hours) is:

Sun Frost
Dr. Larry Schlussler
Box DD
Arcata, CA 95521

Low-flow showerheads
The Incredible Head and Ondine lines of showerheads are now available in hardware stores and home centers nationwide. Other sources are:

NOVA B6401
Ecological Water Products
1341 West Main Road, Dept. GM
Middletown, RI 02840

Water and Power
Conservation Int.
Box 310
Mokelumne Hill, CA 95245

Water-saving toilets
IFO Water Management Products
2882 Love Creek Road
Avery, CA 95224

Eljer Plumbingware
1301 Eljer Way
Ford City, PA 16226
(916) 944-3074

Porcher
13167 Merchandise Mart
Chicago, IL 60654
(800) 338-1756

Universal-Rundle Corporation
217 N. Mill Street
P.O. Box 960
New Castle, PA 16103
(412) 658-6631

U.S. Brass
901 10th Street
Plano, TX 75074
(800) 872-7277

Plastic recycling bins
Rehrig Pacific Company
625 W. Mockingbird Lane
Dallas, TX 75247

Aluminum can crusher
Lakeside Unlimited
#5 Crossbow
St. Louis, MO 63114

Nontoxic home products
Paints, waxes, polishes, varnishes, shellacs, etc.

Livos PlantChemistry
2641 Cerrillos Road
Santa Fe, NM 87501
(505) 988-9111

Unbleached coffee filters
Rockline Inc.
P.O. Box 1007
Sheboygan, WI 53082

Melitta U.S.A. Inc.
1401 Berlin Road
Cherry Hill, NJ 08003

Better buys, earthwise, in toilet paper
Envision
(Fort Howard Corporation)
available through Seventh Generation
(800) 456-1177
Basic 500 (Kimberley Clark)
Scott Tissue
Charmin Free

**Long-life grocery
and lunch sacks**
Made from durable tent-grade
nylon, PermaSax stand up
independently like paper sacks,
guaranteed for long life.
PermaSax
P.O. Box 714
Indian Hills, CO 80454
(303) 697-8089

Windstar Foundation
2317 Snowmass Creek Road
Aspen, CO 81654

**100% cellulose waxed paper
sandwich bags**
Earth Care Company
Box 3335
Madison, WI 53704

Cloth diapers and covers
Biobottoms
P.O. Box 6009
Petaluma, CA 94953
Bumkins
(800) 553-9302

Organically grown food
Many supermarkets now
have organic products.
For listing of mail order
companies, write:

Americans for Safe Food
1501 16th Street N.W.
Washington, D.C. 20036
(202) 332-9110

Consumer action magazines
Environmental Action Magazine
1525 New Hampshire Ave., N.W.
Washington, D.C. 20036
(202) 745-4870

Garbage Magazine
P.O. Box 51647
Boulder, CO 80321-1647

E Magazine
P.O. Box 5098
Westport, CT 06881

The Earthwise Consumer
Box 1506-E190
Mill Valley, CA 94942

**EFFICIENCY IS GOOD BUSINESS
High-efficiency photocopier**
Canon PC-30 Model
Canon U.S.A., Inc.
1 Canon Plaza
Lake Success
New York, NY 11042

Recycled paper
Cross Pointe Paper Corporation
1295 Bandana Boulevard North
Suite 335
St. Paul, MN 55108

P.H. Glatfelter Company
Spring Grove, PA 17362-0500
(717) 225-4711

Conservatree Paper Company
10 Lombard Street, Suite 250
San Francisco, CA 94111
(800) 522-9200

Miami Paper Corporation
P.O. Box 66
West Carrollton, OH 45449
(513) 859-5101

Ward Paper Company
P.O. Box 587
Merrill, WI 54452
(715) 536-5591

100% Recycled Paper Stationery
12 Montcalm Avenue
Brighton, MA 02135
(617) 782-4876

Recycling information
American Recycling Market
Directory
Recoup Publishing
P.O. Box 577
Ogdensburg, NY 13669
(800) 267-0707

National Recycling Coalition
(202) 625-6406

Socially responsible investing
Calvert Social Investment Fund
1700 Pennsylvania Avenue, N.W.
Washington, D.C. 20006
(800) 368-2748

Dreyfus Third Century Fund
600 Madison Avenue
New York, NY 10022
(800) 645-6561

Parnassus Fund
1427 Shrader Street
San Francisco, CA 94117
(415) 362-3505
Outside California:
800-999-3505

**Socially responsible
investment publications**
The Wall Street Green Review:
Environmental Investment
Strategies for the 1990s.
(800) 825-7746

Guide to Social Investing Services
The Social Investment Forum
711 Atlantic Avenue
Boston, MA 02111
(617) 451-3252

Catalogs
Seventh Generation
Products for a Healthy Planet
10 Farrell Street
South Burlington, VT 05403
(Carries products such as Ecover,
a washing powder that breaks
down in 3-5 days.)

Co-op America
Attn: Denise Hamler
2100 M St., N.W. #310
Washington, D.C. 20063

Gardens Alive!
(biological pest control)
Natural Gardening
Research Center
Highway 48, P.O. Box 149
Sunman, IN 47041

**SUSTAINABLE INSTITUTES AND
DESIGNERS**
Ocean Arks International
John and Nancy Jack Todd
10 Shanks Pond Road,
Falmouth, MA 02540

The Land Institute
Wes and Dana Jackson
2440 E. Water Well Road
Salina, KS 67401

Worldwatch Institute
Lester Brown
1776 Massachusetts Ave.,
N.W. #701
Washington, D.C. 20036

Rocky Mountain Institute
1739 Snowmass Creek Road
Snowmass, CO 81654-9199
(303) 927-3128

Institute for Local Self-Reliance
Larry Martin
2425 18th St., N.W., 2nd Floor
Washington, D.C. 20009

World Resources Institute
Gus Speth
1735 New York Avenue, N.W.
Washington, D.C. 20006

Solar Energy Research Institute
1617 Cole Boulevard
Golden, CO 80401

American Council for an
Energy-Efficient Economy
Howard Geller
1001 Connecticut Avenue, N.W.
Suite 535
Washington, D.C. 20036
(202) 429-8873

Windstar Foundation
2317 Snowmass Creek Road
Aspen, CO 81654

Biosphere II
P.O. Box 689
Oracle, AZ 85623
(602) 622-0641

Environmental Defense Fund
Frederic Krupp
257 Park Avenue South
New York, NY 10010

Jim Starry
(Designer of the Starport, water
purification systems, individual/
mass transit hybrid system, and
many other designs.)

Environmental Protection
Designs, Inc.
P.O. Box 1931
Boulder, CO 80306
(303) 939-9825

Natural Resources
Defense Council
Thomas Stoel, Jr.
1350 New York Avenue, N.W.,
#300
Washington, D.C. 20005

E.F. Schumacher Society
R. Swann
Box 76, R.D. 3
Great Barrington, MA 01230

Bioregionalism
Bioregional Project
David Haenke
New Life Farm, Box 3
Brixey, MO 65618

Planet Drum Foundation
Box 31251
San Francisco, CA 94131
(415) 285-6556

NATURE-COMPATIBLE DESIGNS
Gypsum blocks
INFORM
381 Park Avenue South
New York, NY 10016
(212) 689-4040

Turfblocks
Paverlock Company
Cincinnati (513) 874-0306
Houston (713) 691-0022
Atlanta (404) 482-6466

Information:
David Smith
National Concrete Masonry
Association
P.O. Box 781
Herndon, VA 22070

Solar Box Cookers
Solar Box Cookers International
1724 Eleventh Street
Sacramento, CA 95814
(916) 444-6616

Glazings
For a list of suppliers of Heat
Mirror (low-E) windows:
The Southwall Corporation
3961 E. Bayshore Road
Palo Alto, CA 94303

For inert gas-filled
windows, contact:
Robert Clarke
Alpen, Inc.
5400 Spine Road
Boulder, CO 80301

**Houses made from
recycled materials**
Michael Reynolds
World Energy
Box 1041
Taos, NM 87571

**Biological detoxification
system**
Uses microbes in manufacturing
processes to detoxify hazardous
constituents.
Art Gebhardt
Manville, EMI (R-04)
P.O. Box 5108
Denver, CO 80217-5108
(303) 978-5080

Mechanical spray bottles
Peter Gould
Exxel Container Corporation
33 Schoolhouse Road
Somerset, NJ 08873
(201) 560-3655

Interlocking bottles
Michael Sparling
I-Corp
238 Cypress Street
Rochester, NY 14620

Solvent recycling system
Finish Company, Inc.
931 Greengarden Road
Erie, PA 16501

Dumptrike
George Bliss
111 East 12th Street
New York, NY 10003
(212) 505-8276

**INFORMATION
Canada's Environmental
Choice Project:**
Environment Canada
Regional Director General
Ontario Region
25 St. Clair Avenue East (6th floor)
Toronto, Ontario
Canada M4T 1M2

**Environmental Protection
Agency
Pollution Prevention
Clearinghouse and Hotline**
(800) 424-9346

**EPA Community Right-to-Know
Hotline**
Provides Toxic Release Inventory
data for each region and state
(data also available on floppy
disks):
(800) 535-0202
(202) 479-2449

INDEX

ABOUT THE AUTHOR

David Wann is a policy analyst for the Environmental Protection Agency and has previously worked as a public information officer with the EPA and as a water quality specialist for the city of Denver. He has published numerous articles in magazines and newspapers, including *Environment, Environmental Action, High Country News, Denver Post,* and *Christian Science Monitor.* He has produced and/or written scripts for eight environmental videos on architecture, agriculture, transportation, energy, and hazardous wastes. Several of these programs have received extensive television play, illustrating to a diverse audience the central role that design plays in our quality of life.

Wann has a Master's degree in environmental science from the University of Colorado. He has taught at the college level, worked with grassroots groups, and directly experienced the environment by getting his hands into his garden soil. "That's been my real environmental education," he says. "When you genuinely understand how one ecological system works, you can intuitively know others by extension."